THE CHANKAS AND THE PRIEST

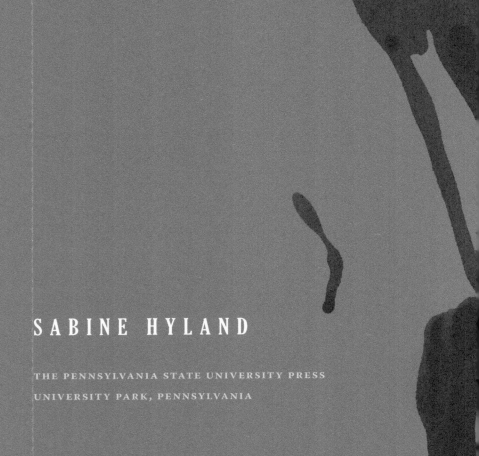

SABINE HYLAND

THE PENNSYLVANIA STATE UNIVERSITY PRESS
UNIVERSITY PARK, PENNSYLVANIA

THE CHANKAS

AND THE PRIEST

A Tale of Murder and Exile

in Highland Peru

Library of Congress Cataloging-in-Publication Data

Names: Hyland, Sabine, 1964– , author.
Title: The Chankas and the priest : a tale of murder and
    exile in highland Peru / Sabine Hyland.
Description: University Park, Pennsylvania : The
    Pennsylvania State University Press, [2016] | Includes
    bibliographical references and index.
Summary: "Presents the story of the Chanka people of
    Peru, from the fifteenth to the eighteenth centuries,
    told through a narrative of the crimes committed by a
    priest, Juan Bautista de Albadán, in the early 1600s"—
    Provided by publisher.
Identifiers: LCCN 2015044963 | ISBN 9780271071220 (cloth :
    alk. paper) | ISBN 9780271071237 (pbk. : alk. paper)
Subjects: LCSH: Chanca Indians—History. | Bautista
    de Albadâan, Juan, 1562–1611. | Chanca Indians—
    Crimes against—Peru—Pampachiri—History. |
    Peru—History—Conquest, 1522–1548. | Peru—
    History—1548–1820. | Pampachiri (Peru)—History.
Classification: LCC F3430.1.C4 H95 2016 | DDC 985/.03—
    dc23
LC record available at http://lccn.loc.gov/2015044963

This book is dedicated

with gratitude to my

teacher and mentor

Richard L. Burger.

CONTENTS

ILLUSTRATIONS

ACKNOWLEDGMENTS

Many people have contributed to the creation of this book. I would like to thank Brian S. Bauer for his initial funding and support for archival research on the colonial Chankas, for his comments on an earlier draft of this manuscript, and for generously allowing me to use his photos. I am grateful for the efforts of Donato Amado Gonzalez, who was an outstanding research assistant in the early phases of this project, and to Miriam Aráoz Silva and Nicole Coffey Kellett for their companionship in the field. Frank Salomon, who served as an outside reviewer for Penn State Press, made extremely helpful comments on the manuscript, as did an anonymous reviewer for the press. Christine Lee provided very useful suggestions for the text and kindly took photos of Pampachiri for me. My gratitude goes to Danielle Kurin for her encouragement of the project, and to Carlos Espinosa, who challenged me to explain why Albadán's story mattered. Monica Barnes obligingly provided corrections to chapter 1. Mario Aguilar graciously shared with me the draft of his manuscript on the liberation of God.

I am deeply grateful to Richard Burger for his continuing support of my work, for his profound insights into the study of anthropology, and for our lively discussions about ethnohistory and the influence of Kroeberian anthropology at Yale. I would also like to thank my colleagues in the University of St. Andrews Department of Social Anthropology for their encouragement and friendship. The librarians and archivists at Sterling Library (Yale University), the Biblioteca Nacional (Madrid), the Archivo General de Indias, the Archivo Histórico Nacional (Madrid), the Biblioteca Nacional (Lima), the Archivo Departamental del Cusco, the Archivo General de la Nación (Peru), the Ministry of Agriculture in Andahuaylas, the Royal Library of Copenhagen, St. Norbert College, the University of Glasgow, and Special Collections at the University of St. Andrews have all contributed greatly to this project.

Additionally, I would like to thank the community of Uranmarca for allowing me to transcribe its colonial manuscripts.

The National Science Foundation and the National Endowment for the Humanities provided generous grants that funded this research and the writing of this book. I owe much gratitude to Ellie Goodman and the production team at Penn State University Press for their excellent work.

My family is the heart of my universe, and I am very grateful for their patience with my labor on this manuscript. Eleanor Hyland provided invaluable assistance with the visual aspects of this book, along with her good-humored support. Margaret Hyland cheered me on when my spirits flagged. Last, but not least, this book would have been impossible without my steadfast and loving husband, Bill, to whom I owe more than I can say: "omnia bona et sancta factis amplius quam verbis [ostendat]" (Saint Benedict of Nursia).

1. SETTING OUT

Introduction

This is the story of terrible crimes. Four hundred years ago, in a remote corner of the Peruvian Andes, a sadistic Catholic priest tortured, sexually abused, and murdered native peoples from the southern region of Andahuaylas, where the ethnic group known as the Chankas lived. During the ten years (1601–11) he ministered to the Chankas around the town of Pampachiri, Father Juan Bautista de Albadán not only amassed a personal fortune but also unleashed a reign of terror that permanently altered daily life for the Chanka people; the effects of this decade of madness would last well into the eighteenth century. Despite efforts to bring Albadán to justice, he managed to subvert any investigation into his crimes. However, his sudden and unexplained death in 1611 raises the possibility that local peoples may well have taken matters into their own hands and finally eliminated him with the help of the local administrator, the *corregidor* Don Alonso de Mendoza Ponce de León.

Although the Spanish Church in colonial Peru is often criticized, many Catholic priests and missionaries were honest, caring individuals who did their best for their native parishioners. Catholic priests in the Andes loaned money to native leaders and petitioned the government for the alleviation of tribute abuses against the native peoples. Many priests in colonial Andahuaylas left substantial sums of money to their Andean parishioners and absolved native chiefs (*kurakas*) of any debts. A typical example of this is Father Joseph Núñes de Guevara, the priest of Talavera and Huancarama in the late 1600s. In his will, Núñes allocated all of the rental income from his estate to the purchase of wine, candles, hosts, and other items for the church, so that the Indians would not have to provide them, "resulting in the universal alleviation of them all." In honor of his patron saint, Saint Joseph, he also left money to pay the choirmaster to teach young Indian boys how to be cantors, thereby enabling the youths to earn a living and avoid labor in the mines. Finally, he willed the paintings and tabernacle from his bedroom to the parish church, with the provision that no future priest could remove them for his personal use.[1]

Some priests were even willing to fight for native rights. For example, on a summer evening in 1656, Father Antonio de Aponte, priest of the Chanka parish of Ocobamba, burst into the bedroom of the local hacienda owner Joseph Gutiérrez with a drawn pistol in one hand and a naked sword in the other. Aponte threatened to kill Gutiérrez and his wife as they lay in bed unless Gutiérrez turned over the title to a cornfield and signed new papers that granted possession of the field to the Indian community of Ocobamba. Aponte maintained that Gutiérrez had obtained the cornfield fraudulently and therefore must return the land to the native community to whom it rightfully belonged. Fearing for his life, Gutiérrez signed the requisite papers, and the Indians repossessed their field.[2]

Aponte's concern for the Indians was by no means unique among the clergy in colonial Peru and serves to highlight the depravity of Father Albadán by contrast. As the following chapters will reveal, Albadán tortured and abused members of the native Chanka population virtually unchecked. This true tale of crime reveals the very real sufferings of the Chanka people and the lasting effects of Albadán's evil activities. It also sheds light on the important question of how these crimes were allowed to happen. Given all of the safeguards against corruption that the Spanish had put in place, how could a priest get away with committing brutal and public acts of torture and sexual abuse for ten years? What does this story reveal about daily life in this rural region of the South American Andes in the early seventeenth century?

Historians and anthropologists have repeatedly analyzed crimes for the insights that such deviant activities provide into the nature of the society under investigation. In the 1970s, 1980s, and 1990s, the most successful works of "microhistory"—the intensive study of small communities at one point of time in the past—focused on crimes and deviance and plumbed archives for the personal insights afforded by witness testimony and confessions. Two of the most acclaimed microhistories ever written—Carlo Ginzburg's *The Cheese and the Worms* and Natalie Zemon Davis's *The Return of Martin*

Guerre—recount specific crimes as a means of gaining unique insights into past periods in European society. *Good Faith and Truthful Ignorance* by Alexandra and Noble David Cook, a highly regarded work of South American microhistory, carefully depicts the world of Spanish conquistadors in sixteenth-century Peru by examining the records of a transatlantic bigamy trial. Such studies of criminal testimony can provide a unique form of social realism in which the underlying themes and contradictions of daily life are revealed through episodes of destructive deviance. By focusing on a specific crime, an author is able to reveal not only the character of the criminal and of his or her victims, but also the nature of the society that gave rise to the atrocities committed.[3] This tale about an evil priest—Juan Bautista de Albadán—and his victims is a window through which we can view life in a highland village in colonial Peru in the early 1600s. Understanding the world of the native chief who unsuccessfully tried to stop Albadán is as important to this story as the description of the mad priest's personality and upbringing. Who was the native Chanka lord Don León Apu Guasco, and how was he destroyed in his attempt to bring Albadán to justice? Who were the Indian women subjected to Albadán's lust, and how were their lives affected by his actions? How did Albadán's counterattack on Don León affect Chanka political and social history for the next 123 years?

The microhistory format typically focuses on one slice of time, projecting the "ethnographic present," as it were, onto an episode in the past. This work attempts to bring the analysis of Chanka society into a more holistic ethnohistorical perspective by placing Albadán's atrocities in the context of the changing nature of Chanka politics and kinship from the fifteenth to the eighteenth centuries. Virtually nothing has been known until now about the intrigues among Chanka elites from the Inka period to the late Spanish colonial period. Based on unpublished documents in archives in Spain and Peru, I analyze how Albadán's actions affected Chanka political life for generations after the priest's death. The revenge that Albadán exacted against the Chanka lord who accused him of abuse exploited an instability in the Chanka political structure dating to when the Chankas were incorporated into the Inka Empire. Thus, this story begins in the fifteenth century, when the Chankas were defeated by Inka troops and made part of the Inka state.

Part I of this book will tell its story through vignettes focused on different aspects of Albadán's life and crimes. During his years in the Chanka town of Pampachiri, as he acquired more and more wealth, Albadán put together the largest library in the entire region. His collection of sixty-three volumes outshone all of the libraries of other priests and hacienda owners throughout the province. Amid the tomes of moral theology and canon law in his library were classical gems such as the Roman satires of Juvenal and Horace. In biting, ribald, and outspoken essays on various topics, Juvenal condemned the corruption and hypocrisy of Roman society in his time. Horace's writings, while gentler, likewise regarded Roman life with a critical eye. Both writers described the world around them through essays on a kaleidoscope of different topics, such as dining with a corrupt patron or the abuses committed by cruel slave owners. In some ways, the essays by Horace and Juvenal serve as inspiration for this work; the troubling story of Albadán's crimes will be narrated through chapters exploring facets of daily life in the highlands of colonial Peru, including hospitality and the circulation of books.

In part II, the narrative turns to focus on the Chankas and their history from the Spanish conquest to the mid-eighteenth century. These chapters examine how Albadán's actions disrupted the Chanka social structure for generations. Most important, in chapter 8 this history is analyzed through the Chankas' own concepts of lineage—the *ayllu*—and of the Andean binary political structure—the *saya* (moieties) of *hanan* (upper) and *urin* (lower). Focusing on these Chanka ethnocategories, rather than on the more familiar Western notions of class division and economic development, provides new insights into change in Andean society throughout the Spanish colonial era. Part II reveals that, contrary to previous assumptions, ayllu and moiety rivalries continued to dominate the politics of indigenous Chanka elites well into the eighteenth century, drawing creole landowners, with whom the Chankas had intermarried, into these native feuds on the eve of the "Age of Andean Insurrection." Because part II is diachronic, covering hundreds of years of indigenous history, this study goes well beyond the normal temporal limits of microhistory; its *longue durée* spans Chanka kinship and politics from the Inka period to the late eighteenth century.

Throughout this work I have tried to adopt a more discursive, narrative style so as to engage a wider audience of readers than is usual for academic monographs on Andean ethnohistory. I found the story of Albadán, of Don León Apu Guasco, and of the subsequent rivalries and intrigues to be riveting, and I hope to convey this interest to the reader. Long discussions of anthropological and postcolonial theory have been left out of this work intentionally, although such theory naturally informs the arguments presented here. I want this text to be accessible to a diverse readership, from the villagers of modern-day Pampachiri to specialists in South American anthropology and history. The book takes a form that is unconventional for anthropology—a narrative spanning centuries—as a way to balance the personal, individual stories of Albadán, Don León Apu Guasco, Don Diego Quino Guaraca, and others against a consideration of broader economic, political, and demographic factors. One of the challenges for recent anthropology has been to discover new ways to represent individual choices within the frameworks of tradition and history.[4] *The Chankas and the Priest* attempts to achieve such a balance by delving into a narrative of crime that changed Chanka life for many decades, a story that elucidates aspects of power and knowledge in the seventeenth-century Andes while showing how older forms of Andean kinship and society evolved within the colonial state. The emphasis on marriage patterns and on the indigenous categories of ayllu and moiety reflect the anthropological concerns that lie at the heart of this study of the Chankas. The use of a narrative style is less common in anthropological monographs. Nonetheless, by focusing on a microhistoric view of how Chanka elites negotiated their changing circumstances over generations, the book reveals the process of cultural change.

The Kingdom of the Chankas

For me, the story of Albadán and the Chankas first began decades ago, when *People* magazine published an article about the exploits of a young American archaeologist in Peru. The cover of the October 20, 1980, issue was graced by a smiling Liz Taylor, wearing an orange chiffon dress, dangling diamond earrings, and a diamond brooch. Inside the issue, whose pages are now crinkling and brittle, was one of the first articles written in English about the quest to understand the Chankas: "An American Woman Discovers an Ancient Empire Lost in the Mountains of Peru."[5]

This multipage article describes the work of American archaeologist Monica Barnes in a remote region of the Peruvian Andes. In 1978, while working in another part of the Andes, Barnes heard rumors about the existence of "a pre-Inca kingdom standing virtually intact in a remote valley high in the central Andes." She set out to learn more: "For three weeks she explored the valley by horse, burro and on foot, stunned by the sheer quantity of plainly ancient artifacts. In one set of tombs she found skeletons, mummy bindings and shards of pottery she believed to be more than 1,200 years old; at another she was astonished to find a town full of circular stone walls—ruins whose architecture certified that they were erected before the Inca empire (1425–1534). But by whom?"[6] Monica soon realized that the ruins she was seeing had belonged to the ancient people known as the Chankas. In

Inka legends, the Chankas were famed as great warriors who nearly over-threw the Inka capital of Cusco, yet scholars in the 1970s knew little about them. Together with Frank Meddens, a fellow student from the University of London, Monica and fourteen crew members (including the fiancés of both principal investigators) settled into the town of Pampachiri as their base (fig. 1), at an altitude of almost twelve thousand feet, and began a grueling period of systematic excavations to uncover the mysteries of this past civilization. The research was not easy:

> The only place for anyone to sleep was on the stone floor of the marketplace. Bedrolls did little to protect the researchers from the subfreezing temperatures at night; during the day they baked in 100-plus degree heat. The closest outpost of civilization was a seven-hour drive away, and their truck was rarely in working order. They often had to walk to sites several miles from Pampachiri carrying equip-ment on their backs. Their diet contributed to regular outbreaks of a particularly virulent diarrhea they called "the Inca two-step." The staple meat was guinea pig, and Barnes still hasn't recovered from eating a cat one night.[7]

Monica and Frank eventually discovered the ruins of ten Chanka settle-ments scattered around Pampachiri, and they uncovered more than twenty thousand artifacts, including ceramic shards, ornate textile fragments, and musical instruments such as lutes, flutes, and drums. Numerous mummi-fied human remains, occasionally with wads of chewed coca leaf still nestled tightly in their skeletal jaws, were found in the course of their investigations. Amid the excitement of these discoveries, the work was not all hardship—close to Pampachiri were regionally celebrated hot springs, and the crew occasionally took breaks to soak in the warmth of the healing waters. The *People* magazine article included a shot of a sexy, blonde Monica wearing a swimsuit in a steaming hot spring bath, accompanied by her fiancé, David Fleming, clad only in his swimming trunks.

Yet, after the fieldwork was completed, the investigators turned to other projects. Monica wound up as a Ph.D. student in anthropology at Cornell University, pursuing a related but different topic. It was there, at Cornell, that I met Monica and David and first heard their stories about Pampachiri and the Chankas. In 1985, I was an undergraduate at Cornell, starry-eyed and filled with dreams of becoming an anthropologist in the Andes. Monica was always a very spirited presence in our seminars and drew upon her years of

FIG. 1 Pampachiri today. Photo by Christine Lee.

field research during class discussions.[8] Her stories about Pampachiri, where she witnessed exotic rituals such as the Yawar Fiesta ("Blood Festival"), in which a condor, representing the Indians, is tied to the back of a Spanish bull and slowly wounds the bull with its talons, were utterly engrossing.[9] Her photos of the ruined circular buildings of the Chankas haunted me. Who were these ancient people? What had happened to them after their double conquest, first by the Inkas and then by the Spanish?

The years passed, and I became involved in other Andean research projects, eventually earning my Ph.D. As I made my way professionally, I never quite forgot Monica's tales about the enigmatic Chankas. So, in 2000, when the Chicago archaeologist Brian Bauer asked me whether I would be willing to work with him on a project to research the history of the Chankas, I was intrigued. Brian had received grants from the National Science Foundation and the John Heinz III Charitable Trust for a five-year, multidisciplinary project to uncover the history and prehistory of the Chanka ethnic group. The Chankas today—for they still exist in a high-altitude Andean landscape dotted with overgrown agricultural terraces and ruined stone buildings from

FIG. 2 View of the town
of Andahuaylas. Photo by
Brian S. Bauer.

their former kingdom—are centered in the Peruvian city of Andahuaylas (fig.
2), in the department of Apurimac, west of the ancient Inka capital of Cusco
(map 1). Brian's project had two parts. He would be in charge of the archaeological survey of the Andahuaylas valley, systematically recording all of the
archaeological remains in the area. I would be responsible for searching for
Spanish colonial documents about the Chankas in archives in Spain and
Peru.

From 2000 to 2004, Brian, a tall, lanky man with a trim brown beard
and a baseball cap glued to his head, shading his blue eyes, led a team into
Andahuaylas every summer. He was accompanied on his long walks along
archaelogical survey lines by a Peruvian codirector, Miriam Aráoz Silva, a na-
tive-born Cusqueña with green eyes, curly hair, and a merry smile; two grad-
uate students, Lucas Kellet and Carlos Socualaya; and a changing band of
local assistants. For the summers that I joined them, I remember seemingly

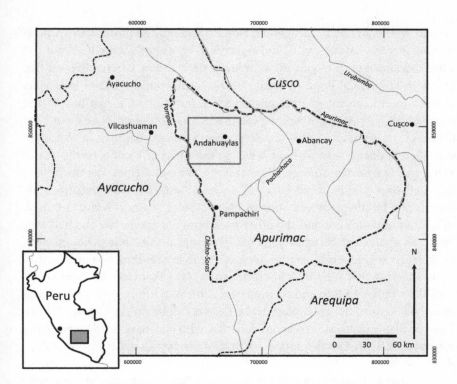

MAP. 1 Map of the Andahuaylas region in Peru. Adapted from Kurin, "Bioarchaeology of Collapse," 11.

endless days of walking through a sun-drenched countryside, starting from the bottom of river valleys, where tropical oranges and lemons grew. Up the dirt roads that climbed the valleys, we encountered typical Andean landscapes featuring adobe houses and potato fields, which culminated in cold, high grasslands (*puna*) with snow-capped mountain peaks looming above. Sometimes, in the evenings, Brian would treat the crew to the favorite local drink—hot tea with rum, cloves, and sugar—at Garabatos, a pub on the main plaza of Andahuaylas. In Garabatos, where the walls were lined with jaguar, bear, and skunk pelts, the tables were tree trunks, and the benches were padded with raw wool, we would gossip for hours.

Most of my time on the project, however, was spent working in archives, such as that of the Ministry of Agriculture in Andahuaylas, which housed copies of colonial documents from the region's indigenous communities. Donato Amado Gonzalez, a Cusco-born historian, served as my assistant in

Peru as well as in Spain. Altogether, Donato and I found more than six hundred sixteenth-, seventeenth-, and eighteenth-century documents about the Chankas, allowing us to gain an intimate understanding of what life was like for them in colonial Peru. In Spain, in the Archive of the Indies in Seville, Donato found the set of unpublished manuscripts that forms one of the foundations for this study. Among them was a five-hundred-page document detailing the great wealth of the Spanish priest Juan Bautista de Albadán, who died suddenly and without a will in the town of Pampachiri in 1611.[10] What was truly extraordinary about this set of manuscripts was that it also included over one hundred pages of personal letters to Albadán from his friends and family members, such as his two older brothers—one in Potosí, in what is now Bolivia, and the other back home in Spain. No one had ever found an equivalent cache of personal letters from the Andean countryside in the early seventeenth century. One of the many revelations contained in these letters is that Albadán's maternal uncle, Fray Francisco de Prado, who was like a father to him and to whom he confessed his evil activities, was a close colleague of the great playwright Tirso de Molina (Fray Gabriel Téllez). Tirso probably heard stories about Albadán, who may have even inspired the accursed cleric in Tirso's famous drama *Damned by Doubt* (*Condenado por desconfiado*).

Albadán's name was familiar to us even before Donato found these documents. In the early seventeenth century, a Peruvian Indian named Don Felipe Guaman Poma de Ayala wrote a 1,189-page letter to the king of Spain in which he described Inka society and narrated both the positive actions of the Spaniards in Peru—such as the holy works performed by many Catholic priests—and the abuses committed against the Indians by their European conquerors. This text, housed in the Danish Royal Library, contains nearly four hundred line drawings, which remain some of our best visual representations of Andean life during the late Inka Empire. Guaman Poma singled out Albadán as a particularly evil Catholic priest who sexually assaulted the young Indian women under his care and publicly and sadistically tortured Indians who opposed him. He described how Albadán manipulated the juridical and political systems in his favor so that he avoided any prosecution for his crimes against the native peoples of Pampachiri and the surrounding region. The colonial documents uncovered during the course of our project, along with the personal letters written to Albadán by his relatives during his lifetime, reveal plentiful evidence that Guaman Poma was writing the truth about the Spanish priest. The letters provide us with an unprecedented and uniquely intimate glimpse into the personal life of a seventeenth-century psychopath. The documents that accompany the inventory of Albadán's wealth also raise the question of whether he died a natural death or was poisoned by the local people.

Moreover, the archival materials reveal that in his effort to avoid justice, Albadán attacked the Chanka leader who accused him of abuse and, in so doing, profoundly altered the Chanka political and kinship structure. Unfortunately for the people of Pampachiri, Albadán had a lasting impact on the Chankas; their history would not be complete without consideration of his actions. By telling Albadán's story, I hope to answer—at least partially—Monica's questions from so long ago: Who were the Chankas, and what happened to them under Spanish rule?

The Chanka Lords

When Albadán arrived in Chanka territory in the late 1500s, he entered an ethnic region that had been conquered by the Inkas at the beginning of the latter's expansion throughout the Andes.[11] According to Inka history, the Chankas, led by two self-styled "brothers," Astoy Guaraca and Tomay Guaraca, besieged the city of Cusco in the early 1400s, during the reign of the eighth Inka emperor, Viracocha. The Inka army, under the command of Prince Inka Yupanqui (later Emperor Pachakuti), repulsed the Chankas, killed both Chanka leaders, and eventually overran and conquered the entire Chanka region, located about two hundred miles northwest of Cusco.

Once the Chankas had been incorporated into the Inka state, they were forced to accept communities of outsiders into their territory. Throughout their empire, the Inkas broke up ethnic groups and resettled their members elsewhere. Within Andahuaylas, the Chankas were joined by communities of Aymaraes (who lived nearby to the southeast), Yungas (lowlanders), and Chachapoyans (an ethnic group from the cloud forests to the north). These colonists—*mitimaes*, as they were called in Quechua—were given land and served as the government's eyes and ears, should the Chankas think of insurrection.[12] Likewise, the Chankas were divided; some were sent to Andahuaylilas, near Cusco, others to Lucanas, near Ayacucho, while still others were made to work in the quicksilver mines of Huancavelica.[13]

Colonial documents can provide us with some hints as to which members of the Chanka confederacy were sent away as colonists. Chanka society, like most Andean groups, divided itself politically, socially, and ritually into two halves, or moieties: an upper half and a lower half. The relationship between the two halves can be thought of as that between an older brother and a younger brother. Thus, the Chanka leaders were spoken of as brothers, although it is unlikely that they were actual siblings. Such was the case with Astoy Guaraca, the leader of the upper half of the Chankas, and Tomay Guaraca, the leader of the lower half. Each was the chief (or *kuraka*, in Quechua) of a type of family group/lineage known as an ayllu. Grasping the concept of the ayllu is fundamental to understanding Andean history. Ayllus are malleable, nested social formations that can be considered as groups of individuals joined by real and imagined kinship; as people who share the same mythical origin place and ancestor; and as people who form corporate groups with rights to communal landholdings.[14] They could be thought of as lineages, but lineages that confer political and ritual duties as well as access to land and water rights. Ayllus can have property rights across a broad stretch of landscape, spanning many villages and settlements.

Under the Inkas, the Chankas comprised ten ayllus; of these, five ayllus belonged to the Upper Chankas and five ayllus belonged to the Lower Chankas. Both the upper half and the lower half possessed a chief who was installed by the Inka authorities. When we look at a listing of ayllus of the Upper Chankas from 1570, we see that the lineage of Astoy Guaraca simply disappears, and that the leader of the Guasco ayllu was made the chief (kuraka) for the entire upper half: "Ayllus of the Upper Chanka: Guasco; Malma; Apes; Moros; Pachacaruas."[15] The chronicler Cieza de Leon tells us that the leader of the Guasco ayllu was the head ("cacique principal" or "apu kuraka") of all the Chankas in the 1540s; the Guascos would remain the head of the Upper Chankas until the late eighteenth century.[16] During the Inka period, the head of the upper half was considered the leader of the entire group, although the chief of the lower half wielded considerable power over the ayllus in his half. It is not known what happened to the ayllu of Astoy Guaraca after the Chankas' defeat. Presumably the members of this ayllu were moved to various locations as colonists, where they no longer had any rights to their ancestral lands.

During the Inka period, the political structure of the Lower Chankas was altered as well. In the ayllus of the lower half, the Tomay Guaracas still existed, but they were no longer in charge. The Inkas appointed the leader of the Guachaca ayllu as the head of all of the ayllus of the lower half, demoting the Tomay Guaracas: "Ayllus of the Lower Chanka: Guachaca, Tomay Guaraca, Quichua, Caha, Yana."[17] The Tomay Guaracas would not forget that they had once ruled over all of the ayllus of the Lower Chankas. Under Spanish rule, their leaders would retain the name "Tomay," which once distinguished them from the Guaracas of the Upper Chankas. Moreover, as we shall see in chapter 8, the Tomay Guaracas would not continue to accept the Guachacas' authority over the Lower Chankas throughout the Spanish colonial epoch. Albadán's interference in the Chanka political structure—an interference that came about as he tried to evade the legal case that the leader of the Chankas, Don León Apu Guasco, brought against him—would greatly intensify the rivalry between the Tomay Guaracas and Guachacas for dominance over all the Chankas, a power struggle that would last for over a century after Albadán, but that had its roots in the Inka reorganization of Chanka political power.

Pampachiri, the "Cold Plain"

Albadán's domain was centered on the town of Pampachiri, located in the southern part of Chanka territory in the Chicha Valley (see map 1). He also ministered to the populations of the nearby communities of Umamarca and Pomacocha, which were part of the *doctrina* (parish). The Chicha Valley marked the southernmost limit of Chanka territory. Pampachiri lay within the portion of the valley that was under the authority of the Chanka kurakas, and that formed part of the *repartimiento* of the Chankas during the Spanish colonial period. The Soras ethnic group inhabited the valley on the other side of the Chicha River.[18] When the Spanish arrived in this area, they found that the Sivi Paucars, who were ethnically "Inka," were the governing dynasty in Umamarca, Pampachiri, and Pomacocha (see chapter 5). However, during the centuries of the Spanish viceroyalty, the Sivi Paucars were under the authority of the Chanka kurakas.

In Quechua, "Pampachiri" means "the cold plain" (fig. 3). Located at a height of almost 12,000 feet above sea level, the air is thin and the nights are cold. The unpaved highway from Andahuaylas to Pampachiri crosses a plain over 13,000 feet high, where flocks of vicuña, the slender cousins of the llama, roam freely, feeding on the tufted *ichu* grass.[19] According to ancient folklore, nests of deadly, mystical snakes had lived on the icy heights overlooking the community of Pampachiri since primordial times. The colonial chronicler Don Felipe Guaman Poma de Ayala recounted that when the snakes saw a person, they emitted an earsplitting sound like the thunder of an arquebus. Then one of the snakes would fly through the air and sink its poisonous fangs deep into the person's skin, burrowing through layers of clothing, if necessary. The only possible cure was through one of the primeval snake's own

FIG. 3 Plains above Pampachiri. Photo by Brian S. Bauer.

eggs, which of course was impossible to obtain without being fatally bitten. Therefore, anyone attacked by these extraordinary shooting snakes would die. Guaman Poma's legend of the primordial serpents is an example of the supernatural myths that were embedded in the Chanka landscape, as elsewhere in the Andes.

Fortunately, we saw no flying serpents; our time in Pampachiri was golden. The sun gilded the village with a special high-altitude intensity that gave beauty to the humble mud-brick and plaster buildings. Just as Monica had described, there were plentiful ruins of circular, non-Inka stone structures throughout the surrounding countryside. During the Wari Empire (A.D. 550–1100), Pampachiri was a wealthy center of llama and alpaca herding;[20] now, however, its farmers barely eke out a living by herding and by growing potatoes, alfalfa, and the prickly pear cactus fruit called *tuna*. When we were there, the façade of the colonial church in the heart of the village was being repaired, but the women in charge of the church allowed us to climb the adobe church tower, which gave us a panoramic view of the main square. Albadán's artists had decorated the outside of the church with strange relief

FIG. 4 The Pampachiri church in 2004 before restoration. Photo by Brian S. Bauer.

sculptures of life-size naked women, which remain (fig. 4). We did find a nearby colonial home with an old stone lintel upon which a cross had been carved; it is possible that this was the rectory where Albadán lived when he was in Pampachiri.

Our crew was among the first teams of researchers in the area since Monica and Frank's expedition decades earlier.[21] In the intervening years, the Chanka heartland around Andahuaylas, including Pampachiri, had become a "red zone" due to the terrorist activities of the Shining Path (Sendero Luminoso) and was closed to outsiders. The Shining Path, a Maoist guerrilla insurgent organization founded by Abimael Guzmán, initiated armed conflict with the Peruvian state in 1980; by the time Guzmán was captured in 1992, it controlled the Andean regions of Apurimac, Ayacucho, and Huancavelica, and carried out successful terrorist attacks as far away as Lima, where it bombed government offices, electricity transmission towers, and shopping malls, resulting in many deaths. Guzmán's capture significantly weakened the insurgency, but hostilities continued in the red zone until 2000 and beyond. In the countryside, the Shining Path's brutality toward landowners, peasants, and popular leaders was matched by the violent abuses of the military forces sent to eliminate the insurgents. The Peruvian Truth and Reconciliation

Commission estimated that 69,280 people died or disappeared between 1980 and 2000 as a result of the conflict. The Shining Path massacred roughly half that number; the armed forces killed about a third; and smaller guerilla groups and local peasant militias committed the rest of the slayings.[22]

Pampachiri did not escape the violence unscathed. For example, the Shining Path murdered 12 community members on July 16, 1984, in a massacre known as the "Express Bus to Death." Prior to the killings, peasants from 25 indigenous communities, including Pampachiri, had formed an alliance against the Shining Path. In revenge, insurgents disguised themselves as Peruvian soldiers, set up a roadblock along a major highway in the red zone, and stopped a public bus filled with passengers. They then executed 102 passengers whom they suspected of being from the communities in question. The families of the Pampachiri victims brought their bodies home for burial; they were exhumed and examined years later by the Peruvian Human Rights Commission.[23]

The civil war isolated the Indian communities in the red zone from the outside world for almost twenty years. This seclusion from the rest of Peruvian society was expressed to us forcefully one afternoon by Filomeno Guaman, a farmer from Uranmarca, a Chanka community northwest of Pampachiri. Only one road ran through Uranmarca, once an important stop on the Inka road from Cusco, crossing the Pampas River and leading to the Inka temple of Vilcashuaman. Brian and I had agreed to sponsor a *rutuchikuy*—a traditional Andean ritual in which a child receives his or her first haircut—for Filomeno's five-year-old daughter, Yenifer. On the day before the ceremony, Brian, Filomeno, and I chatted on the banks of the Pampas River, where Brian had organized a picnic. Suddenly, Filomeno looked at us and said,

> Y'know, during the Sendero years, we would have a kid guard each entrance to the village. Whenever an outsider approached, the kid would signal and all of us would flee into the caves in the mountains, and hide there, even for days, until the outsiders left. If the visitors were Sendero, they would put a gun to your head and make you give them food. Then a week later the military would come through. Someone would say to them, oh, that person is a Senderista, he gave them food. And then the military would take you out and shoot you.

Understandably excited by the possibilities that peace had brought, Filomeno was brimming with plans for improving his fields and growing cash crops that could now be sold to the outside. Yet I found it difficult to comprehend how, in the same years that I was getting married, having children, traveling, and enjoying a middle-class American life, the people in the rural Chanka communities were hiding in caves at the approach of any outsider.

The Chanka people have been no strangers to violence. Sadly, violence disrupted their daily lives in the early seventeenth century, when a Spanish priest appeared in their village with empty pockets and the ambition to live as a rich gentleman, and settled into the rectory near the Pampachiri church. This is his story and that of his victims.

PART I

2. THE CRIMES

The Chronicler Guaman Poma

The fullest description of Father Albadán's crimes comes from the pen of Don Felipe Guaman Poma de Ayala, otherwise known as Guaman Poma, a provincial nobleman from the Lucanas province, next to the Chanka homeland of Andahuaylas. Born in Lucanas around 1535, he spent most of his life there and in the nearby city of Huamanga (Ayacucho), where he learned to write Spanish, although his grammar in this foreign tongue was never perfect. In the 1570s, he served as an assistant to the Spanish priest Cristóbal de Albornos, who was trying to eradicate native Andean religious practices from the communities in the region. Guaman Poma's work with Spanish clerics continued when he assisted the Mercedarian chronicler Martín de Murúa in the late 1580s and 1590s. Murúa authored a chronicle about the Inka past; it is now known that Guaman Poma painted many of the colored illustrations for Murúa's work.[1]

By the mid-1590s, Guaman Poma found employment with the Spanish judge of Huamanga in charge of land titles. Unfortunately, Guaman Poma, who seems to have been an irascible character, made enemies while he worked for the judge. In 1600, all of his property was confiscated and he was banished from the city of Huamanga. It was at this point that he began wandering through the Andes for the next fifteen years, until his death in 1615, describing the glories of the Inka Empire as well as the suffering of the Andean Indians under Spanish rule. In instances where scholars have

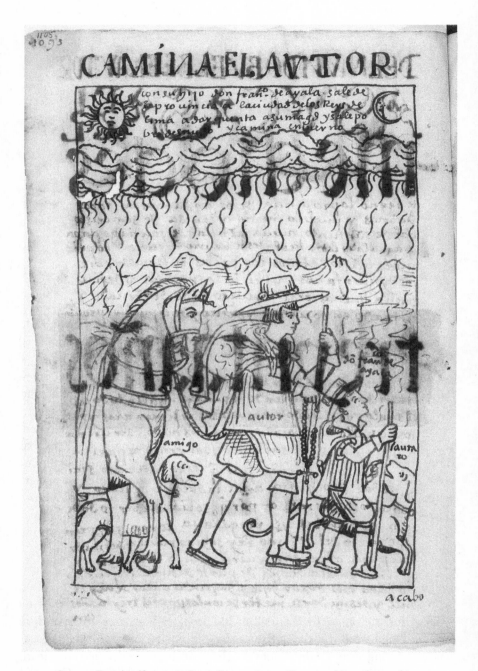

FIG. 5 Guaman Poma's self-portrait. From Guaman Poma, *Nueva corónica y buen gobierno* (1615), p. 1095, no. 385. The Royal Library, Copenhagen, GKS 2232 quarto.

been able to investigate the truth of his accusations against corrupt officials, they have found Guaman Poma's charges to be abundantly supported by evidence.[2]

In his 1,189-page letter to the king of Spain, lavishly illustrated with hundreds of line drawings, Guaman Poma left us an iconic image of himself (fig. 5). In this drawing, we see the chronicler walking with his son to Lima, where he intended to inform His Majesty, King Philip III, about the crimes committed against Andean peoples by the king's officials, Catholic priests, and creole landowners in the kingdom of Peru. Accompanying them are Guaman Poma's two dogs, one (next to the horse) named Amigo (Friend) and the other (frisking in the lead) called Lautaro, after the heroic Mapuche Indian rebel of the sixteenth-century epic *La Araucana*.[3]

Guaman Poma's letter to the king condemned evil Spaniards—"jaguars," "lions," "foxes," and "rats" who "devour the impoverished Indians in this kingdom."[4] Yet the chronicler also praised those righteous Spaniards who strove to live holy lives and to serve the poor and downtrodden. For example, he lauded the life of the humble Catholic priest Diego de Avendaño:

> Oh Christian Father Avendaño! Thirty years you were in your Indian parish without grief, and you died serving God and the poor Indians! . . . You didn't want to see an unmarried woman in your house, nor did you order the young ladies gathered together [for your pleasure]. You served the old women and the sick, while you ministered to strangers and "baptized" them with alms . . . you died in a very Christian manner and very poor; in your house no one could find money or any belongings, just all [holy] poverty. And the poor Indians and all of the province are weeping for their Father.[5]

By contrast, Guaman Poma was not afraid to catalogue the sins of other Catholic clergy in the Andes. He described priests in Indian parishes who seduced young women, who forced women to work without pay in textile sweatshops, and who beat and mistreated their parishioners. For the most part, with certain exceptions, the accusations are general; Guaman Poma usually did not single out particular priests for criticism. Yet, in the case of Juan Bautista de Albadán of Pamapchiri, Guaman Poma could not be silent. "Father Albadán," he wrote, "was a very tyrannical, cruel Father; the things that this priest used to do cannot be described."[6] Addressing Albadán, he proclaimed, "Look here, proud Father! If you proud and tyrannical lords punish rebels [i.e., Indians] unjustly, they will complain afterwards to the judge [i.e., to God]. And thus the lords will be given terrible punishments!"[7] In other words, the cries of the abused Indians will be heard by the heavenly judge, who will one day mete out horrific punishments to tyrants like Albadán—if not in this life, then in the next. Many of Albadán's atrocities, the chronicler stated, were too horrible to commit to paper; nonetheless, those that Guaman Poma could bring himself to describe were chilling.

Albadán's Crimes

The story of Albadán's depravities begins with his sexual abuse of the young Indian girls in his pastoral care. Every morning, he would select some of the attractive young girls in his parish and order them to come to his house. There, he would strip them naked and examine their buttocks and their vaginas. As part of this daily ritual, he would thrust his fingers into their vaginas; then he pushed his fingers four times into each girl's anus. Guaman Poma described it thus: "Father Albadán stripped them naked and looked at their asses and their cunts and stuck in his fingers, and he gave four little thrusts into their anuses; each morning he did this to all the unmarried women."[8]

Among the young women who received his unwanted attentions were the unmarried daughters of an Indian named Don Juan Uacrau. These women complained about Albadán's assaults to the artist who had been hired to decorate the church in Pampachiri. It is not clear whether the artist protested against the women's treatment to outside authorities or simply to Albadán himself. In any event, Albadán had his own unique technique for dealing with anyone who possessed the temerity to criticize him.

The priest ordered his assistants to set up a Saint Andrew's cross—that is, a cross that looked like an "X"—in the town plaza. The artist was stripped naked and tied with leather thongs upside down on the cross. Albadán beat him and then broke out his stockpile of tallow candles; apparently, he went through a large number of them in what was to follow. With the lit candles, Albadán burned the artist's testicles and penis, and then, ripping open the man's anus with his bare hands, continuously thrust the lit candles "up his ass."[9] Guaman Poma emphasized that Albadán burned many candles in his torture of this unfortunate artist.

At the time of Albadán's death in 1611, he possessed more than 180 tallow candles in his house in Umamarca alone.[10] A tallow candle made of sheep's fat has a melting point of around 120 degrees Fahrenheit. Ten minutes of uninterrupted exposure to this temperature will result in third-degree burns, the most severe degree of burn, implying irreversible damage to the skin. The tallow candles used for Mass[11]—the kind that would have been most readily available to Albadán—would have each burned for at least one hour, if not longer. Presumably, Albadán moved the flame from area to area on the victim's body; nonetheless, if the priest were burning these specific areas of flesh for hours, there would have been third-degree burns across the artist's rectum, anus, and genitals.

Tallow candles are notorious for the large amounts of hot wax that they release compared to beeswax or modern paraffin or soy candles. So, in addition to the injuries caused by exposure to the flame itself, Albadán's victim would have suffered hot-wax burns, particularly in the rectum. While suffering through this torture, he would almost certainly have gone into hypovolemic shock ("burn shock") due to loss of fluids; he may also have suffered multiple organ failures from perfusion and inflammatory mediators. If the artist was still alive when he was cut down from the cross, he did not live long. Not only would there have been a near certainty of severe infection throughout the damaged tissues, but the inability to urinate or to defecate due to the location of the burns would have proved fatal in the seventeenth century.

Clouds of black smoke are released by tallow candles, in contrast to beeswax or paraffin candles. Tallow candles also have an unpleasantly acrid odor, particularly if they have become rancid while stored in the candle boxes used to keep pests from eating them. The image of Albadán sexually torturing this poor man in the Pampachiri town plaza—the clouds of black, sooty smoke, the scent of burned flesh mingling with the foul tallow smell, the screams of his victim as the villagers watch in horror—is truly infernal. It is also quite public, which speaks to the power that Albadán was able to wield over the Indians of his parish. Guaman Poma insisted that the artist was not Albadán's only victim. For example, Albadán performed the same sadistic and public tortures on a Pampachiri Indian named Diego Caruas, who had refused to hand his livestock over to the priest. And these atrocities were carried out on other Indians in even crueler ways; as Guaman Poma wrote, "They say that he did other things, much worse, that cannot be written; only God knows them and the other very many injuries and evils that he used to do."[12]

Such public acts of violence traumatize not only the victims, but the entire community of people who witness the brutality and are powerless to stop it. The Indians of Pampachiri would all have known about Albadán's habitual sexual abuse of the young women, whether it occurred in public or in the privacy of his home. Kristine Hagan and Sophie Yohani, who have studied contemporary war rape, note that such publicly known acts of sexual assault are intended to torture the men of the community, who can do nothing as their sisters, daughters, and nieces are being assaulted. The female victims of such offenses frequently suffer long-term psychological consequences, as their sense of control over their bodies and of their personal safety and trust are shattered. Public acts of great brutality, such as Albadán's sadistic torture of the men on the Saint Andrew's cross, create a collective trauma of humiliation and pain for the community. As Hagen and Yohani write, "the [person] lying bleeding . . . is no longer a human being but a symbolic body to inflict hatred, violence and pain upon."[13] The psychological effects of witnessing violence can be similar to those experienced by the victims, including shame and long-lasting psychological distress.[14] Albadán's unpunished brutalities would have reinforced for the people of Pampachiri how complete their subjugation was under Spanish rule.

News of Albadán's acts of horror spread throughout the Andes. In a letter dated March 1, 1609, Albadán's brother Gerónimo, who was a scribe in Potosí, over nine hundred miles away, wrote that Albadán's evil deeds were the subject of gossip there (fols. 84r–87r). Gerónimo proposed an ingenious solution to counter this gossip. He suggested that Albadán buy the office of scribe for Alonso Herrera, Gerónimo's friend, so that Herrera could refute the rumors, telling everyone what a wonderful priest Albadán was. It is worth noting that Gerónimo did not question the truth of the rumors concerning his older brother, but merely devised a way for Albadán to escape any negative consequences. In fact, before Albadán's death, Gerónimo wrote repeatedly to his brother, explaining that he was deeply enmeshed in corrupt behavior himself, especially in activities with women and other vices "that would shock you." Gerónimo begged to be allowed to join Albadán in Pampachiri, where he promised to help him and to "follow your will even in extremely difficult things, at your pleasure."[15] Rather than surround himself with and show favor to strangers, Gerónimo wrote, Albadán should accept his brother's assistance: "You are rich and can do me good, as you do for strangers and for whomever; you will be very pleased if you favor me thus."[16]

The rumors that Gerónimo heard about his brother's new wealth were quite correct. Albadán had received nothing of his inheritance from his parents (see chapter 3) and possessed no business or factory that might have produced wealth. He was quite poor when he entered his doctrina in 1601, where his salary was only 40 pesos annually, roughly equivalent to 7,400 U.S. dollars today.[17] Yet, upon his death in 1611, his estate, including the large gifts that he sent to his family members, was worth over 10,000 pesos, or about

1,850,000 U.S. dollars today (see chapter 3). His extraordinary wealth indicates the scale of his theft from the natives of Pampachiri and its environs, as well as the level of terror that he must have used to compel people to hand over such a large quantity of livestock and other goods.

How Did Albadán Evade Punishment?

Had Pampachiri still been under Inka colonial rule, the families of the murder victims would have presented their cases against the accused to the local chief, or kuraka.[18] While the Inkas allowed local elites considerable latitude in adjudicating crimes within their own ethnic group, a case of homicide had to be brought before an Inka magistrate, called a *tukrikuq*—"he who sees." In the provinces, there was no separate system of legal courts; instead, these magistrates, who were generally responsible for all aspects of local Inka administration, heard criminal cases. The kuraka took a case before the tocricoc, who then listened to evidence from witnesses and from the accused before rendering a verdict. Justice was swift, and a homicide conviction merited the death penalty. Had Albadán's acts of public depravity been committed under Inka rule, the head Chanka kuraka, together with the families of the victims, would have denounced the cleric before the local tocricoc, and Albadán's reign of terror would have come to a quick and bloody end.

Of course, the Spanish colonial government in Peru set up a full administrative system throughout the Andes that was supposed to have been able to punish a Spaniard guilty of torturing Indians to death. How did the system fail so spectacularly in the case of Albadán? A lack of ecclesiastical oversight in remote regions of the highlands, combined with Albadán's own cunning in outwitting the Spanish and ecclesiastical legal systems, allowed his atrocities to go unchecked for ten years. Moreover, as Albadán quickly became one of the richest men in the entire province, his increased wealth enabled him to pay bribes to evade justice.

In the region around the city of Andahuaylas, in the territory of the colonial Chanka ethnic group, there were no settlements of religious orders. In other words, except for occasional Jesuits who passed through on temporary missions, there were no monks or friars in Chanka territory throughout most of the colonial era. It is quite possible that if there had been a religious house near Pampachiri, the local friars would have ensured that Albadán was brought to justice, but such was not the case. All of the Catholic priests in the area were secular clergy, who answered directly to the bishop. Initially,

Andahuaylas and its environs formed part of the Cusco diocese, under the jurisdiction of the bishop of the ancient Inka capital. In 1614, however, when it became clear that the diocese of Cusco was too large to be governed properly, the province of Andahuaylas was added to the newly formed diocese of Guamanga.[19] Thus, Albadán was the priest in Pampachiri when it was still part of the extremely large Cusco diocese; had his parish been closer to the episcopal seat of power, it is possible that the bishop might have decided to investigate the rumors about Albadán's atrocities.

As secular priests, the Andahuaylas clergy experienced less scrutiny than did members of religious orders. Regular priests, such as Dominicans, Augustinians, and Mercedarians, who had taken vows to follow a *regula*, or rule, not only lived in community, where their actions were closely observed by their brothers, but were frequently inspected in formal visitations sponsored by the heads of their orders. According to the canons of the Council of Trent, bishops were required to inspect their diocese every two years. In practice, however, episcopal visitations were much less frequent. Very few ecclesiastical visitations of Andahuaylas are recorded from the period when the region was part of the Cusco diocese. Of these, most were not concerned with examining the conduct of doctrina priests. For example, one early visitation was called by the viceroy to settle a dispute between the priests and the corregidor of Andahuaylas,[20] while almost all of the others focused exclusively on whether the native Andeans were still worshipping their ancient gods.

A continuing problem in Andahuaylas, and throughout the Spanish Empire more generally, in the colonial period was governing the diocese during the frequent periods when the episcopal see was vacant. The appointment of a bishop was a lengthy process. News of the death or retirement of an Andean bishop had to be sent by ship to Spain; the appointment of a new bishop had to be recommended in Spain and confirmed in Rome, and then the individual had to be sent to Peru. Given the slow communications, especially between Peru and Europe, it was quite common for there to be no sitting bishop in Cusco. At such times, the cathedral chapter tried to respond to the needs of the larger diocese; however, given the limited scope of its responsibilities, the chapter was poorly equipped to cope on a regular basis with issues such as diocesan visitations. The two ecclesiastical visitations of Andahuaylas in the sixteenth century called by the cathedral chapter of Cusco were both later accused of serious irregularities.[21] Out of the ten years that Albadán was in power in Pampachiri, there was no bishop at all in Cusco for about three of them, from July 1606 until late 1609.[22]

Likewise, the most important ecclesiastical institution for disciplining clergy, the Inquisition Tribunal, was located in Lima, far from Andahuaylas. Inquisitors argued that bishops, in the interest of avoiding scandal, might fail to punish wayward clergy; therefore, an independent institution such as the Inquisition was necessary to oversee the behavior of priests.[23] John Chuchiak has shown how native Mayans in colonial Mexico repeatedly filed complaints against local priests with the Holy Office of the Inquisition Tribunal.[24] Although these charges did not always result in convictions, they initiated lengthy investigations into the clergy's conduct, often with negative results for the priests in question. In the Andes, branches of the Lima Inquisition Tribunal were established in large cities such as Potosí. Native peoples in these urban areas occasionally filed accusations against priests with the Holy Office. For example, in Potosí in 1580, two Indian women and one mestizo accused the Mercedarian friar Melchior Hernández of sexual abuse.[25] Although Hernández was eventually acquitted on a legal technicality, his order removed him from his ministerial position in Potosí and transferred him far away to Panama as a result of the affair. However, Andahuaylas's remoteness in the Spanish viceroyalty seems to have insulated its priests from the attention of the Inquisition. When the head Chanka kuraka, Don León Apu Guasco, lodged a formal complaint about Albadán's illegal activities, he did so with the royal authorities—the viceroy and his court, the Audiencia—not with church officials.

In general, the secular clergy of Andahuaylas experienced virtually no interference in their daily management of their doctrina. While Catholic priests in Indian parishes had little influence outside of their jurisdiction, they ruled as autocrats within its confines. Most had been trained to hold their clerical authority in high regard, as was common at this time. The famous Peruvian writer Fernando de Avendaño expressed a typical view of sacerdotal authority when he wrote that priests were "messengers of God" whom the Indians must obey at all times.[26] Avendaño, a member of the cathedral chapter of Lima and a professor of theology at the University of San Marcos, knew important churchmen in Andahuaylas and had taught some of the region's priests, such as Francisco de Aldana, the vicar of Pampachiri, in 1621.[27] His beliefs on the absolute nature of clerical authority, along with his unwillingness to acknowledge even the possibility of priestly shortcomings, held wide sway throughout seventeenth-century Peru.

If the Church in seventeenth-century Andahuaylas was ill equipped to deal with Albadán, what about the royal officials? Why didn't the local corregidor or one of the periodic governmental investigators charge Albadán for his crimes? Unfortunately, the colonial system was notoriously susceptible to corruption, and that seems to have been the case for Albadán. The priest was able to evade royal investigations in part through a well-run system of bribes. From Guaman Poma, we know that Albadán regularly ordered the Indians to hand over llamas, handwoven textiles, and fishing nets so that he could give these goods to the local corregidor. He also demanded other items from the Indians: money for the local scribe; lead llamas and carrying sacks for the local lieutenant; and chicken eggs for the Spaniard who ran the local inn. Albadán exacted these items as he addressed the Indians during Mass, adding the following admonishment: "Suc garrotillauan padre canca! Alli oyariuay!" (The Father is ready with the noose! Listen well!).²⁸ Through this system of bribes, Albadán preempted any Spaniard who might have considered lodging a complaint against him. The list of those who needed to be bribed is interesting—the corregidor, the scribe, the lieutenant, and the innkeeper, each with his own ability to influence events. For these men to be bribable, of course, they had to possess a certain level of indifference to the sufferings of Albadán's Indian victims.²⁹

Another way in which Albadán consolidated power was through giving loans. A new corregidor, Don Alonso de Mendoza Ponce de León, arrived in Andahuaylas at the beginning of 1609. On January 18 of that year, Don Alonso took out two very large loans from Albadán, one for 250 pesos and another for 1,128 pesos (fols. 37v–39r), totaling an enormous amount equivalent to over 254,900 U.S. dollars today. As yet unaware of the degree of Albadán's abuses of the native peoples, the new corregidor likely did not completely realize the implications of taking out such large loans from the priest. Any subsequent efforts to bring Albadán to justice would be thwarted by the fact that Albadán could insist on repayment of the loans; if Don Alonso were unable to repay them, he could be sent to jail. At the time of the priest's death in 1611, Don Alonso still owed him this money.

One of the men Albadán bribed must have warned him that an official Church inspector (or "visitor") was going to pass through Pampachiri on a routine investigation into conditions throughout the diocese. In 1607, Father Juan de López de Quintanilla, the "general ecclesiastical visitor" for the diocese of Cusco (fig. 6), arrived in Pampachiri with the intention of questioning the priest and the inhabitants about conditions in the doctrina.³⁰ This was the only ecclesiastical visitation to occur in the Cusco diocese during Albadán's ten years in Pampachiri. Forewarned about the visitor, Albadán made sure that all of the Indians in the community were far off in the countryside when Quintanilla passed through. In his official report, Quintanilla noted that there was no one to be found in the entire village of Pampachiri when he

FIG. 6 The *visitador* Father Juan de López de Quintanilla. From Guaman Poma, *Nueva corónica y buen gobierno* (1615), p. 681, no. 270. The Royal Library, Copenhagen, GKS 2232 quarto.

visited—everyone was absent. He was not able to question anyone, and so he moved on to the next doctrina. Guaman Poma likewise described how Quintanilla—a good and honest man, according to the chronicler—found Pampachiri empty. "In the said pueblo," Guaman Poma wrote, Quintanilla "did not find a living soul, and the said church was locked, all of the Indians hidden in the puna; he did not even find a jar of water."[31] By hiding the Indians, Albadán ensured that none of them could complain to Quintanilla.

The governor and head kuraka over all the Chankas, Don León Apu Guasco, did not stand idly by while Albadán established his reign of terror in Pampachiri. As we shall see in chapter 7, Don León worked tirelessly on behalf of the natives under his jurisdiction. According to Guaman Poma, Don León protested Albadán's abuses, speaking out particularly against Albadán's sexual assaults on young women.[32] Don León lived in the city of Andahuaylas, and there is no evidence that he ever visited Pampachiri, which was located in the southernmost part of his jurisdiction. However, he must have heard numerous complaints against the Spanish priest and believed that an investigation into Albadán's activities would lead to his just punishment and removal from office. According to Guaman Poma, Albadán retaliated against Don León by officially complaining about the kuraka, "saying that [Don León] had hidden Indians from the visitation."[33] The chronicler wrote that Don León was found guilty of hiding potential tributaries, was exiled, and later died of grief.

Archival documents confirm Guaman Poma's account of Albadán's retaliation against Don León. Early in 1606, the viceroy received intelligence from Albadán that Don León had hidden Indians from the 1604 census. A new inspector, a lawyer from the Audiencia, was dispatched to investigate the situation.[34] He found an additional 641 tributary Indians who had been hidden by Don León from the tribute rolls (temporarily saving these men from working in the mercury mines of Huancavelica). In 1607, Don León was deposed, and leadership over all the Chankas was given to the head of the lower moiety (Urinsaya), Luis Tomay Guaraca.[35]

Unfortunately, Don León's efforts to defend his people against Albadán did not have the results he had wished. Instead of seeing Albadán removed from Pampachiri, the kuraka was himself dismissed and his office given to his lineage rival; no action was ever taken on Don León's accusation. In an effort to destroy his opponent, Albadán initiated an inquiry into the Chanka leader's own hiding of Indians from government tribute agents. The ensuing investigation not only led to Don León's downfall, exile, and death, but also kick-started an era of political instability for the Chanka leadership that would last for the next 123 years.

3. THE PRIEST

Guaman Poma described Albadán as an isolated ogre—selfish, sadistic, and cut off from normal human contact—able to wreak terror in the doctrina of Pampachiri because of its remoteness. Indeed, Albadán's letters reveal that he repeatedly refused requests from his close relatives to visit him in Pampachiri; he even went so far as to order his nephew Diego, who had arrived in South America with the sole intention of visiting his rich uncle, to sail back to Seville immediately, sight unseen.[1] Once he became wealthy, Albadán sent large sums of money to his family members and wrote to them regularly, but he absolutely denied their repeated entreaties to spend time with him in his doctrina.

Guaman Poma could not have known that despite Albadán's isolation in the Chanka countryside, the priest was in fact part of a closely knit, transatlantic network of family members and business associates based in Seville. His maternal uncle Don Andrés Núñez de Prado, a prosperous merchant in Seville, had facilitated Albadán's initial arrival in Peru. Don Andrés's business associate Francisco Gutiérrez Coca, a family friend who had been living in Lima since 1559, apparently helped Albadán throughout the priest's many years in the viceroyalty. For example, when Albadán wished to send letters and money home to Spain, he sent his packets to Gutiérrez Coca in Lima, who forwarded them with his shipments of merchandise to Seville (fols. 51v–53r). Albadán kept in contact with numerous relatives in Spain, including his maternal uncle Fray Francisco de Prado, the head of the Mercedarian house in Seville and, later, in Jerez de la Frontera.

Fray Francisco, the brother of Doña Ana de Jesús y Prado, Albadán's mother, was like a father to Albadán. In a letter dated March 2, 1608, Fray Francisco wrote to his nephew, "although my sister is dead, my obligation to you has not died, nor my responsibility that I have as a father [toward you]."[2] Throughout 1607 and 1608, Albadán wrote four long letters to his uncle in which he poured out the anguish of his soul, confessing "everything" and calling himself "lost" and "damned."[3] In these letters, Albadán expressed his unhappiness with his exile in the Indies, "living among barbarians,"[4] and pleaded for permission to return to Spain, where he could rest. Although Albadán's letters no longer exist, we can ascertain their contents by Fray Francisco's responses. In his letter of March 2, 1608, Fray Francisco said, "for the Blood of Christ I beg you to no longer [think] of coming to Spain; you are not a child; here [in Spain] you would have to try to be virtuous and try to earn your living as so many others do. . . . Let there be no more games [in Pampachiri]; rather you should be conscious of saving yourself, remembering that you are the son of good parents, and you should buckle down to contemplate your personal destiny so that you are not completely damned."[5] It is significant that Fray Francisco used the word "games," or *juegos*, to describe Albadán's illicit activities in Peru. *Juegos* was a common euphemism for immoral and decadent sexual activities at this time.[6]

Fray Francisco wrote again on February 3, 1609, after having received another "long account" of Albadán's "work and exile," which Fray Francisco felt "in his soul."[7] In this epistle, Fray Francisco expressed his sympathy for Albadán's continuing exile and desire to retire to Spain, where he could live quietly.[8] Nonetheless, Fray Francisco reiterated that his nephew could not come back to Seville, that he would not be satisfied with the simple way of living in Spain after enjoying the wealth of the Indies (fol. 82v). Finally, in an undated letter written after September 1609, Fray Francisco told Albadán, "if until now I wrote with harshness it was only to wake you up from the dream in which you were living . . . and although I could write much about how I feel, you must stay in your corner [of the world] without trying to come to enjoy this sky and homeland and to see the greatness of this city [once again]."[9] Clearly, Albadán's letters to his uncle described his misery in Pampachiri, his contempt for the "barbarians" among whom he lived, his inability to live virtuously while in Peru, and the evil "games" in which he indulged and which were leading to his damnation. Despite Albadán's pleas, Fray Francisco refused to support his nephew's request to return home, condemning Albadán to remain in Pampachiri until the latter's unexpected death in 1611. In fact, in 1605, Fray Francisco had been the target of a major Vatican investigation of corruption, from which he had barely escaped; he could not risk having a nephew like Albadán living as a priest in Seville under his patronage.

The particulars of Fray Francisco's career with the Mercedarians and the accusations of corruption against him and the Seville house are described in detail by Fray Francisco's fellow Mercedarian Fray Gabriel Téllez, who knew him personally. Fray Gabriel, better known under his pseudonym, Tirso de Molina, is considered one of the three greatest playwrights (with Lope de Vega and Calderón de la Barca) of Spain's Golden Age of literature. Famed as the creator of the archetypal rake Don Juan in his drama *The Trickster of Seville* (*El burlador de Sevilla*), Tirso was extraordinarily versatile, penning comedies, tragedies, *autos sacramentales* (morality plays), biblically based narratives, historical dramas, and hagiographical works, as well as a trilogy of plays dramatizing the conquest of Peru by the Pizarro brothers and the subsequent civil wars among the conquistadors. Between 1637 and 1639, Tirso wrote an official history of the Mercedarian order; however, because of his lack of discretion in portraying some of the disagreements and scandals that troubled the Mercedarians, this work was not published until 1973.[10]

In the second volume of his history, Tirso noted Fray Francisco's rise to positions of high authority among the Spanish Mercedarians, as well as his very close association with Fray Alonso de Monroy, the Andalusian provincial, who was later elected master general of the entire order.[11] Tirso also provided the only extant account of the Vatican investigation of the Mercedarian house in Seville in 1605, when Fray Francisco was in charge of it. Fray Francisco and the men in his house were accused of sexual relations with a secular woman enclosed with the nuns of the Assumption in Seville; of living an overly luxurious life in terms of food, drink, the refurbishment of their monastery and library, and their lifestyle in general; of using violence to give the Mercedarian habit to an illegitimate relative; and of other actions against the Mercedarian constitutions. Tirso explained drily how Fray Francisco and the Mercedarians of Seville countered the charges by sending their own delegation to Rome under the leadership of Fray Hernando de Ribera, who, through his "courtesy and excellent manners" toward the Roman curia, was able to make the charges go away.[12]

Later in his work, Tirso described other events in Fray Francisco's life, such as the time in 1618 when royal troops entered the magnificent Mercedarian house in Seville, demanding that the friars comply with the king's orders concerning their elections. On this occasion, Fray Francisco, once again head of the Seville house, rang the church bell and called a meeting of the friars, only to be told by the soldiers that such a meeting was illegal and that the friars must remain in their cells for fifteen days.[13] Tirso openly criticized Fray Francisco as a man "of little constancy" (de poca constancia) for acquiescing to the royal demands. As one of the most prominent Mercedarians of his day, Fray Francisco was well known to the younger Tirso, who would have heard considerable gossip about him during day-to-day life in the monastery. Tirso came from the Castilian province of the Spanish Mercedarians, who were great rivals of and competitors with Fray Francisco's Andalusian province. Tirso's history documents the acrimony between the two provinces throughout the sixteenth and seventeenth centuries, describing a situation in which rumors about members of the opposite province were rife.

In his letter to Albadán dated March 2, 1608, Fray Francisco thanked his nephew for the generous gift of 100 pesos (equal to two years of Albadán's annual salary as a priest in Pampachiri) to him and to his fellow Mercedarians in the Jerez house. Fray Francisco wrote that his confreres in Jerez would like to know whether there were any gifts from Spain that they could send to Albadán in appreciation of his generosity (fol. 81r). In other words, Albadán's existence and considerable wealth were common knowledge among the Spanish Mercedarians, who were deeply interested in the sources of wealth of other houses, particularly in Andalusia. In fact, Albadán's entire family was well known to the Mercedarians in Seville. The home of his parents in Seville was near the Mercedarian monastery, and the friars often accompanied Fray Francisco on visits there (fols. 180r–181r). His mother's confessor was a Mercedarian, Fray Juan de Chaves (fol. 166v), and her funeral was attended by many of the friars in the Seville house.[14] Fray Hernando de Paredes, the provincial vicar of the Mercedarians in Peru at the time of Albadán's death, went to school with Albadán and his brother Francisco in Seville (fol. 181v) and knew the family well. It is almost certain that Tirso would have heard stories about Albadán and his generosity to his uncle Fray Francisco. It is also quite likely that Tirso heard rumors about Albadán's atrocities in Pampachiri, spread by Mercedarians in Cusco—particularly Mercedarians from Tirso's own Castilian province who were sent to Peru, such as his friend Fray Diego de Velasco.[15]

Only three degrees of separation divide these two great writers and satirists of the seventeenth century, Guaman Poma in the Andes and Tirso de Molina in Iberia: Guaman Poma to Albadán to Fray Francisco to Tirso. Albadán's story is a truly transatlantic narrative, revealing how even a depraved cleric in a remote mountain village in the Andes could be part of a web of personal relations reaching, in this case, to the most exalted literary circles of the Spanish Golden Age.

Albadán's Family and Early Life

Juan Bautista de Albadán was born in 1562 in Seville, the son of Diego de Albadán and Doña Ana de Jesús y Prado. The family lived in the elegant and prosperous neighborhood of La Magdalena, on San Vicente Street, near the Guadalquivir River (fol. 164r). Juan had two siblings: Francisco, who was two years older (fol. 51r), and Gerónimo, who was seven years younger and who would eventually emigrate to South America after Juan. Diego and his family were not newcomers to Seville; Diego's parents, Francisco Núñez de Canaleis and Doña Máxima de Prado, were citizens (*vecinos*) of Seville, as their son (Diego), grandson (Francisco), and great-grandchildren (Francisco's five children) would be.[16] Seville at this time was one of Europe's most rapidly growing urban areas, as people flocked to the city from elsewhere in Spain and from abroad to take part in the economic opportunities created by the trade with the Americas. In its century of expansion, the city grew from a population of 50,000 in 1530 to 150,000 by 1600; this spectacular growth was spurred by its trading monopoly with the Indies from 1503 onward. In that year, the Casa de Contratación (House of Trade) was founded in Seville to regulate all goods exported and imported.

Throughout the sixteenth and seventeenth centuries, the rhythm of life in Seville was dominated by the departure and arrival of the great transatlantic fleets, especially for a family like Juan's, as his uncle's fortune came from trade with Peru. The fleet departed twice a year, in spring and in late August. The city turned out en masse to watch as the harbor became a hive of activity: officials checked cargoes, ships were loaded with food and supplies, and sailors, emigrants, and missionaries prepared to sail away. The arrival of the fleet, after a crossing that could take between three and six months, sparked even more excitement. Precious cargoes were unloaded, loved ones were reunited, and news was exchanged as letters arrived from all parts of the Indies.[17] Reading through Juan's personal letters, one gains a sense of how transatlantic communication was regulated by the slow ocean crossings. For example, a typical letter to Juan from Fray Francisco, who was then living in Jerez, began, "Seeing that the fleet was in, I rushed to come here to Seville to write to you with greater ease and to respond to the three [letters] that I received from you."[18] A letter from Juan's brother Francisco in Seville to Gerónimo in Potosí, dated December 31, 1607, opened in a similar fashion: "In the galleons that just arrived . . . I received your [letter] and with it the kindness that you have shown me."[19]

Diego de Albadán was a scribe and a very successful commodities broker in the city.[20] Francisco referred frequently in his letters to the prosperity that the family enjoyed in his youth. He also commented often on their high social standing, speaking proudly of "our honorable surname, esteemed in this city as very noble and honored . . . it is very advantageous to be an Albadán . . . in the eyes of people of quality, it is well known [as] an Old Christian [name]."[21] Diego's high status was indicated by his membership in the Brotherhood of Mercy (Hermandad de la Santa Misericordia de Nuestro Señor Jesucristo) (fols. 57v–58r), one of the most exclusive confraternities in Seville; Francisco, who would inherit his father's place in it, claimed that it was the most "honorable" brotherhood in the entire city (fol. 58r). Founded in 1247 by King Fernando III, the confraternity administered an important hospital in the city that attended to the needs of the poor and the infirm. It also distributed food, including bread, meat, oranges, lemons, and wheat, to widows and the poor. The confraternity was famed for its role in the Holy Week processions in Seville, in which Diego would have taken part.

Francisco described his father as "deserving of good memories . . . of good nobility and papers."[22] When Francisco was a young man, Diego had insisted that he should not cheat himself by marrying for a large dowry (fol. 54r). One wonders whether this advice from Diego was based on his own assessment of his marriage to the wealthy Doña Ana. In his will, Diego had no word of affection whatsoever for his wife, but wrote very lovingly about his slave women, one of whom shared his wife's given name. At the time of his death, Diego owned three slave women who lived in the family house. Ana, a *mulata*, was an older woman and probably part of the household when Juan was still living in Seville. In his will, Diego freed Ana because she "had served me for many years with much love, good will, diligence, and care."[23] The other two women, Maria and Sebastiana, mother and daughter, were "captive slaves . . . of black color," meaning that they had come directly from sub-Saharan Africa. In his last testament, Diego expressed his "great love and good will" toward them "because of the fine service they have done for me" and asked his heir, Francisco, to treat them well.[24]

Seville was the center of the Iberian slave trade, and around 10 percent of the city's population consisted of enslaved men and women, who were branded and auctioned off on the steps of the cathedral.[25] Among prosperous households in Seville, it was considered normal for masters to have forced sexual relations with their female slaves of color.[26] The most common methods for punishing slaves included whipping, placing yokes on the neck, and "'dripping pork fat' or 'taper wax' onto the skin."[27] Juan probably witnessed slaves being disciplined with burning wax and fat, possibly in his own home by his father or mother. It seems to have been a clear model for how he would later torture Indians to death in the Peruvian countryside. Diego, despite his professions of love and affection for his slave women, may have disciplined Ana, Maria, and Sebastiana in this way. Diego passed away in 1604, when Juan had already been living in Pampachiri for several years. After Doña Ana's large and substantial dowry was returned to her from Diego's estate, the remainder of his wealth was divided equally among the three boys (fol. 49r–v). Juan, however, renounced his inheritance and gave it to his mother, perhaps hoping to win her good wishes (fol. 39r).

Doña Ana de Jesús y Prado, Juan's mother, had three brothers: Don Andrés Núñez de Prado, a wealthy merchant; Fray Francisco de Prado, a leading Mercedarian friar; and Fray Hernando de Prado, a Franciscan friar in Seville. Like her husband, her surname included the honorific "de," indicating high status. Apparently, in her youth, Doña Ana had shared a warm friendship with Francisco Gutiérrez Coca, her brother Andrés's business partner. In Gutiérrez Coca's letter to Juan dated March 22, 1608, in which he accepted the responsibility of sending Juan's large gift of 2,300 pesos to Doña Ana, he wrote, "This task is for me one of great sentiment and pain that I have had, and will have, because of how much I loved Doña Ana for her very noble and excellent demeanor, and the old and decent friendship that we had."[28] Gutiérrez Coca also referred to a tragic fall that Doña Ana had experienced in the past. This helps explain a comment by Francisco that his mother spent the last twenty years of her life bedridden, in considerable suffering and penance (fol. 53r). She died on January 6, Three Kings' Day, in 1608, which would place her fall in 1588, long after Juan had left for Peru, but before Gerónimo emigrated there.

What did Doña Ana think of her difficult son Juan? In many of Francisco's letters to Juan, he says that he does not want to anger his younger brother, or asks Juan not to get angry with him, suggesting that the Juan he grew up with was bad tempered and easily set off. Juan left for the Indies at the young age of fourteen—in Fray Francisco's words, "being exiled almost since you were born, away from your homeland and family."[29] Fray Francisco's use of the word "exile" implies an unwilling emigration to Peru on Juan's part. One of the letters from his older brother suggests that the young Juan had committed some atrocity or barbaric act that forced his family to get him out of Seville quickly. In his letter of April 1, 1604, Francisco reminisced about how the three brothers were once all together, but were now all separate: "as year follows year, I am in this place and of the three that we once were, I remain alone." He continued, "I feel very sorry that everyone who speaks about you is on their side and has so little forgiveness for you."[30] Although Francisco never specified what he meant by this, he seemed to be referring to a horrific act that Juan had committed and that people still remembered and talked about decades later. It appears that Juan's propensity for violence may not have developed suddenly in his years in Pampachiri, but may have been part of his personality from a young age.

Although she did not explain her actions, Doña Ana made her feelings about Juan clear in her will, dictated as she lay dying during the Christmas holidays in 1607 (fols. 162r–171v). In this document, she listed her considerable wealth, including 1,050 ducats of principal, 220 ducats of annual income from rent paid by the dukes of Medina Sidonia, and her furniture, jewels, and personal property.[31] After bequests to various churches and monasteries, she named her son Francisco as her primary heir, because of "the great love that I have for him."[32] She expressed no feelings at all for her two sons "in the Indies," Juan and Gerónimo. Gerónimo inherited roughly a third of her estate (202,287 maravedís, or 539.43 ducats; fol. 171r), but Juan received absolutely nothing, suggesting the depth of her estrangement from her middle son.

At the time of Doña Ana's death, she had not seen Juan for over twenty-nine years. According to the license allowing him to travel to Peru, Juan first left Spain for Peru in 1576, at age fourteen.[33] He traveled through the auspices of Don Andrés, accompanying his uncle's shipment of goods. Don Andrés's business brought Juan back to Seville very briefly the following year, and he left for Peru for the final time on December 3, 1578, at the age of sixteen. It is unknown how he supported himself in Peru between 1578 and 1591, but presumably Francisco Gutiérrez Coca, in Lima, assisted him. In the viceroyalty of Peru at that time, the only place where Juan could have prepared for the priesthood was in Lima. He must have attended either the Jesuit Colegio de San Pablo (founded in 1568) or the Jesuit-run Colegio Real de San Martín (founded in 1582), where he would have studied a humanistic curriculum of Latin and the arts (the famous *ratio studiorum* was not adopted by the Jesuits until 1599). Then he may have taken theology classes at the University of San Marcos in Lima and been ordained in either Lima or Cusco.[34]

In 1591, Juan was granted the doctrina of Kula and Chullisana in the Andahuaylas region for a salary of 50 pesos per year.[35] Given his peninsular status and powerful personal connections, this was a remarkably low-ranking benefice to give him; nonetheless, he was not able to keep it for long, for reasons that remain unclear. San Juan de Kula (Cula) and Chullisana (Chuliçana) are both near San Antonio de Cachi, a small municipality about 25 kilometers

(15 miles) from the city of Andahuaylas. In 1592, Gerónimo left Seville for Peru in hopes of staying with Juan until he found a job.[36] Gerónimo initially lived in Lima with Gutiérrez Coca (fol. 187v) and wrote to his brother from the capital, asking Juan whether he could come stay with him at his home in Kula. The two men had not seen each other since 1578, when Gerónimo was nine years old and Juan sixteen, yet Juan refused to allow Gerónimo to visit him in his new home. In a letter dated March 1, 1609, Gerónimo recalled this exchange: "and I remember when I came as a greenhorn to Lima, I wrote to you, I wanted to come up to Cusco to earn a living if you could help me with that, and you responded to me to not do that because you were poor, and you had no way of helping me because if I came, it would be where people will not see me. And I did as you wished."[37]

Juan clearly preferred that his younger brother stay away from his domain in Kula and Chullisana. Maybe he knew that in Kula the local people would refuse to help a relative of his, or maybe he was involved in activities that he wished to hide from his family members. In any event, Gerónimo left Lima for Potosí, where he eventually became a royal scribe in 1607, after many rough years enmeshed with prostitutes and other "vices of the land."[38] Even when Juan became wealthy in Pampachiri, he refused to allow Gerónimo to visit him, despite the younger man's repeated pleas.

It is unclear how long Juan remained in Kula; however, within a few years he appears to have been residing once again in Cusco, struggling to earn a living for himself without a benefice. Eventually he was able to acquire another benefice in 1601: the doctrina of Pampachiri, Umamarca, and Pomacocha, located more than 57 kilometers (35 miles) away from Andahuaylas, across very rugged terrain. A letter to Juan from Gerónimo suggests that the priest purchased the benefice illegally from the corregidor, José de Billela, for the sum of 100 pesos (fol. 85r). Around this time, Fray Francisco's close friend Fray Alonso de Monroy was made the vicar general for the Mercedarian province of Cusco.[39] Presumably, Juan visited with Monroy in Cusco, just as he would later visit family friend Fray Melchior de Porres in the city. Monroy, incidentally, seems to have angered local Mercedarians in the Cusco province while he was in Peru. According to Tirso, Monroy stripped the Cusco province of much of its wealth, which he spirited back to Seville under a false name.[40] Monroy and Fray Francisco used the wealth from Peru, Tirso explained, to rebuild the Mercedarian house in Seville with extreme opulence, commissioning fine art, gilded furniture, and every type of luxury, including one of the finest libraries in the city.

Albadán in Pampachiri

In Pampachiri, Albadán settled into the rectory, a plastered and painted adobe building near the church on the town square (fig. 7). He was friends with two of the priests in neighboring doctrinas—Francisco Peréz Ramírez in Soras and Juan Núñez de Ilescas Zambrano in Huayana—and visited with them on occasion (fols. 11v–15r). His jurisdiction covered Umamarca and Pomacocha as well, and he enjoyed a prominent residence on the village square in each of these communities. Pampachiri was the largest of the three towns, with a native population of about 1,341 people in 1604: 215 adult men of working age; 98 elderly men; 798 women; and 270 children. Umamarca was smaller, with around 872 indigenous inhabitants, while Pomacocha was the tiniest town, with a native population of only 349 people.[41] The gender imbalance in Pampachiri, which had 313 men and 798 women, was seen in the other two towns as well. Such a predominance of women was common in highland settlements, as adult men gave up their ancestral rights to the land in order to flee the tribute labor requirements (see chapter 7). However, there were able-bodied men in each community who hid from the royal inspector, so the actual number of men in each community, and the total population figures, would have been slightly higher.

The royal official Augustín Arce de Quiroz, who surveyed the region in 1604 and acquired these population figures, spoke to Albadán when passing through Umamarca. He asked Albadán to bring out the books in the church, along with Albadán's records of all the baptisms, marriages, and funerals that he had performed since arriving in the doctrina. According to Arce de Quiroz's account, Albadán simply said that he did not have them; he had not kept records of this information in the entire time he had been there.[42] The royal visitor did not add anything else to the record of his time in the doctrina, so apparently Albadán was not admonished for his lapse.

Albadán traveled on a gray mare, with his goods piled on a chestnut mule (fols. 15r–19v), as he journeyed from one community to the next. The horse was one of three that he took from the Indians Pedro Caquia, Luis Curiguaman, Alonso Condor, and Juan Ticllacuri, and for which he never paid. Martín de Soria, a local physician, witnessed how Albadán simply demanded the horses that he wanted without any hint of payment (fol. 112rv). Soria also testified that he saw Albadán take finely worked bridles and saddles from four Indians in Umamarca—Don Gerónimo Sivi Paucar, Juan Astao Cusi, Francisco Astao Sipa, and Cristiano Bascaya y Toco—again without paying for them (fol. 111r–v). Albadán was able to travel in style thanks to his theft from the local people.

FIG. 7 The Pampachiri church today. Photo by Christine Lee.

Although his annual salary in Pampachiri was among the lowest in the region, Albadán received free housing and donations of food from the local people. Unlike members of religious orders, secular priests—such as Albadán—do not take vows of poverty. Thus, they are allowed to keep any wealth that they inherit or otherwise acquire throughout their lives. Antonio Acosta Rodríguez has demonstrated how secular priests in colonial Peru engaged in a variety of businesses for their personal benefit.[43] In Andahuaylas, the clergy were supported by a combination of yearly salaries, which by 1613 were paid by the Crown, and goods given by the Indians under their care. The salaries were modest and varied from doctrina to doctrina; the following are the yearly salary levels determined by the Audiencia in 1613, which would have been virtually identical to levels in the previous years, when Albadán was there:

Andahuaylas = 80 pesos
San Jerónimo = 30 pesos
Talavera = 70 pesos

Huancaray and Turpo = 40 pesos
Kula and Chullisana = 50 pesos
Huayana, Ulcay, and Curamba = 40 pesos
Pampachiri, Umamarca, and Pomacocha = 40 pesos
Huancarama and Cotarma = 90 pesos
Ongoy, Piscobamba, Omaca, and Ocobamba = 35 pesos
Uripa, Cayara, Cocharcas, Mollepampa, and Uchupampa = 75 pesos[44]

The natives of each doctrina or parish in Andahuaylas were required to provide substantial foodstuffs for their priests. Every three months, the priest was given approximately 13 liters of chili peppers and 12 pounds of salt. Each month, he received 6 bushels of corn, 1½ bushels of wheat, 1½ bushels of potatoes, 1 sheep, and 1 pig. Once a week, the native parishioners contributed 12 birds to the priest's household. During Lent, the Indians had to provide him with 15 eggs and 2 pounds of fish per week. Finally, on a daily basis, the natives had to bring a large pitcher of beer (*chicha*) and firewood to the priest's house, along with fruit when it was in season.[45] It was the kurakas' responsibility to ensure that these products were delivered to the local priest. This could be a source of conflict between the two men, as priests at times accused the Indians of refusing to provide the necessary food. For example, in 1591, Father Fausto López claimed that the Indians of his doctrina, Kula, owed him over 40 cargas, or 8,000 pounds, of food![46]

In addition to the goods for his personal household, the priest collected tithes for the diocese from his indigenous parishioners. Yearly, the kurakas delivered livestock and crops to the priest, who transported these products to the dean of the cathedral chapter of the diocese. The dean then auctioned off these goods, and the money was turned over to the diocese. In 1613, the tithes from the Indians of the entire Andahuaylas region had a value of 1,390 pesos and 2 tomines;[47] by 1633, this number had increased to 1,850 pesos.[48] Beyond interactions related to spiritual issues, the priests and the kurakas communicated regularly about these economic matters, as the local kurakas oversaw the provision of household goods and tithes to the priests.

Albadán would have spent considerable time in his highland home collecting tithes, food, and other goods described by Guaman Poma, all too frequently through the horrific means ("games") also depicted by the chronicler. Testimony collected after Albadán's death reveals that he took time out to visit Cusco frequently, perhaps on shopping trips to buy the paintings, silver dishes and cutlery, tablecloths, books, and other items that graced his houses. For example, on October 17, 1611, an old family friend, Fray Melchior de

Porres, of the order of Our Lady of Carmel, testified that he met with Albadán many times in Cusco during the period that Albadán lived in Pampachiri. Fray Melchior, who was fifty-five years old, knew Albadán's brother Francisco in Spain, along with Francisco's wife and children; his regular meetings with Albadán reveal yet another way in which Albadán maintained his ties to his family in Spain (fols. 211r–212r).

While in Pampachiri, Albadán apparently enjoyed indulging in the finest wine that could be found in the town. The innkeeper in Pampachiri was a Basque named Domingo de Lersundi, from an ancient and noble family in Azcoitia.[49] In April and May 1611, Lersundi petitioned for 30 pesos—nearly Albadán's annual salary—from Albadán's estate to pay his wine bill. Lersundi and his witnesses, who included his servants Diego Tayplantay and Augustín Manta, testified that Albadán purchased expensive grape wine from Nasca and ordered it brought to his house. Once the wine was delivered, Albadán said that he did not have the money to pay for it and that the cost should be added to his tab (fols. 112v–122r). Incidentally, Diego Tayplantay, who testified that he had known Albadán in Pampachiri for over two years, was from Lucanas, Guaman Poma's homeland. He would have had abundant knowledge of the priest's activities in the town to share with the chronicler, both as an eyewitness and through hearing the accounts of others, such as his fellow servant Augustín, who had known Albadán in Pampachiri for over eight years.

Another witness, the local scribe Andrés Bravo, said that he often observed Albadán writing (fols. 121r–122r). The priest kept "a small book of accounts in his own hand and script,"[50] where he recorded debts. Albadán, who could not be bothered to record the births, marriages, and deaths of his parishioners, kept meticulous accounts of what they owed him. In fact, in the hundreds of pages of testimony about Albadán, the only writing of his that is preserved are three pages listing the small debts "owed" to him by forty-four natives in Umamarca (fols. 127v–129v). He would also have been busy composing letters to his relatives in Spain and South America. And it is likely that he spent time reading the books in his well-worn yet extensive library.

During Albadán's years in Pampachiri, he became quite wealthy, despite having no known means of generating income other than theft from the natives, as described by Guaman Poma. The plentiful documentation concerning his estate shows no evidence of industry or trade whereby he could have acquired wealth. Upon his father's death in 1604, he inherited over 500 pesos, but he gave his share of his father's estate to his mother (fols. 39r, 58v). Once he became prosperous, he sent large sums of money to his family members, including 2,300 pesos to his mother in 1608 (she passed away before these funds arrived in Spain), 1,379 pesos (1,000 ducados) to his brother Francisco the same year (fol. 75r), and 100 pesos (800 reales) to his uncle Fray Francisco; he also purchased a scribal office for his brother Gerónimo's friend (fols. 87v–90v). After his death, his belongings were auctioned off, and the value of his goods came to over 6,100 pesos (fol. 100r). His total estate, including the generous gifts that he bestowed, came to over 10,000 pesos, a fortune at that time. In today's terms, Albadán's estate would have been worth over 1,850,000 U.S. dollars—from a salary of 7,400 dollars annually.[51] The size of his estate suggests the scope of his thievery and the terror that he must have inspired among the native Chankas in the countryside to be able to rob on such a grand scale.

The amount of riches that Albadán acquired before his death was considerable, placing him among the wealthiest men in colonial Apurimac. The personal wealth possessed by secular priests in colonial Andahuaylas varied greatly. Some clergymen, such as Father Fausto López of Kula, lived fairly modestly. At the time of his death in 1591, this priest owned a chestnut-colored horse and an unbroken colt; a trunk with lock and key; twelve books, including his missal and breviary; a wooden table with benches; a mirror; two pairs of scissors; five pairs of eyeglasses; four cotton blankets; two hatchets for cutting firewood; two padlocks; three sieves; a sword; and thirty pesos.[52]

Some of the other clergy in the region throughout the colonial period, however, were wealthy landowners from prosperous creole families and were already rich before they became priests. For example, Father Luis Cardenas y Rojas, who served in Andahuaylas in the 1590s, owned the Roccha horse ranch on the outskirts of the city.[53] Years later, in 1660, the priest of Andahuaylas, Father Juan Alarcón y Valenzuela, paid 10,000 pesos in cash for the hacienda of Capacalla.[54] The property belonging to the priest of Talavera in 1591, Father Diego Sánchez Gordillo, included not only fields, land, and a house, but also a black slave named Marcos.[55] One of his successors to the benefice of Talavera, Father Lope de Mendoza, owned the hacienda of Moyoc in Talavera; the orchards, fields, and houses of Yungas in Talavera; the sheep ranch of Palca in Chicimbi; and extensive lands, houses, and a mill in Guamanga. In 1660, he bequeathed all of these properties to his young Indian nurse Francisca Miscua, "for having served him for a long time."[56] The vicar of Huancaray in the 1690s, Father Bartolomé Perez de Lodeña, owned the sugar plantation of Cotaguacho near Talavera.[57] In 1693, the priest of San Gerónimo, Father Francisco de Pedroza, possessed houses, fields, pastures, and baking ovens in San Gerónimo, which he granted to two orphans who, he claimed, had been left on his doorstep and whom he had raised from infancy.[58]

Throughout the eighteenth century as well, some of the large landowners in the region were priests. For instance, the curate of Huancarama, Father Bernardo de Aestre, purchased the wealthy sugar plantation of Pincos in 1712.[59] A priest, Manuel Navarro, owned the hacienda of Tancaillo in Uranmarca in 1726.[60] Father Ignacio Zapatero y Ocaña, the vicar of Ongoy, bought the hacienda of Llocllata in Huancaray from Doña Tomasa Aparco in 1756.[61] Another priest of the city of Andahuaylas, Father Francisco Xavier Alfaro, owned the sugar plantation of Carguayco in Ocobamba, which he rented to one of the vecinos of Ocobamba in 1784.[62] Four years later, the hacienda of Pochocota in Huancaray was purchased by the vicar of Huancarama, Father Ignacio Zapatero y Ocaña.[63] While the vast majority of the priests in the Andahuaylas region did not attain the status of hacienda owner, those who did exercised considerable power and influence. Chanka kurakas, ever in need of funds to meet their tribute obligations, borrowed money from wealthy clergymen, incurring financial obligations to them. Such indebtedness would have deepened the kurakas' responsibility to carry out the will of the local clergy, strengthening the priests' power over the local native leadership.[64]

Albadán and His Relatives

The letters to Albadán from his relatives allow us to flesh out the monster in Guaman Poma's work, showing him to be a member of a family, as well as a tormented man who yearned to put his life in Peru behind him but could not do so. It is quite rare for such a correspondence to have been preserved in a remote highland town in the early 1600s; it was highly unusual—if not unheard of—for a local administrator to enter full transcriptions of personal letters into a case. However, Don Alonso de Mendoza Ponce de León, the corregidor, seems to have had almost an obsession with Albadán. In the inventory that he prepared of the priest's papers on March 29, 1611, Don Alonso provided detailed summaries of all the letters—he clearly had read each one carefully (fols. 37v–40v). The corregidor's relatives moved in the same elite circles in Seville as did Albadán's family members,[65] and Don Alonso appears to have known of them, especially Albadán's mother, Doña Ana, and uncle Fray Francisco. Don Alonso, of course, had also been heavily indebted to the priest for years. After Albadán's death, he would push for the viceregal court to donate all of his estate to charity to "make amends" for the "pain" that Albadán had caused to "the kingdom" (fol. 196r–v). In any event, the letters were duly transcribed into the court documents.

The fullest correspondence occurred between Juan and his older brother, Francisco, in Seville. In Francisco's first letter in the collection (fols. 49r–51v), written on April 1, 1604, he apologized for not having written for a long time, but said that he was afraid of angering Juan by recounting the details of his life to him. He explained that he was forced to write now because of his financial difficulties, as the family had fallen into debt due to their mother's expenses. Francisco had had little success in business ventures; he was quite ill and feared leaving his little children behind in such poverty. In the letter, he hinted that Juan should renounce his share of their father's estate, which, in fact, Juan did. Francisco concluded by expressing his sadness that everyone still spoke ill of Juan and had little pardon for him. "I can say this to you as your older brother," he wrote, "although not by more than two years" (fol. 51v).

Francisco's next letter was written over four years later, on December 22, 1608 (fols. 53r–60v), and is sixteen pages long. In this long, rambling discourse, Francisco thanked Juan repeatedly for the priest's generosity to him and his family, and particularly for the money that Juan had sent to their mother, although she died before receiving it. He ascribed Juan's generosity to their saintly mother's prayers from heaven: "I think her good intercession moved your spirit to replenish my lack." Francisco did not explain that Juan had been cut out of their mother's will entirely, in Franciso's and Gerónimo's favor. Rather, he lied, writing that their wealthy mother had died with many debts; apparently, Francisco did not want to jeopardize Juan's generosity by angering him or by letting Juan know the extent of his inheritance. Francisco wrote movingly and at length about his own poverty, his lost prosperity, and the difficulty he had in trying to keep up their social position. "In this life," he stated, "[I have had] many calamities . . . burdened with a thousand unavoidable obligations, I have become old . . . in the house where there is want, everything is a war."[66] Most of the letter concerned two themes: being left out of his rich uncle Don Andrés's will,[67] and his large family, especially his daughters, who needed money for their dowries.

Francisco had expected that Don Andrés's death in 1607 would provide him a way out of his financial straits, but Francisco and his children received relatively little in the will. Don Andrés's legacy was mainly divided in half between his widow and his illegitimate son. Don Andrés also left a legacy to his brother, the Mercedarian Fray Francisco, who received a generous chaplaincy for life. Juan, Francisco continued, was his closest relative now; as he wrote, "I owe you more than my father . . . and I will pay you back somehow; with such gentlemanliness you gave me so much mercy . . . and great charity and service to God to help your nephews and nieces . . . you are my remedy!"

(fols. 58v–59r). Francisco went on to tell Juan about his children; he hoped that this would not make Juan angry, but since Juan was now like a father to him, and lived so far away, Francisco wanted to introduce the children briefly. Francisco's oldest living child was a son, Diego Tadeo de Albadán, fourteen or fifteen years old, dark and intelligent. He had already gone twice on a voyage to the Spanish Main and would like very much to get to know his rich Uncle Juan in Peru. There was also a twelve-year-old daughter named Doña Ana Marcelina, who was dark like her mother, possessed a lovely body, and had "the best eyes in this land"; a ten-year-old son named Juan, after his uncle in Peru; a thirty-month-old son named Gerónimo; and, finally, a three-month-old daughter named Maria Magdalena, after her mother, Doña Magdalena. As Francisco wrote, "[my wife] is in a time of multiplying because she is young."[68] In this letter, Francisco also explained that Juan's ten-year-old namesake was studying for the priesthood and would eventually take over the chaplaincy that Don Andrés left to Fray Francisco.

The final two letters to Juan from Francisco, written on February 20, 1609, and on December 8, 1609, cover many of the same themes as the previous epistle. Francisco expressed his gratitude repeatedly to Juan in extravagant terms: "I don't deserve the actions of such a brother, when I consider how little I've served you and your powerful hand that has done me such good, I judge that you are very much like Our Lord of whom you are a great imitator . . . I am not your brother but your slave, and I will say this as long as I live, and my wife and children will say the same . . . it is my good luck to have a brother who is a father, and the honor of all our lineage" (fol. 64r). There is much more in this vein, but this excerpt provides an idea of Francisco's language in these later letters. Francisco also complained harshly about Gerónimo (fol. 64v), who had not sent as much money to his family as Juan had, and who had actually needed money sent to him. Finally, in each of these letters, Francisco emphasized how much his oldest son, Diego, wanted to come to Peru to serve his Uncle Juan.

A letter written by Francisco's wife, Doña Magdalena de Castro, accompanied these letters of gratitude. On December 22, 1608, she penned a short note (fols. 68r–70r) to her brother-in-law, whom she had never met. She began by saying that since she was finally alone—her husband had gone out—she had the opportunity to write to Juan and beg him to accept her as a friend and servant. She expressed her gratitude to Juan for all that he had done for her and her children, adding that she would esteem him for her whole life. Doña Magdalena repeatedly asked Juan to come to Seville to live with them, where he could be happy: "life is spent in this place with the greatest peace in one's soul, although our estate is small."[69] She continued, "I would like for God to make me so happy by seeing you in this place; I think that you are so gentle and a good Christian."[70] The letter continues in this manner, its flow interrupted only by complaints about Don Andrés's unjust will and Gerónimo's stinginess and arrogance: "he thinks that by having the office of scribe he owns the whole world!"[71] Doña Magdalena concluded, "I consider your worth and Christianity [to be] very great, and thus I ask you to remember us and to not forget us nor our children, who are many."[72] It must have been very sweet for Juan to read and reread the praise heaped upon him by his sister-in-law and brother—well worth the money he sent to them.

Gerónimo's two letters to Juan, written in Potosí and dated March 1, 1609 (fols. 84v–87r), and September 30, 1609 (fols. 87v–91r), were likewise very flattering and complimentary. In the first letter, Gerónimo explained that he had stopped writing to Juan because he never got an answer to the many letters he had already sent. It was in this letter that he recalled how Juan had refused to allow him to stay with him in the highlands when Gerónimo first arrived in Lima in 1592. He expressed how much it hurt him that they were not close, and how eagerly he sought out information about Juan from people who knew him. He had heard from "some people who know you" how Juan was doing and that he was now very rich, although he had had to pay 100 pesos to the corregidor Billela, presumably for the benefice of Pampachiri.[73] In this letter, Gerónimo stated that there were "some evil reports" circulating about Juan.[74] He suggested that Juan buy the office of scribe for his friend Alonso Herrera, so that Alonso could counter these rumors. In the rest of the letter, Gerónimo referred to the depths of his own depravity and the "vices" that he had entertained before achieving the office of royal scribe. Now he lived with the corregidor and ate at his table, he said, but he would give it all up if only Juan would ask him to come to Pampachiri to serve him. "When I have tried, you have not wanted me to serve you [there]," he wrote. "I will do it better than strangers, whom you always treat well."[75]

The second letter, written five months later, begins with Gerónimo's expression of happiness over having received a warm letter from Juan and proof of Juan's generosity: "Lord brother, you would not believe the pleasure and contentment that I received with your [letter] that came by Alonso Herrera's hand, and for the mercy that you show to me in it."[76] Gerónimo's words imply that Juan did indeed provide funds ("mercy") for the purchase of an office for Herrera. Confirming this, a manuscript in the Archive of the Indies reveals that Alonso Nieto de Herrera was sworn in as "notary of the Indies" soon afterward, on March 22, 1610, in Charcas,[77] in a position that had to be purchased.

Most of this letter is dedicated to asking for Juan's permission to join him in Pampachiri, where Gerónimo would serve and obey him: "You will experience my will in things that are very difficult and to your pleasure."[78] Gerónimo clarified that he was not interested in Juan's money, since he possessed a healthy fortune of over 2,500 pesos himself; his only wish was to enjoy his brother's companionship. After repeatedly saying that he wanted only to live with Juan—"I will only be content if I am with you"—and serve him as his "best friend,"[79] Gerónimo again launched into the theme of his own debauched behavior. He wrote that in "this place I am [so involved] in trade with women and other things that it would shock you."[80] The "evil reports" about Juan's behavior that Gerónimo heard would have been similar to the stories that Guaman Poma reported in his chronicle. Knowing this, it is disturbing to read Gerónimo's letters, in which he expressed his desire to join in on Juan's games—"things that are very difficult and to your pleasure." Gerónimo's emphasis on his own debauchery seems intended to assure Juan that he did not condemn him, but rather sought to share in his vices.

The final series of letters consists of the aforementioned correspondence from Fray Francisco, to whom Juan wrote frequently and at great length. As discussed above, Juan penned a long, confessional letter that Fray Francisco received in March 1608, along with Juan's gift of 100 pesos (800 reales). In Fray Francisco's response (fols. 79r–81r), he begged Juan, "by the blood of Christ," to renounce his dream of returning to Spain; in Spain, Juan would have to live virtuously and earn an honest living, in contrast to his current situation in Pampachiri. Fray Francisco admonished his nephew to give up his "games" in Peru and to think about the fate of his soul, lest he be damned. He also asked Juan to help support his brother Francisco's children by sending dowries to the daughters, so that they could make honorable marriages.

Fray Francisco's second letter (fols. 82r–83v), dated February 3, 1609, was written in response to another letter from Juan—the lengthy account of Juan's unhappy exile "living with barbarians" in Pampachiri. In that letter, Juan had specifically requested that he be given the chaplaincy that Don Andrés had left to Fray Francisco. With this chaplaincy, Juan hoped to be able to give up his life in Peru and live peacefully in Spain. Fray Francisco simply told Juan that he could not do this; Juan had forgotten how things really were in Spain and would not be happy there. "But I do not want to say more," Fray Francisco continued, "because I do not speak to you to reprimand you, but to write to you about how God took Señor Andrés de Núñez de Prado, your uncle."[81] This was followed by a long discussion of Don Andrés's will and the brilliant marriage that Don Andrés's bastard son was able to make because he had inherited so much of his father's estate. Fray Francisco mentioned that his own brother Fray Hernando was living a saintly life in his monastery in Seville. Finally, he closed with the wish that Juan would write to him, because "it will be a great gift to me to know how you are . . . and anyway you live in a place where you have lots of time to write letters."[82]

Fray Francisco's final letter in the collection (fols. 77r–79r), written after September 1609, reiterated that Juan must "wake up from the dream in which he is living" and realize that his exile will not end. He will never see the skies of his homeland or "the greatness" of Seville again. In this same letter, Fray Francisco stated that Juan had made it clear that he did not want the "bother" and "annoyance" of having his nephew Diego Tadeo de Albadán living with him in Pampachiri. Fray Francisco would write to Diego, who was already in Brazil en route to Pampachiri, and tell him to return. The last half of the letter contained the latest news from Spain: the Moriscos had been expelled from the kingdom of Valencia, and all of the ports were choked with Morisco refugees seeking exile abroad. The edict of expulsion was published on September 22, 1609, and within three months 116,000 Moriscos were transported to North Africa.[83] Fray Francisco believed that they would be expelled from Castile and Andalusia soon—a prediction that proved correct. Thus, Juan's complaints about his involuntary exile from Iberia were voiced against a backdrop of forced expulsion of thousands upon thousands of people who would never see their homeland again.

These letters have a freshness and vivacity that can make it difficult to believe that they were written over four hundred years ago. It is interesting to witness the change in how Albadán's relatives addressed him as he became rich and sent money to them. His brothers Francisco and Gerónimo and his sister-in-law Doña Magdalena showered him with praise and flattery, sending wishes for his continued prosperity. Gerónimo probably best understood the extent of Albadán's atrocities, as he heard "evil reports" about what went on in Pampachiri. He is even likely to have heard descriptions of Albadán's activities that were too terrible for Guaman Poma to recount. It is chilling to read his eagerness to join Albadán, his boasting about his own depravity, and his readiness to obey his older brother in "very difficult" things. However, it is difficult to ascertain how much Fray Francisco knew about his nephew's actions. We do not know the extent of Albadán's self-disclosures in his letters to his uncle, in which he confessed "everything." Nor do we see the full extent of Albadán's self-justifications, although we are privy to his deep sense of self-pity for his lifelong exile. Fray Francisco, however, probably also heard stories about his nephew from his confreres who had been in Cusco. Mercedarians traveled between Spain and Cusco with regularity, and Albadán was certainly known among the Andalusian friars.

These letters reveal Albadán's deep ties to Spain, as well as give insights into his psychology. Through the words of his family and friends, we glimpse Albadán's misery, anger, and disdain for the Andean people around him. We read about his admission of his own viciousness, of his inability to live virtuously, of his sense of exile and deep longing for his homeland. "To be rooted," Simone Weil once wrote, "is perhaps the most important and least recognised need of the human soul."[84] Edward Said, in his essay "Reflections on Exile," suggests that the pain of involuntary exile is much deeper than is generally acknowleged. Unlike the émigré, who chooses to live in an alien land voluntarily, the exile experiences "an unhealable rift forced between a human being and a native place, between the self and its true home." Said criticizes the self-indulgent trope that characterizes all modern life as a form of exile: "Anyone who is really homeless regards the habit of seeing estrangement in everything modern as an affectation, a display of modish attitudes." The "essential sadness" of exile, Said opines, "can never be surmounted." The trauma of permanent homelessness may create a psychological state in which the exile "can make a fetish of exile, a practice that distances him or her from all connections and commitments." This was certainly true in the case of Albadán, who denied the humanity of those around him at its most fundamental level. Moreover, Said continues, "exiles are cut off from their roots, their land, their past. . . . [They] feel, therefore, an urgent need to reconstitute their broken lives. . . . The exile's new world, logically enough, is unnatural and its unreality resembles fiction."[85]

Albadán's unbalanced and mentally disturbed reaction to his exile consisted of extreme violence and a sadistic delight in sexually molesting and torturing the people around him. The following chapters will explore how he tried to reconstitute his world through his books and through his table. Part II will then turn to a consideration of the Chankas and how they were affected by Albadán and Spanish rule.

4. THE LIBRARY

In his novel *The Mysterious Flame of Queen Loana*, Umberto Eco imagines the life of a man whose knowledge of himself is reduced to only the books he has read. Giambattista Boldoni, an antique book dealer in Milan, suffers from a rare form of amnesia after a stroke. He cannot recognize his wife or daughters, and remembers nothing of his parents or his childhood, although he remembers every printed work that he has ever read. His entire sense of being is condensed to the library that he carries in his head of the books he has consumed throughout his lifetime. It is a conceit that many of us who love books share in a more modest form: What will people think of us when they view the books in our library? What do our books say about who we are as people? Do they reveal something essential, something hidden, about our innermost selves?

Albadán's library of sixty-two volumes was a collection of considerable size for his time and place.[1] Most of his books, according to the auctioneer's descriptions, were worn and well read, having been thumbed through many times. Books clearly played a key role in his self-identity, as he attempted to set himself up as a wealthy Spanish gentleman, cultured and generous. Albadán's uncle Fray Francisco de Prado built up the magnificent library of the Mercedarians in Seville,[2] and Albadán followed his example, albeit on a smaller scale. What books did he collect, and can they tell us anything about Albadán the man? How did Albadán's library contrast with the main form of literacy in the rural Andean highlands, which was primarily a notarial literacy? And how did his library compare to the books owned by other priests and landowners in seventeenth-century Apurimac? While there have been numerous studies of the colonial book trade in the cities of South America, much less has been known about the reading habits of people in the rural Peruvian highlands at this time.

Books in Seventeenth-Century Apurimac

Celebrated as the Golden Age of Spanish literature, the seventeenth century marks a high point of drama, novels, and poetry in the Iberian world. For example, one of the greatest works of Spanish letters, Miguel de Cervantes's classic novel of chivalry, satire, and romance *The Ingenious Gentleman Don Quixote of La Mancha*, was first published in 1605 (part 1) and 1615 (part 2), and its popularity grew rapidly as booksellers disseminated copies to the reading public. Men such as Tirso de Molina, Lope de Vega, and Pedro Calderón de la Barca wrote brilliant plays and novels mingling romance, comedy, and biting social commentary; these likewise became popular with the explosion of printing and literacy that accompanied the baroque age of Spanish literature.[3] Novels were widely enjoyed by men and women of the upper and middle classes, despite the efforts of some priests and churchmen to curb the general interest in romantic fiction. In Iberia, this era was noted for its flourishing literature; it was a time of cultural achievement that produced gems, like *Don Quixote*, that are still read and beloved today.

Likewise, in the urban centers of colonial Latin America, there existed a great desire for books from Europe, resulting in a vigorous trade in printed works in Lima and Cusco. Irving Leonard, in his classic *Books of the Brave*, demonstrated the thriving import trade in books from Spain in Lima throughout the sixteenth century. Chivalric romances, as well as more sober works of history and devotion, were regularly shipped to Peru, where they were sold in Lima or carried to Cusco and sold there. Leonard's research reveals the eclectic reading tastes of city dwellers in the South American colony.[4] In 1583, a Lima bookseller, Juan Jiménez del Río, drew up a list of 135 titles that he commissioned his buyer to purchase in Spain and bring back for sale in Peru; ordering multiple copies of many titles, this came to about 2,000 volumes. This list provides rare insight into the colonial literary tastes of Lima. As Leonard notes, of the 135 titles, only 44 percent are ecclesiastical works; 32 percent are nonreligious nonfiction works, such as histories, law manuals, and treatises on science and medicine; and 24 percent are fiction. The fiction read in Lima included classical literature, in this case Ovid, Cicero,

FIG. 8 The quiet man's library. From Alciato, *Los emblemas de Alciato traducidos en rhimas españolas* (1549). Glasgow University Library, SM32. By permission of the University of Glasgow Library, Special Collections.

Homer, and Vergil, along with chivalric novels by authors such as Amadís de Gaula, Belianis de Grecia, La Celestina, Lazarillo de Tormes, and Orlando; even Contreras's *Jungle of Adventures* (*Selva de aventuras*) was read, despite being on the Spanish Inquisition's index of prohibited books.

While religious orders and schools acquired significant libraries during this period, individuals purchased most of the books sold. Possession of a private library in seventeenth-century Latin America was the mark of being a learned and cultured man. The "emblem book" of Andrea Alciato, owned by Albadán, contains a charming illustration of a European gentleman in his study, surrounded by books. This image, intended to display the virtue of silence, also modeled a common ideal of the civilized life of the reader of books (fig. 8). The study containing Albadán's books probably looked similar to this illustration, although his floor would have been beaten earth and not tile. Albadán must have gone to considerable trouble and expense to purchase his books in Cusco and Lima; however, it is unknown whether he felt quite the same about them as a bibliophile from Aragón in 1519, who wrote in his will, "and no one should marvel at all the diligence I have taken over my books, because, according to my affections, they are worth more to me than all my other belongings."[5]

While Albadán's library was quite sizeable for the Andahuaylas region during the colonial period, the largest private library in the entire New World existed in the viceregal capital of Lima and was inventoried only thirty-seven years after Albadán's death. Francisco de Avila, the secular priest, missionary, and writer famous for his role in preparing the Quechua collection of myths known as the Huarochiri manuscript, owned a personal library of 3,108 volumes in his home in Lima.[6] Within this enormous collection were religious works (theological, patristic, homiletic, spiritual, and moral), legal tracts (canon law, civil law, and political), humanistic books (philosophy, history, and fiction), scientific works (medicine, mathematics, and natural science), and Americana. Although the religious works dominated the library, popular novels such as Ariosto's *Mad Orlando* also found their way onto Avila's shelves. Among Avila's Americana were numerous works specifically about Peru, including Garcilaso de la Vega's *Comentarios reales*, Pablo de Arriaga's *Extirpación de la idolatria*, and Fernando de Montesinos's account of the auto-da-fé celebrated in Lima on January 23, 1639, by the Spanish Inquisition, in which ten convicted Jews were burned at the stake.[7] The breadth of Avila's library gives insights into the intellectual richness that was potentially available in the Peruvian capital in the middle of the baroque era.

However, throughout Andahuaylas in the seventeenth century, in both the towns and the countryside, printed books were few and far between. Those printed books that did exist in the countryside, as we shall see, were almost exclusively in the hands of Catholic priests and clerics. Literacy was pervasive in the countryside, but it was a notarial literacy reflected in handwritten documents such as deeds, wills, court orders, and marriage contracts, assisted by scribes and notaries. Angel Rama once famously distinguished between "la ciudad letrada," the "lettered city"—the concentration of men in urban colonial Latin America who wielded dominion over the official channels and instruments of communication—and the rural backwater that was left without access to literacy and the power it commanded. Yet Kathryn Burns, in her study of colonial notaries in Cusco, has revealed that a wide array of people from the countryside came to rural urban centers such as Cusco to use the services of notaries, thereby joining in on the benefits of literacy. As she writes, "the world of literacy extended well beyond those who were in technical command of its forms. Through what [Armando] Petrucci calls 'delegated writing,' notaries' workshops were the gateway through which others made their way into the record, the courts, the archives."[8]

Just as tellingly, Frank Salomon and Mercedes Niño-Murcia have documented how fully the indigenous Andean peasantry engaged with literacy in the countryside in the colonial period. Even today, remote communities throughout the central Peruvian highlands conserve bundles of colonial-era documents created by their ancestors. These administrative papers include account books, receipts, land boundaries, church inventories, and other sorts of notarized manuscripts, often carefully bound in goatskin for protection.[9] The literacy seen in handwritten Spanish-language accounts and notarial texts flourished throughout the rural Andes in the seventeenth century. Bills of sale, land titles, dowry agreements, censuses, baptismal records, and indulgences are just a few of the types of handwritten documents that represent the rural literacy of Andahuaylas during that time. The Chanka kurakas were heavily involved in the production of notarial documents in the late sixteenth and early seventeenth centuries. These leaders commissioned censuses and visitations of their people; lodged complaints against corrupt administrators and priests; and dictated and signed marriage contracts, dowry agreements, and wills (see chapters 7 and 8).

There is no direct evidence that the Chankas, including the people of Pampachiri, also kept *khipus*—the system of multicolored, knotted cords used by the Andeans to record information (fig. 9). However, khipu records were still created and maintained in neighboring areas at that time.[10] For example, on the Maldonado hacienda outside of Cusco, native workers kept khipu records of the loads of maize, chaff, and salt produced on the hacienda annually, along with the amounts subtracted for tithes and the prices at which each load was sold. In 1614, the owner of the estate, Juan Arias Maldonado, sued his administrator Juan de San Pedro, charging that the latter had been cheating him out of profits.[11] In the course of the trial, the four native khipu makers (*khipukamayuq*) on the estate—Lorenzo Astuya, Diego Cusirimache, Diego Tantacache, and Juan Guara Guanca—read pertinent information off of their khipus, covering the economic data as well as details about the weather for the years 1604 to 1613. Similar scenes played out in other trials in the colonial highlands, where khipu testimony was read in court.[12] Recent radiocarbon evidence has revealed that many of the khipus extant today date

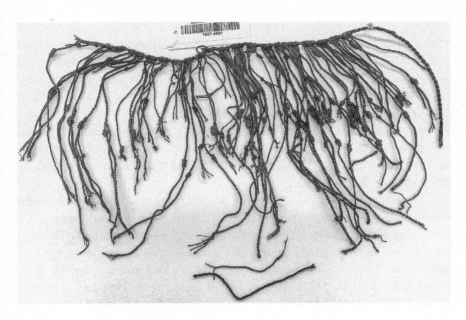

FIG. 9 Andean khipu. Yale University Art Gallery, 1937.4591.

to the Spanish colonial period, suggesting that Andeans continued to use khipus throughout the Andes during that time.[13]

Whereas wealthy and middle-class individuals in colonial Lima owned printed books, wealthy elites in the countryside appear not to have done so. When one reads through the wills of wealthy and not-so-wealthy landowners from the Andahuaylas region in this era—highly detailed documents that list each and every item owned by the deceased, whether a blanket, a leather chair, a piece of crockery, or a pair of scissors—it is rare for a printed book to be mentioned. For example, when every item from the Yaramay hacienda in Huancarama was auctioned off in 1694, there were no printed books among the landowner's belongings. Yaramay was a moderately wealthy sugar plantation that boasted one house, two sugar fields, a building with two cauldrons for processing sugar, a mill, a potter's workshop, eighteen horses, and ten mules. Among the lists of household items—beds, chairs, linens, blankets, and so forth—there were three paintings, including a portrait of the owner, and a chest filled with documents; yet there were no books.[14]

The dearth of printed books in the Yaramay inventory is typical of landowner inventories and wills. When books *are* mentioned in landowner inventories from seventeenth-century Apurimac, it is always in conjunction with a chapel on the estate. If a sugar plantation was wealthy enough to have its own chapel, a missal was usually mentioned as part of the chapel's furnishings. This was the case for the extensive hacienda of Pincos in Huancarama, for instance. The chapel there, inventoried in 1700, contained a copper bell, eight religious paintings—including a five-foot image of Christ crucified—richly dressed statues of the Virgin of the Purification and of Saint Anthony, and priest's vestments of purple damask, in addition to a printed missal to be used in saying Mass.[15] No other book is mentioned among the household belongings of the hacienda.

Wills of wealthy merchants, of indigenous elites, and of other secular individuals reveal the same paucity of printed books. For example, when a rich merchant named Francisco López died in Andahuaylas in 1679, the court inventoried all of his goods so that they could be turned over to his heir, his natural son Andrés, who was still a minor. In the long and detailed list of his belongings, many of which were imported from Spain, there are no printed books.[16] The same is true of the wills of indigenous elites such as the native nobleman Don Fernando Naucayalli, governor and cacique of Cayara. Born in the seventeenth century, Don Fernando dictated his will as an old man in 1725, signing it in his own hand. As an upstanding Christian, he stated that he wished to be buried in the shrine to Our Lady of Cocharcas near Andahuaylas. His will lists all of his goods, from his fields, to his oil paintings of Saint Cajetan, the Virgin, Saint Peter, and Saint John, to his hat of white vicuña wool, to an old blanket; again, however, no printed books are listed, not even a devotional manual.[17]

One might suppose that perhaps printed books were simply ignored when notaries and auctioneers made out wills and death inventories, but that would not be correct. In addition to appearing in chapel inventories, printed books were included in the personal wills of priests. While it was rare for a priest to possess as many books as Albadán did, printed books nonetheless appear to have been the domain of Roman Catholic priests in rural Apurimac.

Even the humblest Catholic priest in colonial Apurimac owned at least a missal and a breviary. Weak-eyed Father Fausto López of Kula, who died in 1591 owning little more than the clothes he wore and a broken-down horse, left behind twelve books, including his missal and breviary, along with five pairs of eyeglasses for reading them.[18] The missal—a liturgical book containing all of the readings and instructions necessary for saying Mass throughout the year—is the priest's guide for public worship. The breviary, on the other hand, is his guide for his daily private prayers—the hymns, psalms, prayers, and readings that he is obliged to read throughout the day as part of his daily Liturgy of the Hours. Together, the two books form a powerful model and explanation of sacred time, one that every Catholic priest would have needed to know and to communicate to the Indians in his doctrina. Father Fausto's other books included a volume of Aquinas; the collected works of the fifteenth-century Dominican theologian and historian Saint Anthony of Florence; all of the Quechua-language catechetical works published by the Peruvian council of bishops; and two more small breviaries.

Most secular priests in Andahuaylas had similarly small, though sometimes slightly larger, libraries. For example, licenciado Don Pedro Berrocal y Valenzuela, the priest in the town of Talavera (now a suburb of Andahuaylas), possessed a collection of twenty-five books, "some large and some small," at the time of his death in 1687. He also owned a small, colorfully painted wooden writing desk, inside of which were a "handful of papers," including vouchers for 175 indulgences purchased by Don Felipe Topa Guasco, the kuraka of the Upper Chanka..[19] Don Felipe would have been forcibly obliged to sell these indulgences to the Indians under his care, to remit the eternal punishments for their sins.

Only one priest in the Andahuaylas region in the seventeenth century owned a library that rivaled that of Albadán—Father Joseph de Vargas, priest of the wealthy neighborhoods of San Gerónimo on the outskirts of the city of Andahuaylas.[20] Scion of a wealthy and noble creole family that owned farms and property throughout Andahuaylas, Father Joseph was a leading citizen of Andahuaylas and its environs. Before he was priest of San Gerónimo, he was in charge of the parish of Talavera, home of Don Pedro Berrocal y Valenzuela. Father Joseph built the church in Talavera and granted it, along with all of its internal furnishings, to the town as a gift.[21] The church, a solid stone building with a large bell tower and a charming inner courtyard garden, is still used for Mass today.

Over sixty years after Albadán's death, Father Joseph owned a library of fifty-one volumes, or thirty-one different titles. Of these thirty-one titles, only three were nonecclesiastical: two calendars, a book detailing the privileges of the Vizcayan nobility of Spain, and the Latin dictionary compiled by Ambrogio Calepino in two volumes.[22] All of the other volumes treated religious topics of one kind or another. There were, for example, numerous books on Jesuit theology and scriptural commentary, including *The Metaphysics* by Francisco Suarez, SJ; the *Summula casuum conscientiae* by

Antonio Escobar y Mendoza, SJ; *The Moral Commentary on the History of the Gospels* by Diego de Baeza, SJ; *The Itinerary That a Man Must Take to Get to Heaven* by Alfonso de Andrade, SJ; *On the Difference Between the Temporal and the Eternal* by Juan Eusebio Nieremberg, SJ; and *Disputations Concerning the Sacrament of Marriage* by Thomas Sánchez, SJ. Twenty-five percent of the titles in Father Joseph's library were written by Jesuit authors; presumably he had close ties to the Jesuits, perhaps having been educated at their school in Lima. There were also two historical works: *The History of the Pontiffs* by Gonzalvo de Illescas and *The Ecclesiastical Monarchy, or Universal History of the World* by Juan de Pineda. Most notable are Father Joseph's four collections of sermons in twelve volumes: (1) sermons for Lent by the Franciscan Gabriel de Rivera; (2) sermons on the Gospels by Saint Peter Chrysologus ("Golden Word"); (3) nine volumes of sermons by Manuel de Nájera, SJ, professor of sacred scripture at the University of Alcalá; and (4) sermons on the Gospels for Lent by Cristóbal de Avendaño, preached before the Royal Court in 1626. Father Joseph expended no small energy and expense acquiring these volumes, which would have provided him with sermon models of the highest caliber. His parishioners in rural Peru could hear sermons modeled on homilies delivered in the royal court of King Philip IV and his queen consort, the beautiful and popular Elisabeth of France. The early church father Chrysologus, famed for his golden speech and brevity, apparently inspired other sermons, as did the works of Manuel de Nájera, the erudite biblical professor from Alcalá. If we take his library as an indication of his interests and aspirations, we can assume that Father Joseph's sermons rang out from his pulpit in the remote Andean highlands with eloquence and learning.

Father Joseph's library contained only three books on American themes: the decrees of the Council of Lima;[23] the life of Saint Rose of Lima;[24] and a Spanish/Quechua devotional manual from 1641.[25] The Third Lima Council in 1583[26] set the basic legislation for the Roman Catholic Church in the Andes throughout the colonial period, so the appearance of its decrees in the library is not unexpected. Saint Rose of Lima (1586–1617), a quiet mystic and lay Dominican from Lima, was the first person born in the Americas to be recognized as a saint by the Catholic Church. This shy girl served as a powerful icon of the emerging creole identity in Peru, the class to which Father Joseph belonged.[27] Father Joseph's final book of Americana—the Spanish/Quechua devotional manual composed and translated by the Jesuit Father Pablo de Prado—was one of the more elaborate works of catechesis for Indians prepared in colonial Peru. This book contains Quechua translations of the standard catechetical materials, such as the Lord's Prayer, the Ten Commandments, the act of contrition after confession, sermons, and so forth. However, it also includes lovely litanies in Quechua, as well as a lengthy section of Quechua devotional songs composed by Jerónimo de Oré in 1598 and an original Quechua composition by Prado in honor of the crucified Christ.[28] This single volume would have provided Father Joseph with all of the basic Quechua texts necessary for ministering to the indigenous Chanka population in San Gerónimo and Talavera.

From his sermon collections to his bilingual catechism, Father Joseph's books included an emphasis on pastoral care, as befitting a man who generously donated a portion of his personal wealth to building the church that still stands in Talavera today. It is worth noting that his library also contained books emphasizing religious tolerance. Among his thirty-one titles was Erasmus's unyielding defense of religious toleration *Apology Against the Spanish Monks* (1527).[29] Juan de Pineda's *Universal History of the World* is famous for its glorification of Jews and Christians of Jewish descent; Pinedo argued that such individuals "without a doubt were from the greatest lineage of the world," having descended from the house of Israel, Abraham, Isaac, and Jacob, and been linked to the lineage of Christ himself. The toleration expressed in these works speaks well of their owner. As we shall see below, Albadán's library, while containing some great works of literature, such as Horace, Juvenal, and Garcilaso de la Vega (El Inca), also hosted books by writers of a very different ilk.

Albadán's Library

Albadán's library of 62 volumes, or 50 separate titles,[30] included some of the works that we've encountered elsewhere in seventeenth-century Peru: the ubiquitous breviary and missal; reference works such as dictionaries and calendars;[31] and solid tomes of scholastic theology. Among the latter, Albadán owned works by the Dominicans Saint Thomas Aquinas and Bartolomeo Fumus (d. 1545), by the Franciscan theologians Miguel de Medina (1489–1578) and Luis de Carvajal (1500–1548?), and by King Henry VIII of England. Henry's polemical work against Luther, *The Defense of the Seven Sacraments*, written before the king's break with Rome, was popular throughout Catholic Europe, going through numerous editions in Latin.

The Spanish priest also possessed an edition of the *Epistles* of Saint Jerome, the fourth-century hermit, theologian, and translator whose letters seem remarkable today for their vitriol against women and women's sexuality. These letters repeatedly devalue women; Saint Jerome "constantly paints pictures of the worthlessness of a woman's life."[32] For him, the only possible value that a woman could have was in her virginity. Women who were unchaste, who lost their virginity outside of marriage, merited disgrace and punishment. Saint Jerome's viewpoint was not uncommon in the cultural world of colonial Iberia, although he was one of the most vituperative exponents of such opinions. When Albadán forced the young girls of Pampachiri to disrobe and peered at their private parts, was he examining them for what he perceived in his tortured mind to be their lapses against virtue? It is, of course, impossible to say. Young women in the pre-Columbian Andes considered it normal to enjoy sexual relations before marriage; the Jesuit chronicler José de Acosta explained acidly, "Except for the virgins consecrated to the Sun or the Inca (the *aclla*), all other women are considered of less value when they are virgin, and thus whenever possible they give themselves to the first man they find."[33] Perhaps Albadán did justify his behavior to himself as punishment for the young women's real or imagined lack of chastity. In any event, he maintained a clear enough sense of his own wrongdoing to try to hide his misdeeds.

Helping Albadán in his efforts to evade criminal prosecution in ecclesiastical courts, his library boasted the *Practica criminalis canonica* by Juan Bernardo Diaz de Luco, the bishop of Calahorra. This work, first printed in 1581, quickly became the standard reference on the criminal aspects of canon law in Spain and Spanish America. It provided detailed descriptions of how bishops and other Church authorities, most notably the Holy Office of the Inquisition, investigated priests' crimes. The *Practica criminalis canonica* also outlined the range of punishments that the Inquisition and bishops could mete out to convicted clergy. Unfortunately, however, this seems not to have deterred Albadán from his acts of brutality against the people of Pampachiri.

Albadán possessed the decrees of the Council of Trent, the mid-sixteenth-century Church council that reformed earlier Church practices and laws. This legal reference book was common; a copy of Trent's decrees existed among Father Joseph's books in San Gerónimo, for example. Another of Albadán's legal works, the *Práctica criminal* by Juan de Robles in seven volumes, was not commonplace in the New World, however. Juan de Robles (1492–1572), a Benedictine abbot from the Monastery of San Vicente in Salamanca, was a Spanish reformer known for the hard line that he took toward the poor.[34] At a time when there was considerable controversy in Spain about how to deal with the indigent, Robles's primary concern was with the maintenance of public order. He believed that begging should be made illegal and that those who gave alms to beggars should be punished. The poor, he advocated, should be forcibly detained in public hospitals, so that their presence would no longer inconvenience the public. Robles's writings reveal little sympathy for the poor, whom he saw as responsible for the spread of disease and sexual immorality.

Apart from these rather grim tomes about social problems and canon law, Albadán appears to have enjoyed works of visual puns and artistry. He owned two "emblem books," one by Andrea Alciato, first published in 1531, and the other by Sebastián de Covarrubias Orozco, published in Madrid in 1610.[35] Emblem books are books of images, usually representing clever wordplay, with a moral lesson attached.[36] There was a rage for emblem books in Europe throughout the sixteenth and seventeenth centuries. Alciato's *Emblemas* was the first of the genre ever produced. It consisted of a series of "emblems," each of which comprised three parts: a motto, a corresponding picture, and a brief poem illustrating the theme represented by the other two elements. The meaning of the trope—the object of the sign—should be neither too obvious nor too obscure; there should be an air of mystery about the emblem, but it should be resolvable in the end. For example, emblem 18 in Covarrubias's *Emblemas morales* shows a pair of eyeglasses with multiple planes of glass (fig. 10). The poem underneath the image explains that the glasses make a hundred things out of one, just as false opinions do. The next page explains the image and the poem in greater detail, stating, "Truth does not have more than one face; it is always one, and it is firm, although it suffers a thousand adversities caused by calumnies and lies. The Gentile Philosophers went around to seek for this truth, and could not find it, not having known the true God, who is the ultimate truth. And thus they divided into different sects and opinions."[37]

One of the most intriguing aspects of the emblem books of the early modern world is that their designs became used in all facets of personal and architectural decoration. The images from these works "were painted, carved and etched both onto decorative objects, such as tankards and furniture, and in architectural spaces, including churches, town halls, manor houses and hospitals."[38] Albadán's emblem books may, in fact, help solve one of Pampachiri's great mysteries: the source of the strange erotic images surrounding the doorway of the village's colonial Catholic church. On either side of the large wooden door are larger-than-life carved stone statues of naked women, one standing on top of the other (fig. 11).

CENTVRIA. I.

OBRAS·SON·DE·LA·VERDAD
COM

EMBLEMA. 18.
Los antojos de lunas quadreadas,
De vna sola cosa, hazen ciento,
Todas, tan igualmente pareadas,
Que echarle mano, a de ser a tiento:
Las falsas opiniones, disfraçadas
Al no aduertido, sacaran de tiento,
Representando por verdad constant.
La mentira, que engaña al mo ate.

FIG. 10 Emblem 18 (front).
From Covarrubias Orozco,
Emblemas morales (1610).
Glasgow University Library.
By permission of the University of Glasgow Library,
Special Collections.

The caryatids on the bottom are bare-breasted and wear flowing skirts, in a manner vaguely similar to the later depictions of sirens on Andean churches from the eighteenth and nineteenth centuries. The women standing on top are completely naked; one has her hands clasped to her chest, while the other clasps her hands in front of her. Each woman stands on an elaborate platform of rectangular and circular forms and has oddly shaped designs above her head. Images of bare-breasted sirens occur occasionally in churches as representations of sinfulness, but never in prominent positions such as this; nor does one find images of completely naked women as church portals. In contrast to the Pampachiri statues, the later Andean caryatids usually have fish tails—reflecting legends about fish-women thought to live in Lake Titicaca—or are fully clothed.[39] Local people and visitors frequently speculate about the origin of the strange imagery in Pampachiri. Yet it is very

FIG. 11 Entrance to the
Pampachiri church. Photo
by Christine Lee.

similar to the borders in Covarrubias's emblem book. In fig. 11, the border consists of a bare-chested woman dressed in a flowing skirt on each side of the image. Fig. 12 (emblem 19) features naked figures, one standing on top of the other. In fig. 13 (emblem 25), a naked woman wearing only a fig leaf stands shyly on a pedestal, with an elaborate architectural motif above her head, on either side of the image.

Borders are similar to doorway portals; they both mark the boundaries where one passes through to another state or reality. It appears that Albadán, under whose supervision the Pampachiri church was decorated, chose these emblem book borders as his models for the church exterior.[40] It was common practice to use emblem book images in this way, although it was quite unorthodox to select anonymous naked women for such prominent decorations on the exterior of a Catholic church. The modeling of the Pampachiri

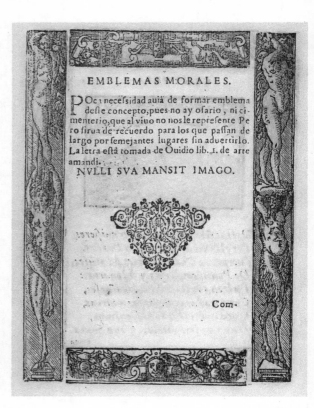

church sculpture is much cruder than that of the engravings in the emblem books. However, according to Guaman Poma, Albadán tortured to death the artist he had hired to work on the church. Perhaps the priest was forced to rely on the services of a less talented artisan because he had murdered the more skilled sculptor.[41]

Not only does Albadán's library reveal his delight in clever imagery, but it also shows his love of classical and Renaissance literature. Among his volumes we find the *Epistles* of Angelo Poliziano (1454–1494), the gossipy and romantic letters of one of the greatest scholar-poets of the Italian Renaissance. Poliziano's letters provide an intimate glimpse into the world of Renaissance Florence, from the pen of a man who was the friend, protégé, and possibly lover of Lorenzo de'Medici. Another classical work in Albadán's library was *Aesop's Fables* in Latin. These charming stories, short and unaffected, featuring talking creatures and plants and always ending in a moral, were very

FIG. 13 Emblem 25 (front).
From Covarrubias Orozco,
Emblemas morales (1610).
Glasgow University Library.
By permission of the University of Glasgow Library,
Special Collections.

popular throughout the Middle Ages and Renaissance. In fact, their popularity was so great that numerous authors wrote new sets of fables, while still attributing them to Aesop.[42] By the early seventeenth century, there were many different editions of Aesop's fables, each containing different tales. Without more information about a publisher or editor, it is impossible to know which fables Albadán may have amused himself with while reading in his house in Pampachiri.

Albadán also seems to have had a fondness for Roman satire, owning the works of both Horace and Juvenal. Given Guaman Poma's depictions of Albadán's crimes, the priest may well have enjoyed reading Juvenal's descriptions of Roman decadence, perhaps deriving a perverted inspiration from the satirical portraits of upper-class cruelty. Satire XIV, for example, portrays the sadism of a patrician named Rutilis; the verse's reference to "seared flesh" is an all-too-appropriate description of Albadán's treatment of Indian men:

Does he hold that slaves are fashioned, body and soul, from the same
Elements as their masters? Not on your life. What he teaches
Is sadism, pure and simple: there's nothing pleases him more
Than a good old noisy flogging, no siren song to compare
With the crack of the lash. To his quaking household he's
A monster, a mythical ogre, never so happy as when
The torturer's there on the job, and some poor wretch who's stolen
A couple of towels is being branded with red-hot irons. What
Effect on the young he must have, with his yen for clanking chains,
For dungeons, and seared flesh.[43]

The homoeroticism evident in Albadán's tortures, as described by Guaman Poma, may have also found a reflection in Juvenal's works. Although homosexuality was strictly condemned in colonial Peru, two of Juvenal's satires (II and IX) focus on the prevalence of homosexuality in the classical world. Juvenal paints an image of Rome in which male homosexuality was common, describing anal sex between men with a bluntness shocking even to modern sensibilities. Juvenal's intention, of course, was to condemn homosexuality, along with the multitude of other so-called perversions he encountered in Rome. Who can say how his satires may have appeared to the mind of a madman? It almost seems as if Albadán adopted the negative aspects of Juvenal's satires as a model for living, instead of viewing them as condemnations of behavior to be deplored.

Americana was well represented in Albadán's library. Seven out of the fifty titles, or 14 percent of the total, were books on the Americas. The first was an unusual book for Peru: the *Itinerarium Catholicum, or Catholic Itinerary for Missionaries Who Go to Convert the Infidels* by Juan Focher (Seville, 1574). Focher (Jean Foucher) was a French Franciscan who spent most of his adult life in Mexico. This work, edited by Focher's native disciple Diego Valadés, describes how to administer the sacraments to indigenous Mexicans; it contains sermons in the native languages, as well as twenty-eight pages describing the Chichimeca people of Mexico. It is most notable, however, for presenting an impassioned justification for Spain's war against the Chichimeca, which raged from 1550 until 1590.[44] In the early 1570s, Viceroy Enríquez de Almansa hosted a series of debates about whether to end the war against the Chichimeca; Focher was the leader among those who called for prolonging the war. In this book, he reiterates his arguments about the need to subjugate native peoples militarily. While he presents unique ethnographic data, Focher is not overly sympathetic to indigenous society, nor does he value the peaceful conversion of Amerindians to Christianity. One suspects that Albadán would have been a receptive audience for such opinions.

The second work of Americana in Albadán's library is not known to have existed elsewhere in South America at this early date. The inventory of his goods lists the *Libro tercero de los retablos de Testera*—that is, the *Third Book of Testera's Images*. This book would have presented the type of visual puns and wordplay developed in Mexico in the sixteenth century and frequently attributed to the Franciscan friar Jacobo de Testera. Pictographic catechisms use symbols and rebus writing or visual puns to represent prayers and basic Christian doctrine. For example, a full or half circle indicates heaven. To represent the phrase "Pater noster" (Our Father) for a Nahuatl-speaking audience, the catechism depicted an image of a banner—*pantli*—and a nopal fruit—*nochtil*.[45] Only thirty-five pictographic catechisms from Mexico are known to exist today, all produced between the sixteenth and eighteenth centuries, and none have been found in Peru. In Peru and Bolivia, a particularly Andean form of pictographic catechism developed in the nineteenth century, but its symbols are distinct in many ways from those of its earlier Mexican predecessors.[46]

The Spanish priest also possessed works related to Peru. Like Father Joseph de Vargas, Albadán had a volume containing the decrees of the Third Lima Council, which laid the canonical foundation for the Roman Catholic Church in the colonial Andes. Unlike Father Joseph, Albadán also owned a copy of the *Royal Commentaries of the Incas*, the eloquent account of Inka Peru penned by the famous mestizo Garcilaso de la Vega, son of the Spanish aristocrat Sebastián Garcilaso de la Vega y Vargas and the royal Inka princess Palla Chimpu Ocllo. Although no date is given for the book in the inventory, Albadán would have owned the first part, on Inka life and customs, published in 1609; the second part of the *Royal Commentaries* was not published until 1617. The *Royal Commentaries* presents a highly positive view of the Inka Empire, one that Garcilaso learned from his mother's royal relatives as they looked back with nostalgia on the world destroyed by the Spanish conquest of the Inkas. If he read this work, Albadán would have learned about the Inkas' worship of the Sun God in the Sun Temple—Coricancha—in the Inka capital of Cusco. Garcilaso recounted in some detail how the beautiful Virgins of the Sun cared for the golden image of the Sun God in Coricancha. He also described the worship of the Sun God by the Inkas in their major festival of Inti Raymi, during the winter solstice in June.

Additionally, Albadán owned three bilingual catechetical works in Spanish and Quechua: (1) a catechism; (2) a guide to hearing confessions;

and (3) a sermon collection. The Third Lima Council, held in 1583, had produced all three of these works to assist with the Christianization of the Andean people. It was not considered sufficient for the natives to renounce their local gods and to undergo the rites of baptism, confirmation, marriage, and so forth. The theologians of the Third Lima Council, such as the Jesuit José de Acosta, inspired by the humanism of sixteenth-century Spain, wanted to ensure that Andeans had an intellectual and heartfelt understanding of their new faith. Therefore, the Council went to extraordinary lengths to prepare substantial bilingual catechetical materials—one set in Spanish and Quechua, and another set in Spanish and Aymara—for distribution throughout the Andes.[47]

The sermon collection *Tercer catecismo y exposición de la doctrina christiana por sermones* (1583) comprised thirty-one sermons covering the basic tenets of the faith, the sacraments, the commandments, prayer, death, and judgment, all in Spanish and translated into Quechua by a team of skilled linguists. The first sermon begins with the affectionate Quechua phrase "Greatly beloved sons of mine" (Ancha munascay churiycuna), translated as "My very beloved brothers" (Hermanos míos muy amados); the words "beloved sons of mine" (munascay churiycuna) are terms of endearment repeated throughout the Quechua texts. The first sermon reminds its native listeners that those who are good will enjoy eternal rest, while the wicked will suffer. Amid the sermons on standard Christian doctrine, sermon 18 exhorts the Andean people to cease worshipping the sun, explaining, "Listen: the sun is not God, but only a creation of God" (Uyari: intica manam Dioschu, Diospa rurascanmi) and "The sun does not feel, does not think, does not recognize anything, and does not know anything" (Intica manam animayocchu, manam yuyayniocchu, manatac ymactapas riccinchu, imaytapas yachanchu).

Albadán, Father Fausto López, and Father Joseph de Vargas all possessed Quechua-language sermons and other catechetical works, but how were these texts actually used in the countryside? We don't know about Fathers Fausto and Joseph, but Albadán's Quechua sermons were a far cry from the humanistic idealism of José de Acosta and the Third Lima Council. Guaman Poma presents a bitingly satirical view of Albadán's pastoral care, recording one of the priest's Quechua sermons. It begins with the familiar and affectionate term found in the Third Lima Council's sermon collection: "churiycuna," or "sons of mine." From there, Albadán's sermon becomes a list of items that he intends to extort from the Indians under his care, ending with a threat in bumbling, ungrammatical Quechua[48] to murder those who do not comply:

My sons, do you have the dried white potatoes?
    No, Father.
Is there fish?
    No, Father.
Is there wool?
    No, Father.
Are there dried potatoes?
    No, Father.
Do you have the llamas for the Corregidor?
    Yes, Father.
Do you have the woven cloth for the Corregidor?
    Yes, Father.
Do you have the silver for the scribe?
    Yes, Father.
Do you have the llama harnesses and sacks for the lieutenant?
    Yes, Father.
Do you have the chicken eggs for the Spaniard who runs the tambo?
    Yes, Father.
Isn't there any water for the Father?
    No, Father.
Isn't there silver, or blankets, or straw, or firewood for the Father?
    No, Father.
The Father is ready with the noose. Listen well![49]

As with the emblem book borders and Juvenal's condemnation of sadism, Albadán takes inspiration from his books in a skewed way—one that feeds his own evil desires, rather than one that truly listens to what the books have to say.

There is one last book to consider in Albadán's library. Unlike the other books listed in the inventory of the priest's goods, this particular set of three volumes was found in Albadán's bedroom, by his bed, at the time of his death. *The Spiritual Exercises for Every Day in Lent* by Pedro de Valderrama, OSA (1550–1611), was written in Spanish and published in Seville in 1603. Albadán was apparently reading this spiritual text before his final illness. Was he using these exercises to repent of his atrocities against the native peoples? Perhaps, but it is unlikely that this particular work would have inspired such sentiments. The first decade of the seventeenth century witnessed a rapid increase in the violent persecution of *conversos*—people of Jewish descent—in Spain, and this was one of the books responsible for this wave of violence and abuse.⁵⁰ The third volume of the *Spiritual Exercises* is devoted to enumerating the "sins" of the Jews, beginning with their supposed murder of Christ and continuing through long lists describing their alleged perfidy and immorality. For Valderrama, the root cause of the Jews' supposed dedication to evil was their sun worship, learned from the ancient Egyptians while the Jews were captive in Egypt.⁵¹ Chapter after chapter describes the moral failings of people who adore the sun instead of the true God, emphasizing that such groups should be cast out and destroyed for the common good. The sermons of the Third Lima Council and the *Royal Commentaries* both allude to the Andean worship of the sun; it would not be a far stretch for Albadán to have seen the local Chanka people as substitutes for the Jews in Valderrama's diatribes about diabolical sun worshippers.

Albadán's books seem to have been a part of himself that he attempted to inscribe on the world, whether through the crudely naked statues around the door of the Pampachiri church or through Quechua sermons that quickly left behind any semblance of Christian instruction. His library, the largest and most comprehensive in the entire region, could have been a beacon of learning and Renaissance culture for those interested in such things. He may well have imagined himself as the dispenser of wisdom and wit as he perused his volumes of emblems, satires, fables, letters, theology, and canon law. Given his abusive treatment of the native people, few would have been granted access to his library, other than the natives who carried out his orders, described in the next chapter. Moreover, not all of the volumes in his library represented great works of classical humanism. As we have seen, he also selected books that advocated imprisoning the poor (Robles); that argued for warfare to spread Christianity among Indians (Focher); and that promoted deadly persecutions of conversos and Moriscos (Valderrama). The library suited the man, although the acts of barbarism that he carried out were ultimately his own, and not the fault of his books.

After Albadán's death, his goods were auctioned off in Andahuaylas under the watchful eye of the corregidor, Don Alonso de Mendoza Ponce de León. Forty of his books were sold to the local clergy; the vicar of Andahuaylas, Father Diego Arias de Sotelo, purchased the largest number, including the four volumes by Aquinas, Robles's *Práctica criminal*, and Luco's *Practica criminalis canonica* (fols. 93r–95v). A local priest, Father Gregorio Fernández de Salcedo, purchased the Roman breviary, the *Vocabulario eclesiástico*, and the three books in Quechua and Spanish: the catechism, the confessional, and the *Tercer catecismo*. Albadán's successor in Pampachiri, Father Alonso de Sigura, bought a book on the Lima councils and another one on the Council of Trent, along with a tin box covered with small, decorative silver seals. After the sale, twelve volumes, including Horace and Juvenal, remained, and they were packed up and carried to Lima, where they were sold by weight. Albadán's carefully collected library was gone, dispersed throughout the viceroyalty. The clergy who remained in Apurimac possessed far fewer books than he had, and these apparently consisted entirely of sermons, devotional literature, canon law, and theological works; there is no record of the other colonial clergymen in the region owning Roman satires or fantastical emblem books.

5. THE DINNER PARTY

Juvenal's satire about the rich man's dinner party (Satire V) opens with a rhetorical question: Is it worth swallowing your pride to have an opulent feast with your patron? Wouldn't it be better to "share in a beggar's mat . . . shivering cold on a diet of mouldy dog's bread" than to endure the insults heaped upon you by your patron at the dinner to which he has invited you? Juvenal creates a vivid picture of the sensual delights enjoyed by the rich man at his table: fine wine so old that the date on the bottle is obscured by the dust of time; savory breads made of the whitest wheat flour; delicate fish, goose livers, and a ham so succulent it might have come from the legendary Calydonian boar hunt. The vessels from which the patron drinks are made of precious metals encrusted with jewels. Yet the hungry dinner guest who has performed errands for the rich man, "cutting his sleep short, hurrying out in the dark with his shoelaces trailing" in the hope of reward, will taste none of these delicacies.[1] While the patron dines in luxury, his lowly guest will be expected to be grateful for hard, stale bread; a single shrimp served with half an egg; fish from the sewer; "some dubious toadstools"; a rotten apple like those gnawed upon by trained monkeys; and wine so sour that it wouldn't even be used to disinfect wounds, served in a battered and broken cup.[2]

Juvenal explains that the patron treats his henchman this way not out of poverty, but for the pleasure of witnessing his subordinate's pain: "What farce or pantomime could be a bigger joke than your empty, rumbling belly?"[3] The patron hopes to entertain himself by watching his subordinate pour out his anger in tears, clenching and grinding his teeth impotently throughout the meal. One can imagine Albadán in his study, perusing his well-worn copy of Juvenal and chuckling in pleasure as he reads these lines.

Guaman Poma likewise presented a satirical view of the rich feasts given by corrupt Catholic priests in the Andes as a reward for their subordinates—and of the disreputable Indians who attended them. In a drawing, he showed the unshaven priest—it could well be an image of Albadán himself—seated at the head of the dinner table, flanked by his henchmen, including a Spaniard with a flowing beard and two lowborn natives wearing the headdresses of chiefs (fig. 14). The drawing bears the caption "The Father invites low Indians, mestizos, *mulatos* to the drunken fests to take part in robbing the Indians" (Conbida el Padre a los borachos yndios uajos, mestizos, mulatos para tener parte de rrobar a los yndios pobres).[4] The native chronicler lamented how the legitimate Andean lords have been cast aside and exiled by corrupt priests. Meanwhile, he continued, these debauched Catholic priests elevate base-born Indians and men of mixed descent to the level of "hidalgo," calling them "Don Juan," "Don Pedro," and "Don Juan the World Upside Down" (Don Juan Mundo al rreués), and inviting them to eat and drink at the priests' table. It is through these assistants that the priest is able to carry out his immoral sexual relations and his rampant theft from the local people, according to the chronicler.

In the drawing, the priest and the larger native chief drink out of European-style silver goblets, while the smaller Indian has to content himself with drinking from a native-style beaker. A tablecloth is draped over the dining room table, on top of which sit a Spanish-style knife and dishes. A cooked fowl, probably a chicken, is on the table, ready to be eaten, along with a piece of fruit. The native manservant, tiny in relation to the gentlemen around the table, pours grape wine from a leather pouch; were he serving *chicha*, an Andean alcohol, he would employ a ceramic serving vessel known as an *aryballo* (fig. 15). In his illustrations, Guaman Poma is careful to distinguish between the pottery used for serving native beers and the leather bags for decanting Spanish-style wine.

Albadán was well equipped to host elegant dinner parties for visiting Spanish officials, such as the corregidors Billela and Mendoza Ponce de León; for priests from the neighboring doctrinas, such as his friends Francisco Pérez Ramírez in Soras and Juan Núñez de Ilescas Zambrano in Huayana; and for his native allies. The opulence and richness of his table was extraordinary for seventeenth-century Apurimac. According to the inventory of his goods prepared after his death, Albadán set his table with dishes of pure, solid silver—twenty-two large silver plates and twenty-four small silver plates,

FIG. 14 A corrupt priest with his drunken cronies. From Guaman Poma, *Nueva corónica y buen gobierno* (1615), p. 603, no. 240. The Royal Library, Copenhagen, GKS 2232 quarto.

FIG. 15 Inka aryballo. Peabody Museum, Yale University, YPM ANT 257148.

silver drinking cups, silver candelabras, silver salt cellars, silver pitchers, and pure silver forks, knives, and spoons. Pedro Guamancusi, Albadán's manservant, dished out food from two matching serving bowls of pure silver. Linen tablecloths imported from Spain also graced the table. Large stores of food—including butchered sheep, smoked pork shoulders, dried chicken, dried fish, sacks of wheat flour for bread and cakes, loaves of sugar, wheels of cheese,[5] jars of butter, olives, orange and lemon marmalade, peach conserve, raisins, brandy, and many bottles of wine—suggest that Albadán ate well. Francisca Tocto, his Indian cook and Guamancusi's wife, prepared the dishes that were served by her husband. According to Guamancusi's testimony after Albadán's death, the priest never paid them during the four years that they worked for him. Guamancusi and Tocto requested four years' salary—two hundred pesos, or twenty-five pesos a year per person—from his estate.[6] Apparently, they never felt empowered to demand their wages while Albadán was alive.

Albadán's house in Pampachiri contained three old oil paintings on canvas—a large Crucifixion, a smaller painting of the Virgin Mary with Jesus and John the Baptist as children, and an image of Saint Christopher. One or more of these venerable paintings would have decorated the walls of his dining room. If the priest's guests decided to spend the night at his house—perhaps they had imbibed too much wine at dinner—his storeroom contained piles and piles of woven blankets, similar to the ones he demanded from his native parishioners, for the weary guests to use.

Notably, the foods that were in Albadán's storehouse at the time of his death, and that made up his menu, were primarily European in origin, with the possible exception of the dried fish. Sheep, hogs, chickens, wheat, olives, sugar, peaches, oranges and lemons for marmalade, grapes for raisins, brandy, and wine represent animals and crops that had been imported from the Old World. By the early 1600s, these domesticated animals, grains, and fruits were all produced in Peru. They were both more expensive and more prestigious than the South American llamas and guinea pigs, quinoa and potatoes, cherimoya (custard apple) and tuna (prickly pear cactus fruit), and maize beer consumed by the local people.

It was not a matter of chance that a Spanish priest in colonial Peru maintained such a European larder. As historian Rebecca Earle has explained, diet "was central to the colonial endeavour" in Spanish South America.[7] Spanish explorers and settlers in the Indies expressed great anxiety about breathing the American air and drinking its water. Columbus, for example, claimed that the Europeans could not thrive in the Caribbean because of the "change in water and air"; the settlers could maintain their health, he wrote, only if provided with "the foods we are accustomed to in Spain."[8]

Throughout the sixteenth and seventeenth centuries, it was believed that the indigenous American diet could alter the very bodies of the Europeans, making them more "Indian." European medical texts of the time conceived of the body as essentially porous, in active dialogue with the environment around it. The American climate was thought to be harmful to Spanish settlers because of its excessive "dampness"; the primary way in which European colonists could protect themselves from this malignant influence was by consuming a diet as European as possible. If the colonists subsisted on only the native foods, their bodies might become more like those of "Indians." According to the tenets of humoral theory, the Indian constitution was "phlegmatic," like the constitution of women. The phlegmatic nature of their bodies was due to the combination of the damp climate and an inadequate diet, which made the native men like women, as evidenced by the former's lack of beards. Gregorio García, writing in the seventeenth century, suggested that the Spaniards might even lose their beards in the New World, given that the hot, moist climate supposedly impeded the growth of facial hair. García hastened to reassure his readers, however, that as long as they kept to a diet of "good foods and sustenance such as lamb, chicken, turkey and good beef, [wheat] bread, and wine," their facial hair would be saved. This list consists almost entirely of Old World foods unavailable in the Americas before the European invasion. To García, it was no wonder that the Indian men suffered from an "unmanly" lack of beards, since their diets consisted of potatoes and other foods of "very little nourishment."[9]

Earle notes that Europeans did, in fact, adopt native foods, such as maize, and even praised a select few crops, such as chili peppers, cacao (for chocolate), tomatoes, and avocados. Nonetheless, illness among Europeans was often blamed on eating an "Indian" diet, and therefore Spaniards "went to great lengths to obtain health-giving Old World foods, in particular . . . wheat bread and wine." These two items held a special place in Spanish cuisine. Wheat bread was regarded as the most nutritious food, while grape wine was considered to be "supremely healthful."[10] More importantly, wheat bread and grape wine played a central role in the Catholic Mass. Only wheat bread could become the body of Christ and only grape wine could become the blood of Christ in the Eucharist. According to scholastic theology, no other food or drink could be employed in the Mass, even in regions far from wheat fields or vineyards. For example, if a priest in Peru tried to use corn beer and maize cakes for the Eucharist, the process of transubstantiation—whereby these foods were transformed into the body and blood of Christ—simply would not occur. Moreover, the priest who ventured such an experiment would be disciplined for his illegal act.

Spanish colonists in Peru planted grape vineyards along the coast soon after their arrival in the New World.[11] The oldest vineyard in South America still functioning today is the Tacama winery in the Ica Valley, established in the 1540s. The desert oases on the Peruvian coast in the valleys of Ica, Pisco, and Nazca possessed an ideal climate for growing grapes by traditional methods. In the 1560s, trade in Peruvian coastal wines flourished and production continued to increase; by 1600, virtually no wines were imported from Spain because the local Peruvian wine industry could supply the needs of the Spanish and creole communities in the viceroyalty.[12] Albadán's favorite wine came from the Nazca Valley and was widely considered to be the finest wine produced in South America at the time. In the words of the traveling missionary monk Antonio Vásquez de Espinosa, the wine from Nazca was simply "the best in the Kingdom."[13]

For Albadán to serve grape wine from Nazca and wheat bread to his guests was a sign of power and prestige. Not only were these foods harder to obtain than the native beers and grains, but they were also imbued with symbolism, representing European civilization and Roman Catholic Christianity.

When consumed in one's daily meals, they had the power to create and maintain European bodies; when consumed in the Mass, they literally brought the believer's lips and mouth into physical contact with Christ.

Andean chicha, on the other hand, was one of the primary gifts presented to the Andean gods, and continues to be so even today. In highland villages, one must first offer drops of alcohol to the Earth Mother, Pachamama, by sprinkling them reverently on the ground, before drinking anything oneself. In many communities, it is also proper to flick some chicha into the air as a gift to the mountain spirits. Anthropologist Catherine Allen has described how this homemade maize liquor has long been central to community life in Andean villages.[14] Drinking chicha together is a core aspect of festivals and work parties. Typically, a single cup is passed around to all the participants in turn, symbolizing the united spirit behind the act of sharing the chicha. In some celebrations, the *alcalde*—the municipal administrator—shares one cup with the men, while his wife distributes a separate cup to the women. The living earth and the sacred places, such as mountain peaks, receive offerings of alcohol throughout the celebration. Allen explains that pouring chicha on the ground or flicking it into the air is called *saminchay*—"to offer *sami*." Sami is "a kind of ebullient, nourishing spirit inherent in alcohol, coca leaves, food and medicinal substances . . . through repeated offerings of chicha, the powerful and omnipresent Earth and sacred places are satisfied, placated and drawn into the festivities. Their participation is crucial."[15]

It is no wonder that Guaman Poma carefully distinguished between Indian chicha and Spanish grape wine in his drawings. The former is always shown stored in a ceramic aryballo, while the latter is poured from a leather decanter. Each drink symbolically delineated a separate social and spiritual world in the Andean highlands during the 1600s. In Guaman Poma's illustration of the corrupt Catholic priest serving a meal to his cronies, the drink is carefully shown to be grape wine served in separate cups; the priest rewards the lowborn natives in the drawing for their collaboration by drawing them into his European sphere of power and food.

Albadán's Assistants

Who were the men who helped Albadán carry out his abuses of the Indians? If Guaman Poma's drawing was actually depicting Albadán, who were the other guests at the dinner table, keeping company with the unshaven Spanish priest? The men to whom he gave bribes, as listed in Guaman Poma's satirical sermon, may well have sat at Albadán's table, eaten his food, and drunk his wine. They would have included the Spanish corregidor José de Billela, the local scribe, the lieutenant, and the Spaniard who ran the local inn ("tambo") in Pampachiri. Billela, who illegally sold the benefice to Albadán for 100 pesos, may have ridden on horseback to Pampachiri to enjoy the priest's hospitality. There he would have witnessed the ostentatious wealth amassed by Albadán during his years in the doctrina. According to Guaman Poma, Albadán gave the corregidor llamas and textiles, all stolen from the natives. Albadán's largesse, provided by the unwilling courtesy of the local people, also included silver for the scribe, harnesses and sacks for the lieutenant, and chicken eggs for the local innkeeper, Domingo de Lersundi. Giving gifts to these men helped create a network of reciprocity whereby Albadán was able to avoid legal punishment for his crimes.

Yet who were the native individuals who assisted Albadán in his day-to-day affairs, which included exploiting the native peoples? In the text accompanying his drawing of the corrupt priest's dinner party, Guaman Poma explains that the legitimate Andean lords were deposed by the debauched clerics. In place of the highborn kurakas, lesser chiefs and lowborn men were granted power to assist the priest—a power represented by having a seat at the priest's table. This certainly appears to have been true in Albadán's case. The head Chanka leader, Don León Apu Guasco, would have been an unlikely guest at the priest's dinner parties. As we saw in chapter 2, Albadán engineered Don León's fall from power in retaliation for the kuraka's formal complaint against Albadán's abuses.

Handwritten documents found posthumously among Albadán's papers, and diligently recorded by the corregidor's scribe, reveal that the priest's right-hand man in dealing with the natives was Don Alonso Sivi Paucar (fols. 127v–129v). Don Alonso was a kuraka from Umamarca, one of the three settlements that composed Albadán's parish (the others being Pampachiri and Pomacocha). In the early 1600s, Umamarca's adult population was about half the size of Pampachiri's; the official census from 1606 shows that about 680 adults lived in Umamarca, while Pampachiri boasted an adult population of around 1,200.[16] It is not surprising that Albadán worked with the head kuraka from the lower-ranking community of Umamarca, rather than with the higher-ranking head kuraka of Pampachiri, also from the Sivi Paucar dynasty.[17] In a pattern found throughout the colonial Andes, high-ranking kurakas often refused to collaborate with corrupt priests. Such kurakas feared "the unwelcome demands of the colonizers, which jeopardized the Indians' well-being and discredited the officials in the eyes of native subjects."[18]

Don Alonso worked with the native alcaldes of Pampachiri and Pomacocha in carrying out Albadán's orders. These three alcaldes were not part of the kuraka hierarchy of the region, but were commoners promoted to positions of power. Most likely, they were invited to eat at Albadán's table, along with Don Alonso. We know that these men were collaborators with the priest because of a document written in Albadán's own hand, found in a little notebook among his papers. This document listed the Indians who owed Albadán money for the indulgences, or Bulls of the Holy Crusade (Bulas de la Santa Cruzada), that he had forced the natives to buy. What is remarkable about this list is not that he coerced them to purchase indulgences—such a practice was legal in the Andes—but that he sold the indulgences at almost double their legal price and made each of the Indians buy multiple indulgences. Albadán would have enjoyed a healthy profit from these transactions; he would also have been able to use the Indians' indebtedness to force them to work for him. According to the document, Albadán had elevated Don Alonso to the position of "administrator and treasurer of the Holy Crusade." It was therefore Don Alonso's task to force the native population to comply, using whatever means necessary. Don Alonso himself distributed bulls among the people of Umamarca, and he gave his subordinates bulls to sell: the alcaldes of Pomacocha and Pampachiri received sixty-nine bulls and two hundred bulls, respectively. He likewise gave ninety bulls to the "alcalde of the Chankas," twenty-five bulls to the alcalde of the Chankas of Pampachiri, and fifty bulls to the alcalde of the Inkas of Pampachiri (fols. 127v–129v).

Bulls of the Holy Crusade

As another concrete instance of theft from the natives—one that has not been well understood in the colonial Andean context—it is worth pausing to explore what these bulls were and how they were distributed. The Bulls of the Holy Crusade were papal indulgences granted to the faithful for their financial support of the wars against infidels.[19] Papal indulgences remit the temporal punishment for sin that has been forgiven; in other words, they remit the punishments suffered by souls in Purgatory. Plenary indulgences commute the entire temporal punishment so that no further expiation is required in Purgatory. Partial indulgences, on the other hand, remit only a portion of the penalty in Purgatory, shortening the sinner's time of penance by a certain number of days or years.[20] Bulls of the Holy Crusade were first granted in the Middle Ages to encourage men to fight in the crusades against the Turks and

Moors, in the Holy Land or in Spain. Those individuals who could not fight in the wars were allowed to purchase a bull to support the crusades, thereby acquiring the indulgences granted to the Christian crusaders. Pope Clement IV issued the first general bull for all of Spain in 1265, when the kings of Aragon and Castile battled to recapture Murcia. In 1573, Pope Gregory XIII granted the Spanish Crown the right to issue bulls in the New World. While Pope Gregory's concession is generally considered the first Bull of the Holy Crusade issued for the New World, Hernández Méndez has found evidence of these bulls in the Americas by the 1530s.[21]

Alms given for this bull were initially used to finance wars against infidels; however, these funds were eventually employed to cover the costs and repair of cathedrals and other pious works. When each campaign for the Holy Crusade was announced in Spanish America, every diocese received printed bulls, whose distribution was overseen by a member of the cathedral chapter. Priests within the diocese had two years to distribute the bulls among the faithful. By the early seventeenth century, the Spanish government decreed that one half of the money collected during each campaign for the Holy Crusade should go to the diocese, and the other half should be sent to the Crown.[22] Apparently, bishops often failed to keep good records of the funds collected. Reina Maldonado (1599–1660), a cathedral canon and author of a book on the duties of bishops in colonial Peru, emphasized the need to create good accounting systems for handling this money so that fraud could be eliminated.[23]

The official presentation of the bulls in Indian communities was intended to be an impressive ceremony. The priest formally accepted the bulls on the altar of the pueblo's church, "receiving them with a solemn procession, a lively pealing of the bells, [with] flutes and trumpets, [and] a concourse of the magistrates, Spaniards, and the rest of the people who are found in each doctrina, with all of the Indians, confraternities, and banners."[24] The procession wound its way from the church to an outdoor shrine or oratory, where the priest delivered a sermon exhorting his flock to purchase the bulls.[25] During each campaign, previously issued bulls were suspended, requiring the faithful to purchase bulls anew. The price of the bulls varied according to one's station in life. High dignitaries, such as bishops, cathedral canons, presidents, *oidores*, and corregidors, paid 10 pesos for each bull; kurakas paid 1 peso; and ordinary Indians paid 2 tomines (each tomin equaled one-eighth of a peso). Indians were permitted to pay with credit, and to pay in produce, rather than in cash.[26]

Kurakas who were indebted to priests participated in distributing the bulls among their subjects. For example, in the late 1600s, the kuraka of Uripa,

Don Juan Guaraca, borrowed heavily from the priest of Huancavelica, Father Bartolomé Lodeña y Espinosa, to pay the tribute. Don Juan was unable to repay this loan in his lifetime. When his son Bernabe Guaraca became kuraka, he inherited his father's large debt of 150 pesos; Father Lodeña's will reveals that Don Bernabe, in debt to the priest, agreed to be responsible for distributing bulls among the Indians of Uripa.[27] Likewise, Don Felipe Topa Guasco, the head kuraka over all of Hanansaya, accepted 175 bulls from the priest of Talavera, Father Pedro Berrocal y Valenzuela, to distribute among the Indians of Hanansaya.[28] Testimony from a priest in the 1700s suggests that native peoples, who generally did not appreciate the benefits conferred by the bulls, often resented having to purchase them.[29] Nonetheless, the wealth of the secular clergy, combined with the kurakas' pressing need for funds to pay the tribute (see chapters 7 and 8), created a situation in which native leaders could be obliged to collaborate in the sale of bulls to the Indians under their care.

As noted above, Albadán relied upon a lower-ranking kuraka—Don Alonso Sivi Paucar from Umamarca—and on native alcaldes to enforce the distribution of bulls among his flock. Albadán's handwritten list of the Indians who owed money for bulls provides concrete evidence of how he cheated his parishioners. In his transcription of Albadán's "little book" of debts, the local scribe Andrés Bravo wrote that the bulls found in the priest's possession were each worth 2 tomines (1 tomin = 1 real; 8 reales = 1 peso). However, in Albadán's handwritten list of the people's debts, the priest noted that each bull was sold for 3½ tomines. Almost every individual in the community of Umamarca purchased two bulls, for a total price of 7 tomines per person, resulting in a profit for Albadán. Presumably, some of this illegal profit was shared among Don Alonso and the alcaldes who collected the money. But it is possible that the fear of Albadán, coupled with a chance to dine at his table and be seen as his ally, would have sufficed to encourage cooperation with the priest.

When the new corregidor, Don Alonso de Mendoza Ponce de León, settled Albadán's estate in 1611, he originally intended to ignore the list of Indian debts for the bulls (fol. 126r–v). However, his local advisors remonstrated with him, explaining that he needed to enter these debts into the legal record so that they would not be forgotten. Andrés Bravo wrote that, "attentive to [the fact] that the corregidor cannot come to do [proper] diligence [in this matter] because he entered this jurisdiction a very short time ago," they determined that the list should indeed be transcribed in the legal record.[30] Clearly, Don Alonso's local advisors, such as the scribe and the innkeeper Domingo de Lersundi, wanted to keep a record of the Indians' obligations, probably as a means to compel the Indians to work for them.

FIG. 16 Inka site of Sondor. Photo by Brian S. Bauer.

Andean Hospitality

Albadán may have followed the example of Juvenal's rich patron and given measly and insulting portions to his guests, while enjoying feasts of smoked pork and cheese, buttered bread, raisin cakes, and wine by himself. Yet, given his generosity to his relatives—to whom he sent large sums of money once he became rich—it is more likely that he provided lavish meals for his followers. Serving fine food was part of the life of the Spanish gentleman, the model to which Albadán aspired. It was also a central aspect of Andean governing and so would have resonated powerfully with his Andean subjects.

As many scholars have noted, ceremonial feasts in the Andes tradition-ally enacted unequal alliances.[31] A kuraka was expected to host sumptuous banquets for his subordinates, who, by accepting this largesse, enhanced his status. Likewise, during the Inka Empire, representatives of the state rou-tinely held rich feasts for subject kurakas at Inka administrative sites, such as Sondor, outside Andahuaylas (fig. 16). At ceremonial banquets in the Andes, both past and present, the host serves the guests in their order of impor-tance, so that the proper hierarchy among his subordinates is made manifest.

FIG. 17 Andean girl with pack llama. Watercolor by Pancho Fierro. Yale University Art Gallery, 1967.36.15.

As a special treat, the foods served at feasts in the Andes were often baked in earth ovens, in a labor-intensive style of food preparation known as *pachamanca*, which locked in more flavor than was found in the boiled foods eaten every day. The foods consumed included tubers such as potatoes, a grain-like seed called quinoa, beans, guinea pigs, camelids (llamas, alpacas, vicuñas, and guanacos), wild fish, and birds. Food was seasoned with hot chili peppers and salt, and fruit was plentiful. The primary non-Andean food that was eaten was maize. Originally from Mesoamerica, maize was common in the Andes by 1000 B.C. It was consumed in a variety of ways: as corn on the cob; in corn flour dumplings, bread, and cakes; and, most importantly, as chicha.[32] Pack llamas carried food and other products from one region to the next along Inka roads; this traditional Andean form of transport continued well into the twentieth century in rural Apurimac (fig. 17).

In his only other illustration of Spaniards eating, Guaman Poma reiterates the theme of reversal (fig. 18). This drawing depicts the Spanish corregidor enjoying a banquet with lowborn mestizos, mulatos, and Indians. As in Guaman Poma's depiction of the dinner party hosted by the evil priest, the

FIG. 18 The corregidor's dinner party. From Guaman Poma, *Nueva corónica y buen gobierno* (1615), p. 505, no. 204. The Royal Library, Copenhagen, GKS 2232 quarto.

appropriate line of authority has been badly disrupted. The "true" indigenous lords of the Andes—of whom Guaman Poma was one—have been passed over in favor of native commoners more pliable and vulnerable to the will of the colonizers.

The Bezoar Stone

In Satire X, Juvenal advised, "The most popular, urgent prayer, well-known in every temple, is for wealth. *Increase my holdings, please make my deposit account the largest in town!* But you'll never find yourself drinking belladonna from pottery cups. The time you should worry is when you're clutching a jeweled goblet."[33] Among Albadán's possessions were numerous bezoar stones (fol. 92v)—the valuable, mystical object with the power to neutralize any poison that one imbibed, or so it was believed in seventeenth-century Europe. A person who thought that they had ingested poison would lick the stone so that the poison would do no harm. Bezoars, therefore, were often fashioned into rings so that they would be close at hand. Alternately, they were dipped into cups of alcohol that were suspected of being poisoned, as it was thought that this would also neutralize the poison. Often framed in silver or gold, bezoars might be kept on the dinner table close to the cutlery, where they would be immediately available to a diner who suspected that a dish had been poisoned. The stones were so valuable that Queen Elizabeth of Bohemia guarded two bezoar stones among her diamonds and pearls; Queen Elizabeth of England treasured a bezoar stone set in gold as part of her Crown jewels.[34]

A hard, calcified mass found in the intestines of ruminants and composed of things that cannot be digested, such as hair, bezoar stones were precious commodities in colonial Peru and, indeed, throughout all of Europe. In his *Naturalis Historia* (A.D. 77–79), Pliny the Elder noted the bezoar's efficacy against poison, and this belief was repeated by writers throughout the Middle Ages.[35] By the time the Spanish arrived in Peru, there already existed a well-established European trade in bezoars from Asia. However, the highly influential medical treatise *Historia medicinal*, written by Nicolás Monardes in the sixteenth century, lauded the superior efficacy of Andean bezoars from vicuñas, llamas, alpacas, and other Andean camelids, as compared to Asian bezoars from wild goats or deer. Monardes considered Peruvian bezoars to be unsurpassed as an antidote to poison. A brisk trade in the precious Peruvian bezoars soon ensued. The Peruvian viceroy Francisco de Toledo even presented bezoar stones embellished with gold and silver ornamentation to King Philip II; some of the hardened, gray Andean stones were encased in delicate gold boxes.[36]

The presence of bezoar stones among Albadán's belongings suggests that he may have feared being poisoned. He did not possess just one of these valuable objects; rather, he owned an entire bag of bezoar stones weighing a pound altogether (fol. 92v)! Moreover, he had at least one bezoar stone in each of his three residences; there was a bag of bezoars in his Pampachiri house and large bezoars in his homes in Umamarca and Pomacocha. He kept these precious stones in the kitchen with the stores of food so that they would be accessible when he dined. Given his torture of the native people around him and his large-scale theft of Indian property, Albdadán certainly accrued enemies who wished him ill. It would have been quite reasonable for him to fear poisoning. Recent investigations into the curative properties of bezoars have revealed that they do, in fact, have the ability to neutralize arsenic-based poisons.[37] However, for all other types of poison, including those most commonly used in the Andes, their protective powers are woefully inadequate. If Albdadán was using bezoar stones to protect himself from poison, it is unlikely that they served him well.

6. THE FUNERAL

On Sunday, March 20, 1611, the church bell in Umamarca tolled mournfully throughout the morning, announcing the funeral Mass for the former priest Juan Bautista de Albadán (fols. 102v–104v).[1] A slow procession carrying Albadán's open coffin brought him to the door of the adobe church, Our Lady of the Snows, on the plaza of the high mountain village (see fig. 19). At the church entrance, Father Juan Núñez de Ilescas Zambrano, from the Chanka village of Huayana, sprinkled the coffin with holy water while intoning the *De Profundis* and the *Miserere* in Latin. The coffin containing Albadán's putrefying corpse, dressed in beautiful vestments imported from Spain—a stole, maniple, and chasuble of crimson damask with red velvet trim, over a robe of colorful French cotton—was placed in the sanctuary with the feet pointing away from the altar. Six expensive beeswax candles decorated the altar for Albadán's funeral Mass; their warm, clean scent could not have masked the odor of his decaying flesh. During the liturgy, a trained Andean choir intoned solemn Spanish and Latin hymns. At the end of the Mass, Father Núñez de Ilescas passed the thurible with smoking incense over the body, sprinkled holy water again, and prayed the antiphon *In Paradisum*: "May the angels lead you into paradise, may the martyrs receive you at your coming and lead you to the holy city of Jerusalem, may the ranks of angels receive you . . ." Albadán was then buried in the church sanctuary. There is no evidence that Albadán ever actually taught the Christian catechism, but if he did, his parishioners might have reflected on the words of the Lima catechism (1584) as they watched his interment: "[After death] the evil people will come back to life with their bodies, with their souls, all of the evil ones, not dead, will be in the fire with devils, it is proclaimed, suffering greatly forever" (Mana alli runacuna vcucunahuan, animacunahuan, mana tucuc, mana huañuc ninapi çupayhuan huaqlla viñaypac ñacaricucapac cauçarimpuca).[2]

Albadán had died on the previous Thursday, March 17, around 10 o'clock in the evening (fol. 11r–v). According to custom, he should have been buried in Pampachiri the next day. However, the corregidor, Don Alonso de Mendoza Ponce de León, who had arrived in Pampachiri on Tuesday, March 15, spent the day following Albadán's death gathering testimony from the local priests who had attended the dying man. Albadán died without a will, so Don Alonso interviewed Fathers Núñez de Ilescas, Juan Clavero (the priest of Turpo), and Francisco Pérez Ramírez (the vicar of Soras) about whether the deceased had family members to inherit his fortune.[3] On Friday, March 18, the day after Albadán died, the corregidor also inventoried all of Albadán's goods in his house in Pampachiri and auctioned off a portion of the food and textiles (fols. 15r–19v; 24v–27r). The following day, Saturday, March 19, the corregidor traveled with his retinue of servants, scribes, and priests to the small hamlet of Pomacocha, delaying Albadán's funeral yet another day. In Pomacocha, Albadán's belongings were inventoried and all were auctioned off (fols. 27r–28r).

Due to the hostility of the local people, Albadán's funeral could not be held in Pampachiri; the corregidor had to arrange for it to take place on Sunday in Umamarca, the home of Albadán's most important native ally, Don Alonso Sivi Paucar. On the morning of the funeral, as the church bells rang, the corregidor ordered an inventory of Albadán's goods in his house in Umamarca (fol. 30r–v). As in his home in Pampachiri, the deceased priest's belongings in Umamarca included an astonishing variety of fine silver goods—solid silver plates, silver candlesticks, silver serving dishes, silver jars, and so forth. Immediately after the inventory, and before the funeral Mass, the corregidor held an auction of many of the perishable foodstuffs and items of lesser value (fols. 28r–30r). Among the latter were more than 180 tallow candles that sold for five pesos; one can imagine the feelings of the audience as they saw Albadán's instruments of torture on the auction block.

March in the Andes falls at the end of the rainy season, and the weather for Albadán's funeral would probably have been cold and wet. The harvest would not occur until May, so food stores in the villages were getting low. Albadán died during Lent; March 27, one week after his funeral, was Palm Sunday and the beginning of Holy Week. Nonetheless, the corregidor ordered that there be a great feast for everyone in Umamarca after the funeral,

FIG. 19 Christian burial procession. From Guaman Poma, *Nueva corónica y buen gobierno* (1615), p. 619, no. 246. The Royal Library, Copenhagen, GKS 2232 quarto.

supplied by the foods in Albadán's ample larder (fol. 104r–v). Wine, slaughtered alpacas, wheat flour, and sugar for bread and cakes—all of these goods were transported to Umamarca from Pampachiri on Saturday. On the day of the funeral, native women would have been up at dawn, roasting cuts of alpaca, preparing savory meat stews with dumplings, making fry breads sizzle on the griddle, baking sweet sultana cakes, and filling the air with the rich scents of cooking food. March 21, the Monday after the funeral, was traditionally a festival day known as Paucar Huaray, the "Mantle of Flowers." On this day, the equinox, shamans made offerings for a good harvest to important *huacas*, while women decorated the ground with carpets of flowers, a custom that has continued to this day during Holy Week.[4] In Umamarca in 1611, the celebrations began a day early.

When he died, Albadán was only forty-eight or forty-nine years old. The witnesses interviewed by the corregidor described his last days in detail, yet oddly no one ventured a diagnosis of the cause of his death at such a relatively young age—not even his doctors, Martín de Soria and Juan Guanca Pomachuco. Albadán fell ill suddenly on Wednesday, March 9, in Pampachiri and was unable to speak. Some native members of the community—their names are not known—decided to walk the day's journey to Soras to alert Albadán's longtime friend and neighbor (fol. 12v), the vicar Francisco Pérez Ramírez. The Indians arrived in Soras with their news on Thursday; Father Pérez left immediately, entering Pampachiri on Friday, March 11 (fols. 8r–9r). He found Albadán in his bed, very ill. Later that day, Father Pérez "heard" confession from the dying priest. Because Albadán could not speak, the confession was done through signs and signals; Father Pérez asked questions, and Albadán indicated his response by nodding or shaking his head. That evening, Father Pérez wrote letters to two other priests who knew the sick man— Diego Arias de Sotelo, the vicar of Andahuaylas, and Juan Núñez de Ilescas Zambrano, the priest in Santiago de Huayana. He told them that Albadán was dying in agony and that it would be a miracle if he were to survive (fol. 6r–v). In his letter to Father Arias de Sotelo in Andahuaylas, Father Pérez specifically asked the priest to inform the corregidor of Albadán's illness and to send physicians.

Father Pérez said that Albadán seemed to improve after his arrival on Friday; once under his care, Albadán briefly became stronger and more aware of his surroundings. On Sunday morning, March 13, Father Pérez gave Albadán the Eucharist. That same day, Father Núñez de Ilescas arrived in Pampachiri from Huayana around noon (fols. 9r–10r). The thirty-eight-year-old Father Núñez de Ilescas had known Albadán for years as a neighbor and had spoken with him in a friendly fashion many times (fol. 14v). He found "the said Father Juan Bautista de Albadán lying in his bed, very sick and almost outside of his senses, because he could hardly speak or know what was going on."[5] He remained at Albadán's bedside around the clock until Wednesday, when he was called away to give testimony to the corregidor.

Don Alonso de Mendoza Ponce de León reached Pampachiri on Tuesday, March 15, with servants and his scribe, Andrés Bravo, in his retinue, along with two doctors and Father Juan Clavero. Don Alonso had been informed about the gravity of Albadán's condition by Father Arias de Sotelo, who did not himself go to Pampachiri to say farewell. Forty-seven-year-old Father Clavero, who insisted in his testimony that he was *not* a friend of the deceased, joined the corregidor's entourage when the latter passed through the village of Turpo, where Clavero lived (fol. 10r–v). The following day, on Wednesday, March 16, Don Alonso interviewed the attending priests about their arrival and Albadán's condition. Meanwhile, the two physicians, Martín de Soria and Juan Guanca Pomachuco, tended the sick man, assisted by Albadán's unpaid servants, Pedro Guamancusi and his wife, Francisca Tocto, Albadán's cook. Albadán declined rapidly under their care and passed away on Thursday evening, still without having spoken (fol. 11r). Crowded around his deathbed at the end were Andrés Bravo, Father Pérez, Father Núñez de Ilescas, Father Clavero, Martín de Soria, and Juan Guanca Pomachuco, along with the two domestics, Pedro and Francisca.

From this distance in time, it is impossible to say for certain what caused Albadán's illness and death. The symptoms of speech loss and confusion leading to death suggest a possible stroke, although the vast majority of strokes occur in people over the age of sixty-five. However, given Albadán's apparent fear of poisoning, it is possible that his death may have been due to ingesting a deadly substance, one administered to him deliberately. Spanish chroniclers recount that Andean herbalists were skilled poisoners and had a large array of fatal brews at their disposal.[6] According to Inka historians, for example, the sister of the early Inka king Capac Yupanqui poisoned her brother by adding deadly herbs to his food. A secondary wife of Emperor Topa Inka was executed for killing her husband with poison. The soldier and chronicler Pedro Pizarro wrote that one of Emperor Atahuallpa's half brothers died several months after being poisoned. Spanish observers noted that native people throughout the Andes continued to be skilled poisoners well into the colonial era. Malevolent herbalists were able to create a variety of effects with slightly different poisonous recipes. They could use poison to disfigure the victim, making him or her "half-witted and repulsive, being covered with patches and blotches." They were also skilled at varying the time it took for a person to die from the poison: "there were also men and women who gave poison which killed either suddenly or by slow degrees, or stupefied whom they wished, or drove them out of their senses."[7]

According to the colonial sources, Andean herbalists knew how to brew slow-acting herbal concoctions that could kill through the symptoms that Albadán exhibited, including the inability to speak, mental confusion, eventual coma, and death. The chroniclers provide little information about the substances used; however, it appears that most deadly Andean poisons in the colonial period were based on an extract of *Datura stramonium*, to which other substances were added. Datura, a tall shrub with lovely trumpet-shaped, cream-colored blooms, is a powerful hallucinogen that can cause brain damage and death in high concentrations. When combined with other substances, datura can induce a slow demise with symptoms of speechlessness, stupefaction, mental distress, and coma before death.[8]

If Albadán was indeed poisoned, it is not difficult to find suspects or motives. His two servants, Pedro and Francisca, had witnessed his violence and greed firsthand; they were also owed four years' wages, which they were given by the corregidor after the priest's death. Pedro and Francisca both had ample opportunity to secretly feed deadly substances to Albadán, either in his food or his drink. The corregidor also possessed a strong reason for wanting Albadán out of the way. Since January 1609, Don Alonso had owed the priest 1,378 pesos, a sum roughly equal to 254,930 U.S. dollars today.[9] A codicil in the loan agreement stated that after three months, Albadán could demand repayment of the full amount at any time (fol. 40v), leaving the corregidor vulnerable to the priest's good will. If Don Alonso were to assist in any prosecution of Albadán, he would risk going to prison for nonpayment of the loan. In fact, as we shall see, after settling Albadán's estate, Don Alonso attempted to redistribute all of the priest's wealth in charity to the native peoples of Pampachiri, Umamarca, and Pomacocha, making "amends" (enmendar) for the "suffering" (dolores) that Albadán had inflicted on the kingdom (fol. 196r–v). Albadán's physician Martín de Soria was at the corregidor's right hand during the initial phase of the attempted redistribution, testifying in court to thefts that he had seen Albadán commit. If Pedro and Francisca induced Albadán's initial illness through poison, Martín de Soria and Juan Guanca may have been asked by the corregidor to make sure that Albadán did not recover.

Whatever the true cause of Albadán's death, Don Alonso needed to settle the priest's considerable estate before trying to give the wealth back to the people of the doctrina. On Monday, March 21, the day after the funeral, the corregidor ordered that all of the silver items from Albadán's residence in Umamarca be brought out to the central plaza. Each item was officially weighed in preparation for a later auction in Andahuaylas (fol. 30r–v). Don Alonso and his retinue returned to Andahuaylas that same Monday, carrying with them the cartloads of goods from the priest's homes in Pampachiri and Umamarca (all of Albadán's possessions in Pomacocha had already been auctioned off on March 19, the day before the funeral).

On the following Sunday, March 27, in Andahuaylas, Don Alonso held an official weighing of all the silver from Albadán's house in Pampachiri. Each object of solid silver—such as a large, ornately decorated serving bowl and a plain pair of candlesticks—was publicly weighed, and the results were entered into the court record (fols. 31r–33r). On Monday, March 28, in the city's central plaza, under the auspices of the local auctioneer Santiago Puma, all of the silver items, including those from Umamarca (fols. 33v–37r), were auctioned off. However, according to the court records, no one showed up to bid on any of the pieces (fol. 34r)! It is difficult to believe that this was an accident; had the auction been properly advertised, many wealthy landowners in the Andahuaylas region would have been eager to purchase the pure silver dishes, goblets, bowls, and other items at a discounted price. In the absence of any buyers, Don Alonso ordered that each piece be valued by its official weight: ornamented silver was valued at 9 pesos per mark;[10] gilded silver at 9½ pesos per mark; and plain silver at 8 pesos per mark. The total—1,422 pesos—was entered into the list of Albadán's assets (fol. 99r). Although the court record does not state what happened to Albadán's silver after this abortive auction, presumably Don Alonso sold the silver pieces for an amount greater than the assessed value, making a profit for himself. In any event, three weeks after this auction, Don Alonso was able to repay his loan from Albadán, adding his repayment to the value of the priest's estate (fol. 99v).

In April, the rest of Albadán's belongings were auctioned off in the Andahuaylas town square over three days—April 5, 15, and 17 (fols. 91r–96v). These auctions were well attended, and all of Albadán's goods, from his tablecloths to his old shirts of imported French cotton, were sold. Most of the buyers were Spaniards and creoles, but some of the Chanka elites attended. Don Gerónimo Sivi Paucar from Umamarca purchased Albadán's three oil paintings—the Crucifixion, Saint Christopher, and the Virgin Mary with Jesus and John the Baptist; he also bought a large padlock and key.[11] Don Juan Topa Guasco bought a steel ax and a small devotional image (*retablo*) of the Virgin Mary. Don Luis Tomay Guaraca, who became the new head of the Chanka nation after the Guasco family was ousted from the top leadership position, purchased two heavy bronze seals and another steel ax.

Between auctions, Don Alonso found time for other business related to Albadán's death. The corregidor quickly appointed Father Alonso de Sigura as the successor to the benefice of Pampachiri, Umamarca, and Pomacocha. The corregidor also read carefully through all of Albadán's personal letters, which he described with admirable accuracy and ordered to be transcribed into the court documents "for clarity" (por claridad), along with the priest's other papers (fols. 37v–38v). It is because of Don Alonso's remarkable diligence that we have access to the priest's personal letters today. The corregidor seems to have been fascinated by the stories about Albadán's relatives contained in these letters, especially as some of them were neighbors of Don Alonso's family in the elite neighborhood of La Magdalena in Seville.

Before the last auction of Albadán's goods was held on April 17, the corregidor began hearing claims for reimbursement from the priest's estate. One of the first to present a claim was Don Juan Topa Guasco, the head kuraka of Hanansaya, the upper half of the ten Chanka ayllus. On April 2, he presented a claim in court on behalf of the community of Pampachiri (fols. 104v–108v). Apparently, Albadán had been buried in vestments belonging to the Pampachiri church. Don Juan asked that the church receive compensation for these luxurious garments of crimson damask and velvet, all imported from Spain. The corregidor concurred and ordered the officers of the court to purchase similar high-quality Spanish cloth from Francisco Hernandez de Figueroa, a merchant in Andahuaylas who sold goods from Spain. On May 4, the fabric for the replacement vestments, which cost ninety-eight pesos, was given to Don Juan in front of the new priest in Pampachiri, Father Alonso de Sigura. Over the next two weeks in Andahuaylas, the corregidor heard and paid out additional claims against Albadán's estate. Then he journeyed back to Umamarca and asked the community there whether anyone wished to claim compensation. Various native community members, such as Don Gerónimo Sivi Paucar, Juan Atau Cusi, and Francisco Atau Sipa, responded with claims for items that Albadán had taken from them, and for which they received full compensation from the corregidor. The next day, the corregidor rode out to the Chanka community of Turpo, where he heard claims by Indians such as Juan Ayquispa for goods likewise stolen by Albadán. By the following week, Don Alonso was back in Andahuaylas, where he continued to hear native claims, including that of Pedro Caquia, Luis Curiguaman, Alonso Condor, and Juan Ticllacuri, who said that Albadán had demanded their horses and never paid for them. For most of these cases, the doctor Martín de Soria served as a witness (fols. 111r–112v) in support of the villagers' claims against Albadán. In general, Don Alonso quickly accepted the claims and provided full compensation to those whose property had been stolen by the priest.

However, at this point, Don Alonso seems to have become alarmed at the number of potential claims by the natives against Albadán's estate; hearing all of the complaints against the deceased priest would leave the corregidor unable to attend to other business. He thus appointed a local landowner, Hernando de Candidato, as a temporary judge to help him settle the claims against Albadán. Candidato, however, did not make it possible for the natives to bring their claims to court. Instead, he spent weeks on only one case— that of the Basque innkeeper in Pampachiri, Domingo de Lersundi, who wanted compensation for the wine that Albadán had taken from him, which Candidato eventually granted (fol. 123v).

It is unclear whether the corregidor was frustrated by the slow pace of adjudicating the compensation claims, or whether many of the native people themselves were reluctant to bring their claims to court. At any rate, by the end of May 1611, Don Alonso had developed a different strategy for returning Albadán's ill-gotten wealth to the people of Pampachiri, Umamarca, and Pomacocha. Rather than continuing to hear individual cases from natives who had the time and resources to go to court, he decided to petition the royal court—the Audiencia—in Lima to give the entire balance of Albadán's estate to the "caja de comunidad" (the community chest) of the three villages.[12] There, the money would be used for local projects to benefit the people of the region, as well as serve as a resource to help the most needy. Don Alonso knew perfectly well that Albadán had two legitimate heirs, his brothers Francisco and Gerónimo, but he argued that since Albadán had died without a will, the court had the power to give his wealth to charity.

To argue the case in Lima, Don Alonso enlisted the assistance of Domingo Gómez de Silva, the official in charge of settling the estates of the deceased (the *defensor de los bienes de los defuntos*) in Cusco. De Silva was well qualified to carry forward Don Alonso's plan to compensate the native peoples of Pampachiri and its environs.[13] He had been working in the viceregal courts since 1600, when he was appointed as the general defender of minors in the city of Lima. In fact, posterity owes a considerable debt to de Silva. He authored one of the most important civic practice handbooks for the colonial Andes, instructing native leaders on how to bring lawsuits to court. This work, the *Práctica y instrución para albaceas, tutores y curadores*, would become the bane of colonial administrators and landowners who wanted native leaders to keep quiet about injustice. De Silva was partly responsible for the flood of lawsuits and complaints from the indigenous Andean population after 1640, when the book was published. The *Práctica y instrución* was written explicitly to assist individuals not versed in the law— especially indigenous Andean leaders—in bringing cases to court. By the time he took Don Alonso's case in 1611, de Silva had already completed a first draft of his book, but it would take him decades to obtain permission from the viceregal government to publish it. In any event, de Silva possessed ample experience with the Lima courts to press Don Alonso's argument that the people of Apurimac should benefit from Albadán's estate. It is also possible that, as an official in Cusco, de Silva had already heard rumors about Albadán's excesses and may even have helped Don León Apu Guasco lodge his complaint against the priest during the administration of the previous corregidor.

FIG. 20 The president and judges of the Audiencia in Lima. From Guaman Poma, *Nueva corónica y buen gobierno* (1615), p. 484, no. 197. The Royal Library, Copenhagen, GKS 2232 quarto.

On August 3, in Lima, Domingo de Silva, in the name of Don Alonso de Mendoza Ponce de León, presented his case to Dr. Hernando Arias de Ugarte,[14] who sat on the Audiencia, the highest court in the land (see fig. 20). De Silva requested that, because Albadán had died without a will, the remainder of his estate (5,716 pesos after expenses and compensation) go to the community chest of Pampachiri, Umamarca, and Pomacocha (fols. 130v–131v). In de Silva's official petition, Albadán's lack of a will was the only reason given for donating the priest's estate to the community. De Silva seems to have privately discussed Albadán's abuses against the native peoples with Arias de Ugarte, because the judge would later refer to the need for Albadán to make amends for the suffering he had caused. At this stage, however, there was no mention of Albadán's atrocities or the state of his soul.

Arias de Ugarte simply granted de Silva's petition the same day, specifying that the monies should go to the community chest (fol. 132r–v).

However, Gerónimo de Albadán could not let matters rest there (fols. 171v–172r). On September 3, a month after Arias de Ugarte's decision, Gerónimo presented his own petition in Lima in his and his brother Francisco's names. In this document, Gerónimo argued that as Albadán's legitimate brothers, he and Francisco should be permitted to inherit and divide the estate between them. In the following days, Gerónimo brought numerous witnesses to court to testify that they had known Diego de Albadán and his wife, Doña Ana, in Seville, where they were married and had raised three legitimate sons: Francisco, Juan Bautista, and Gerónimo. Among the witnesses to testify on Gerónimo's behalf were Fray Hernando de Paredes, the Mercedarian provincial vicar for Peru (fols. 180r–182v), who went to school with Francisco and Juan Bautista as a boy and, as an adult, dined frequently at Doña Ana's house; Anículas de Valeras, an elderly resident of Lima who had been friends with Diego and Doña Ana in Seville and corresponded regularly with Don Andrés Núñez de Prado, Doña Ana's brother (fols. 183r–184v); Hernando de Antezana, a forty-two-year-old resident of Lima who grew up in Seville knowing Juan Bautista and Francisco well, though he was never friends with them (fols. 185r–186r); Francisco Gutiérrez Coca, the younger, who frequently stayed with Don Andrés Núñez de Prado in Seville and knew Francisco and Gerónimo well (fols. 186v–189r); and Cristóbal de Vargas, a public scribe in Lima who grew up in the neighborhood of La Magdalena in Seville and knew the three brothers (fols. 189v–191r). It is instructive to read through the testimony of these witnesses, as it reveals the close ties maintained by Sevillians in Peru and in Spain. Each witness stated under oath that Diego and Doña Ana had been legitimately married and that the three brothers—Francisco, Juan Bautista, and Gerónimo—were legitimate sons.

Faced with this overwhelming evidence of legitimate heirs, Arias de Ugarte reversed his earlier ruling. On September 23, the judge declared that Albadán's estate would be divided equally between Gerónimo and Francisco (fol. 192r), a judgment that Gerónimo formally accepted (fol. 192v). However, on October 7, Arias de Ugarte made the extraordinary decision to expend the royal fifth of Albadán's estate—the government's sizable inheritance tax—on "masses and pious works for [Albadán's] soul."[15] The viceregal administration relied on taxes such as this one for its operating funds, so donating this amount to "masses and pious works" was not a step taken lightly. Nonetheless, this was seen as necessary to make "amends" for Albadán and for the "pain" that he had inflicted (fol. 196r–v). Such was his degree of concern that Arias de Ugarte even composed the list of priests in Lima who would be paid to say masses for the sake of Albadán's soul (fols. 194v–195r). The judge chose five of the most notable and powerful clergymen in Peru, including the head of the Mercedarians, Fray Paredes, as well as the head of the Franciscans in Peru, Fray Gerónimo de Valera, brother of the radical Jesuit Blas Valera.[16] The rest of the royal fifth would be devoted to charity in Pampachiri and the neighboring communities.

This new ruling did not please Albadán's brother Gerónimo. The very next day, October 8, Gerónimo petitioned the court to dedicate the rest of the royal fifth to founding a permanent chaplaincy in Spain to pray for Albadán's soul, instead of giving the money to the people of Albadán's doctrina (fol. 197v). The priest who held this chaplaincy would receive a permanent income to say Mass daily for Albadán's salvation. Gerónimo explained that he had already paid for more than fifty masses to be said for his brother in Cusco and another fifty in Lima, but that many more were necessary for Albadán's redemption. De Silva, however, did not want to accept Gerónimo's new petition, preferring that the money go to the people of Pampachiri. Over the next few weeks, both Gerónimo and de Silva presented witnesses who testified before the court. De Silva brought forward Andrés Fernández de Córdoba, a former judge in Seville, now resident in Lima, who testified that courts held the power to give the royal fifth to charity (fol. 206r). De Silva argued rather cynically that most priests in rural Andean doctrinas committed many sins and, out of fear of purgatory, donated considerable amounts to charity in their wills; if a priest died before making a will, it could be assumed that he had intended to give money to charity, and so the court should donate wealth "in restitution" to those who were harmed by the priest (fols. 199r–201r).[17]

Gerónimo presented many of the same witnesses as before, who spoke about the poverty of Francisco's family and how Francisco's daughters needed large dowries to make marriages appropriate to their noble status. Fray Melchior de Porres of the Order of Our Lady of Carmel also testified on Gerónimo's behalf on October 17. Fray Melchior lived in Cusco but was from Seville and knew Albadán and his family well. According to his testimony, Fray Melchior met Albadán frequently in Cusco, where they dined together. At these dinners, Fray Melchior stated, Albadán spoke often about Francisco and his daughters and declared his intention to leave all of his wealth to them because they had no one else to help them (fols. 211r–212r).

Again, Gerónimo's witnesses included one of the most powerful members of Peruvian society, Fray Paredes, who was a friend of the viceroy, the Marquess of Montesclaros,[18] as well as a former schoolmate of Albadán and a close personal friend of Doña Ana, Albadán's mother. Faced with testimony from these witnesses, the judge ruled in favor of Gerónimo. On October 26, 1611, Arias de Ugarte presented the final judgment on the question of how Albadán's wealth would be distributed (fol. 215r–v). As before, Albadán's estate would be divided between his two brothers, Gerónimo and Francisco. Part of the royal fifth would pay priests in Lima to say masses for Albadán's soul, while the remainder would go to Seville, where Francisco would use the money to found a chaplaincy to pray perpetually for Albadán's salvation. In his letters to Albadán, Francisco had described how his son Juan, Albadán's namesake, was studying for the priesthood and would have the chaplaincy endowed by their uncle Don Andrés Núñez de Prado (the chaplaincy that Albadán had wanted for himself). Undoubtedly, Juan would also be given the chaplaincy dedicated to saying masses for his uncle who died in Peru. Despite Don Alonso and de Silva's best efforts, all of Albadán's inheritance would go to his family and to prayers for his soul.

Albadán's "Madness"

Albadán's behavior was clearly considered aberrant by those around him. There existed well-defined areas in colonial Hispanic society where torture and violent discipline were allowed, such as in Spanish Inquisitorial interrogations and in the punishment of African slaves. However, such violence was not regarded as normal in daily life; priests in rural Andean parishes did not routinely and publicly torture natives at will. While other forms of exploitation, such as forced labor and rape, were known to exist in Andean doctrinas, Albadán's sadistic abuses were considered truly exceptional. Albadán's uncle Fray Francisco de Prado emphasized to his nephew that such depraved behavior would not be allowed in Spain. In Pampachiri, Albadán was able to avoid punishment for his atrocities only because he knew how to manipulate the unequal power relations implicit in colonial society to his advantage. Is it possible that he suffered from a mental illness that compelled him to commit acts of murderous aggression and sexual violence?

It is notoriously difficult to analyze categories of mental illness across cultures. While many anthropologists agree that a few core mental illnesses, such as depression and schizophrenia, appear to be universal, others maintain that all definitions of mental illness are culturally relative.[19] Nonetheless, if Albadán had lived today, it is likely that he would have been diagnosed as a psychopath—that is, an individual who is incapable of empathizing with the feelings of others, who lacks a moral compass, and who has little ability to feel shame, guilt, or disgust.[20] Unlike sociopaths, who lack empathy yet rarely commit criminal acts, psychopaths often commit violent crimes and delight in torturing their victims. Psychiatric clinicians commonly use several professional checklists of traits to determine whether a person is a psychopath, such as the Psychopathy Checklist Revised (PCL-R) and the Psychopathic Personality Inventory (PPI).[21] These checklists have a core set of traits, which Albadán exhibited. The first is that the psychopath is coldhearted, with a callous disregard for the feelings of others. Allied with this lack of empathy is a deficient sense of disgust; psychopaths have a high threshold for disgust, as "measured by their reactions when shown disgusting photos of mutilated faces."[22] Albadán certainly seemed to care little for the feelings of his victims of torture, while burning and mutilating them to a horrific degree. Like many psychopaths, Albadán exhibited deviant sexual behavior, molesting young women; his torture of male victims had a strongly sexual component. Psychopaths are said to lack social emotions such as shame, guilt, and embarrassment. According to Willem Martens, they may periodically become aware of the effects of their behavior on others and can be genuinely unhappy, at least temporarily, with their inability to control their behavior.[23] They can also suffer from depression due to their lack of lasting relationships with other people. However, even when saddened and depressed by their actions, they typically blame others for events that are actually their fault. Fray Francisco's responses to Albadán's letters show that, while Albadán seemed unhappy with the situation he had created in Pampachiri and the neighboring towns, he blamed his actions on his surroundings and on the "barbarians" around him, rather than on himself. He seemed to imagine that if he could escape to Spain, he could put his evil activities behind him; Fray Francisco had to rebuke Albadán sharply, telling him that he should control his bad behavior while still living in Peru. Psychopaths are also generally irritable and violent and exhibit these traits at a young age; this calls to mind the unknown antisocial act that led to Albadán's exile in Peru at the age of fourteen, an act for which people still blamed him decades later. Even when he was an adult, Albadán's brother Francisco repeatedly expressed in his letters his fear of angering Albadán. Additionally, psychopaths have unrealistic and often grandiose plans for the future, at variance with reality. According to the testimony gathered by Don Alonso, up until the time he died, Albadán talked frequently about how he would be retiring to Spain soon (fols. 11v–15r). Despite the evidence of Fray Francisco's letters, in which he repeatedly told his nephew that he could never return and that he must give up all dreams of living in Spain,

Albadán informed his friends that he would soon return to Spain to take up his uncle's chaplaincy there. As "his friend and neighbor of many years," Francisco Pérez Ramírez testified that Albadán "spoke of this many and various times . . . that he wanted to go to the kingdom of Castile and go off with a chaplaincy."[24] Yet Fray Francisco could not have written more clearly and plainly to Albadán that the chaplaincy from Don Andrés Núñez de Prado was not for him, and that he must remain in the Indies.

One other characteristic of psychopaths is that they have a shallow sense of word meaning.[25] In other words, they have little emotional response to the meaning of words and have difficulty understanding the connotative, rather than the literal, significance of words. Psychopaths, when compared to control groups, are more likely to group words by their literal meaning, instead of by their figurative sense. They also have greater difficulty in comprehending metaphors; they are more likely to believe that metaphors describe literal facts. One is reminded of Albadán's reading of Juvenal—was he unable to understand Juvenal's use of satire and irony? Did Albadán take Juvenal's satirical accounts of torture and sodomy as models of behavior? If this was the case, what did the priest make of the fantastic images in the emblem books? Did he wish to make these strange visions literal and concrete? If so, no wonder he wanted to copy the emblems onto the physical world around him, decorating the church façade with crude copies of Covarrubias's borders of naked women.

Albadán was not insane in the legal sense; that is, he clearly understood that his actions were illegal, and he took great lengths to avoid punishment for them. In fact, he was quite adroit in eluding retribution for his murders, torture, and theft, unless his death itself was due to poisoning by his enemies. Although not legally insane, he would likely be diagnosed with psychopathy—one of the most intractable of all psychiatric conditions—if he were living now. Some research suggests that psychopathy has a moderately strong genetic component, with psychopaths exhibiting a distinctive neurobiology.[26] Symptoms of psychopathy often manifest at a young age, as parents and relatives find themselves struggling to deal with an aggressive, callous child who has no regard for the feelings of others. In Albadán's case, his family's solution was to send him into exile in the Andes while he was still a teenager.

Today, most violent psychopaths are incarcerated in prisons or in mental hospitals. The disease is considered to be particularly resistant to treatment; however, researchers report some success when patients are provided with a combination of pharmacological treatments (usually lithium, antidepressants, or anticonvulsants) and group psychotherapy.[27] Yet recidivism rates for the disorder are high. In part this is because the patients who receive treatment generally get it in a restricted environment such as a hospital or prison, where they are kept away from alcohol and drugs. Numerous studies have shown that psychopaths are more likely than nonpsychopaths to have lifetime diagnoses of alcoholism or drug abuse, and that these addictions probably contribute to their violent behavior. Once the psychopath is again in an environment with easy access to alcohol and drugs, he or she is more likely to relapse into destructive and deviant activities. In Albadán's case, he consumed large quantities of wine, with his storehouses in Pampachiri and Umamarca containing dozens and dozens of empty wine casks. Quite possibly his drinking played a role in his abuse of the native peoples around him.

Psychopathy today is seen primarily as a medical issue—treated through drugs and therapy—that can become a criminal concern if the psychopath commits violent acts. In Golden Age Spain, by contrast, it was viewed mainly as a moral issue of sin, which could have criminal ramifications. Mental illness was recognized in seventeenth-century Spain, but psychopathy would not have been regarded as a psychiatric disease.[28] Tirso de Molina, the great Mercedarian dramatist who described Fray Francisco de Prado so well in his history of the Mercedarian Order, explored the moral dimensions of psychopathy in his famous play *Damned by Doubt* (*Condenado por desconfiado*).[29] This drama tells the story of two men: Enrico, a dashing criminal who gains salvation at the end though his sincere contrition and love for his father, and Paulo, a cynical hermit who, believing himself already lost, gives himself up to his most base and cruel impulses. Paulo, convinced that an angry God has preordained him to damnation, becomes a mountain bandit, committing untold acts of cruelty, violence, and theft. He has no feeling for his victims, such as the innocent shepherd whom he cruelly murders. His intention is to kill without remorse, filling the branches of a metaphorical tree of evil with the heads of his victims. Upon Paulo's death, when he finds himself in an eternal hell of fire and snakes, he weeps that his damnation was due to his belief that his soul was already lost and to his lack of faith in a merciful, forgiving God. This play is generally viewed as a meditation on grace, predestination, and free will in human salvation, in which Tirso expressed the ideas of the Jesuit Luis de Molina, whose theology emphasized human free will.[30]

As we have seen, the ties between the Mercedarians in Seville and Albadán and his family were very close. Fray Francisco, one of the most powerful Mercedarians in Spain, knew the story of his nephew's abuses. He and his confreres not only dined regularly at the house of Doña Ana but also attended her funeral, where Fray Francisco wept openly. When word of Doña

Ana's will circulated, Fray Francisco's fellow Mercedarians must have wondered why Albadán had been cut out of it; they would have been eager to hear the tale. Fray Paredes, who knew Albadán as a schoolboy and was close to Albadán's uncle and mother, testified in the court case over Albadán's inheritance. He would have heard the ensuing discussion about Albadán's need for restitution and redemption, as would have other Mercedarians in Lima and Cusco, some of whom were allied to Tirso's faction in the order. Given the rivalries among the Mercedarians at the time and the general atmosphere of suspicion and gossip among them, Tirso undoubtedly heard stories about Albadán's wickedness. It is possible that Albadán inspired the character of Paulo, the callous and uncaring sinner whose atrocities went unredeemed through his lack of faith. Albadán, like Paulo, seems to have considered himself lost, with no ability to stop what he was doing in Pampachiri. Albadán did perform a mute confession of sorts on his deathbed, nodding and shaking his head. If his contrition was sincere, then this confession would have been considered efficacious, and Albadán would have been condemned in the afterlife to a terrible and lengthy purgatory, after which he would be released to heaven through God's mercy. Even a sinner as wicked as Albadán could find divine forgiveness if his repentance were genuine. In this case, the many masses that were said for him would have helped ease his pains in purgatory and shorten his stay there, according to Roman Catholic teachings. But if he did not repent in that very questionable confession, he would have been condemned to eternal damnation, according to the theology of the time. In this case, he could well have thought the same words that Paulo did upon discovering that he was damned: "Today God's judgment arrived, and God told me, 'go down, damned priest, to the angry heart of the dark abyss, where you will be suffering.' Cursed be my parents a thousand times because they begot me!"[31]

Albadán's story and that of his family illuminates the life of one of Tirso's most important Mercedarian contemporaries, Fray Francisco, who was described in Tirso's brilliant and irreverent history of the order. The windfall of unpublished documents and personal letters presented here also provides an added depth of appreciation for Guaman Poma's account of clerical misconduct in the Andes. Behind Guaman Poma's few paragraphs about the evil priest is a much larger narrative of exile, suffering, deception, and murder— one that sheds light on life in the rural Andes in the early 1600s. Although this account of Albadán's life is not a pleasant tale, it is essential for understanding Chanka history in colonial Peru. The Spanish priest's murders, thefts, and abuses are part of the story of the Chankas; his victims should not be ignored or forgotten. Moreover, when Albadán engineered Don León Apu Guasco's fall from power, he upset the Chanka political balance and sparked 123 years of intense lineage rivalry. In Part II, I will explore the nature of Chanka life in the world of colonial Apurimac—first examining the life and career of Don León Apu Guasco, who was destroyed in his attempts to stop Albadán's abuse, and then describing how the lineage rivalries between the Tomay Guaraca and Guachaca families (ayllus) dominated Chanka politics throughout the seventeenth century and beyond.

PART II

7. THE KURAKA

Introduction

Who was Don León Apu Guasco, the native kuraka who tried to stop
Albadán's abuses, and who was deposed and exiled for his efforts? Don León
rose to power as governor and head of the entire Chanka nation in the late
1590s, ruling for approximately ten years before he was removed from office
in 1607.[1] His grandfather Don Diego Apu Guasco, who governed the Chanka
people throughout the 1550s, had fought side by side with Guaman Poma's father on the royalist side against the rebellious armies of Francisco Hernández
Girón. Guaman Poma left us a portrait of Diego Apu Guasco in the heat of
battle next to the chronicler's father, Don Martín de Ayala, who is depicted in
the foreground wearing a decorated tunic and holding a spear. Behind them
is Juan Guaman Guachaca, the head of the lower Chanka moiety (fig. 21).

Both of the Chanka kurakas[2] and Guaman Poma's father supported the
royalist side during the revolt of Hernández Girón (1553–1554). Guaman
Poma's artwork provides a vivid illustration of the companionship between
his father and the Chanka lords, who fought victoriously together in battle. Diego Guasco, in particular, is shown with a very distinctive face and
an expression of resolute courage. Curiously, in the text accompanying this
illustration, Guaman Poma mistakenly refers to Diego Apu Guasco, his father's fighting companion, as "Don León Apu Guacso," substituting the contemporary leader for the historical one.[3] Guaman Poma probably knew Don
León personally, given the close ties between the two families, and seems to

FIG. 21 Don Martín de Ayala at the battle of Chuquinca, with Don Diego Apu Guasco beside him and Guaman Guachaca behind. From Guaman Poma, *Nueva corónica y buen gobierno* (1615), p. 432, no. 174. The Royal Library, Copenhagen, GKS 2232 quarto.

have been thinking of him when he drew this illustration. It is quite possible that this drawing was modeled on Don León's face, rather than that of his grandfather.

Don León inherited his position as head of the upper moiety, Hanansaya, and governor of the Chanka nation from his father, who was named Don Diego Apu Guasco after Don León's grandfather.[4] During Don León's tenure in office, he worked closely with the head of the lower moiety, Luis Tomay Guaraca. The people governed by Don León lived in dispersed communities within a roughly triangular region, with the city of Andahuaylas near the center.

Our understanding of the extent of the Chanka region has varied greatly throughout the last century.[5] For the Spanish colonial era, the limits of

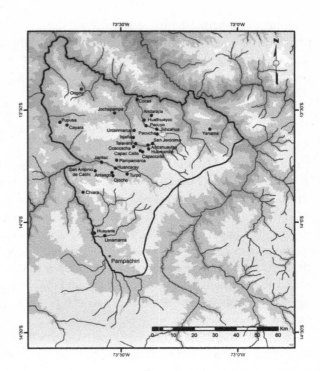

MAP. 2 Map of the Chanka repartimiento, 1536. Adapted from Bauer, Kellet, and Aráoz Silva, *Chanka*, n.p.

Chanka territory can best be determined from a 1539 document listing the communities under the control of the Chanka leaders, in conjunction with the results of Brian Bauer's archaeological survey of the Andahuaylas valley.[6] As map 2 reveals, the Chanka territory extended to Yanama in the east, Ongoy in the north, and Pupusa in the west. Pampachiri lies in the Chicha Valley in the southernmost portion of Chanka territory, with the neighboring town of Umamarca slightly to the north.

This is an area of great agricultural richness; in the sixteenth and seventeenth centuries, the fields of the Chanka heartland produced a wide array of crops and pastured both European and Andean livestock. Don León, as the leading Chanka kuraka, enjoyed access to wealth far surpassing that of the head kurakas of other Andean ethnic groups. This affluence in the late sixteenth and early seventeenth centuries was not due entirely to the agricultural bounty of the region, however. Much of the Chanka leaders' prosperity came from rents on their extensive properties and landholdings in Cusco, which they acquired in the 1570s. While there were numerous demands on this income (see chapter 8), the remainder allowed Don León to enjoy the trappings of wealth. To understand how the Chanka leadership obtained their houses, shops, and plots of land in the ancient imperial city of Cusco, one must go back to the sixteenth century, when the labor of the Chanka people was granted to the Spanish conquistador Diego Maldonado.

Diego Maldonado and the Chanka Encomienda

Since the time of Columbus, the Spanish Crown gave leaders of expeditions in the Indies control over a limited number of labor-service grants, known as *encomiendas*.[7] These grants were to reward service to the Crown, usually in military affairs. Through this system, different native groups were assigned to specific Spaniards. Legally, the Spaniard was to provide protection and religious instruction to the indigenous people under his or her care, while the natives had to give specific goods and labor to their newly assigned overseer. The encomienda was primarily a grant of labor, not of land; nonetheless, many Spaniards were able to use the wealth generated from their encomienda to purchase large estates.

On April 15, 1539, Francisco Pizarro granted the Chanka ethnic group inhabiting the region of Andahuaylas to Captain Diego Maldonado as an encomienda, along with the labor of the people from the village of Vilcaparo, near modern Andarapa.[8] Maldonado, a principal member of Pizarro's expeditionary force, had already been given a large lot on the central plaza of Cusco as well as several other grants of land around Cusco.[9] In fact, he would become one of the wealthiest *encomenderos* in all of Peru, earning the title "Maldonado the Rich."

Diego Maldonado administered his encomienda in Andahuaylas primarily from his luxurious homes in Cusco and Lima. In addition to his profitable Andahuaylas *repartimiento*, he owned the large estates of Guanchac, Tiobamba, Quispiquilla, Conchacalla, Guamanchaupa (which produced salt), and Limatambo, a sugar plantation in Nazca (which included African slaves); extensive property in Cusco, including an entire city block of houses and shops just off the Plaza de Armas; and homes and fields in Lima.[10] The extent of his holdings in Andahuaylas was somewhat reduced in Viceroy La Gasca's redistribution of the encomiendas after 1548, yet his properties were still substantial and extremely valuable.[11]

When Maldonado died on March 2, 1569, his entire estate passed to his Spanish-born widow, Doña Francisca de Guzmán.[12] The marriage of Maldonado and Doña Francisca had produced no children. Maldonado specified that his property should go to Juan Arias Maldonado, his illegitimate son by his long-standing mistress, an Inka princess named Doña Luisa Palla.[13] In his last testament, Maldonado emphasized that because of his great love for Juan Arias, he wanted Juan and Juan's future descendants to enjoy his wealth. As the captain's widow, Doña Francisca held the inheritance in trust for Juan Arias; legally, under normal circumstances, she would not have been allowed to dispose of the bulk of the captain's estate if this would diminish Juan Arias's inheritance. However, Doña Francisca did dispense of much property. When she died in 1579, the Chanka repartimiento of Andahuaylas reverted to the Crown, falling under the direct administration of the corregidor in Andahuaylas; it remained a royal estate throughout the colonial era. Juan Arias Maldonado did not inherit the Chanka repartimiento, although he became the owner of the rest of his father's wealth.

Although Captain Maldonado's will seemed straightforward, leaving his property to his beloved illegitimate son Juan Arias, it contained a short clause that would have a profound effect on the lives of the Chanka leaders for generations. In his will, the captain dictated that he wished for his widow, his executor, and the archbishop to make restitutions to the Indians of his encomienda in whatever manner and amount they considered appropriate: "I would like and it is my will that the restitutions that the said Lord Archbishop and Doña Francisca de Gúzman and Gaspar de Sotelo [Maldonado's executor] have to make and will make to discharge my conscience and my soul . . . to the Indians that I have in my encomienda . . . [will be] in the quantity and manner and order that seems appropriate to them."[14] The captain then cautioned that the restitutions should not be so large as to endanger the wealth that would be passed on to Juan Arias and his descendants.[15]

Doña Francisca, however, seemed determined to ensure that the illegitimate son of her husband's Indian mistress would inherit as little as possible. As an elite woman in colonial Peru, she would have expected her husband to carry on extramarital liaisons.[16] Her apparent hostility toward Juan Arias Maldonado may have been inspired by jealousy toward her rival, particularly of Doña Luisa's ability to bear a son. Or she may have found Juan Arias himself to be personally odious.[17] At her instigation, Juan de Palomares initiated an official investigation of the illegal labor service and goods that the captain had demanded from the Chankas.

The investigation began in 1570 and lasted for years.[18] In the resulting report, there seems to be a discrepancy between the findings against Maldonado, whom historian Steve Stern called "a generous and redistributive patron,"[19] and the compensation offered from Maldonado's estate.

Palomares could find no evidence of any kind of physical abuse by the encomendero against the Chankas. The inspector documented the most outrageous case of verbal abuse that he encountered: on one occasion, the captain stated that, "in general, all the Indians of this kingdom are foolish drunks . . . without honor."[20] While Maldonado's statement was unkind and untrue, it hardly seems unusual in the colonial context. Palomares did document some specific instances in which Diego Maldonado exacted excessive native labor for his textile workshops and agricultural fields. He also uncovered evidence that the captain had taken native livestock to which he had no clear legal right; however, the question of Maldonado's rights hinged upon a fine point of law that was open to divergent interpretations. Legally, the Chankas owed tribute from their own property to their encomendero, which Maldonado took mainly in the form of livestock. Palomares judged that the livestock taken by the captain had belonged to the former Inka estates in Andahuaylas and not to the Chankas; therefore, the captain had no right of possession. To compensate the Chankas, as she interpreted Diego's instructions in his will, Doña Francisca gave most of Maldonado's extensive Cusco properties to the Chanka chiefs, thereby depriving Juan Arias of ownership.[21]

The property that Doña Francisca presented to the Chankas in restitution consisted of numerous houses and shops throughout Cusco. The Chankas were not permitted to rent or to sell these properties themselves; legally, they had to hire a Spanish administrator to manage their property. Collecting the rents that were due to them became a continual concern. For example, in 1587, Don León's father, Don Diego Guasco, went to court to remove Alonso de Mora as the administrator of their properties.[22] According to the testimony of the vicar of Andahuaylas, Father Bartolomé Ximénes, Mora refused to turn over to the Chankas the rents that were owed to them. When the rents were given to the Chanka leaders, they often equalled over 6,500 pesos yearly, a significant amount.[23] Doña Francisca's generosity in carrying out her husband's dying instructions provided abundant financial resources for the Chanka lords.

Advantages of Being a Kuraka

The kuraka,[24] whose title is variously translated as "chief," "lord," or "ruler," was originally an official within the Inka Empire who held a role similar in some ways to that of a magistrate, although with additional symbolic and ritual importance. Kurakas served as key mediators between the people they represented and the superhuman forces, or *huacas*, who controlled the people's prosperity and good fortune. They were responsible for the well-being of their followers, resolving disputes, coordinating work parties, adjudicating land and water distribution, and coordinating relations with the representatives of the Inka government. It was the kuraka's task to ensure that the ethnic group's labor tribute was turned over to the Inka state. In turn, the Inka state treated kurakas to elaborate feasts and granted them marks of high status, such as the right to wear special fabrics, to wear gold and silver jewelry, and to marry multiple wives. The emperor would reward a particularly fortunate kuraka with an *aclla*—a beautiful, young virgin girl—as a sign of great favor.[25] In general, the role of the kuraka was hereditary, although it would be granted to whichever son or nephew of the reigning kuraka was most fit for the task. There are also occasional references in the colonial documents to female kurakas who governed as equals to men.

Generally speaking, the Inkas allowed autochthonous rulers from local ethnic groups to serve as kurakas. We see this in the case of the Chankas, for example (see chapter 1): under Inka rule, the leader of the Guasco ayllu was made the head kuraka for Hanansaya (replacing the Astoy Guaracas), and the leader of the Guachaca ayllu was promoted to head kuraka for Urinsaya (replacing the Tomay Guaracas). Yet, in other cases, the imperial government would appoint an ethnic Inka lord to serve as a kuraka. The Sivi Paucars who governed in Umamarca and Pampachiri, for instance, were described in Maldonado's 1539 document as "orejones" or "big ears," indicating that they were ethnically Inka.[26]

Local kurakas were expected to support the worship of their ancestral huacas. Huacas are material manifestations of the superhuman; they can be found in mountain peaks, caves, rock outcrops, and "any number of humanly made objects in shrines: effigies, human mummies, oracles and so forth."[27] Huacas ranged in importance from major oracles and deities to small carved stones that were believed to guard a household. From 1569 to 1571, a Spanish priest named Cristóbal de Albornoz led a campaign to extirpate native religious practices throughout this part of the Andes.[28] He personally visited Andahuaylas and reported destroying more than two thousand shrines and huacas in the region. His account provides us with the names of three of the holiest huacas for the Chankas. The first two, Uscovilca and Ancovilca, represented the ancestor of each moiety. Uscovilca was "the huaca of the Hanan Chankas; he is stone shaped like a clothed man. He has a temple in the town of Andahuaylas." The other ancestral huaca, Ancovilca, "was the huaca of the Hurin Chankas; he was a stone that they carried with them wherever they went and he had a temple." The third principal huaca was a female deity named Llahapalla, or "Lady of Increase,"[29] who "was a clothed stone with a hole in her shoulder and she had a temple."[30] A primary duty of the Chanka kurakas was to participate in worshipping these beings. Tragically, Albornoz smashed these three holy statues and confiscated the rich offerings in each shrine. It is not known whether Don León Apu Guasco took part in any clandestine ceremonies in honor of the ancestral huacas, who were often re-shaped from remaining fragments by their devotees; however, such rituals did occur in the colonial period, so it is quite possible that Don León may have secretly worshipped local Andean huacas.[31]

Under Spanish colonial rule, the institution of the *kurakazgo* continued, although it was transformed. After the Spanish invasion, the kurakas learned to protect their followers in the courts, to promote Christianity, and to main-tain their community's fragile socioeconomic order in the face of rapid popu-lation loss. The kuraka also had to meet the Spanish labor and tribute duties, serving as the go-between linking the native society with the emerging colo-nial order. This was an often difficult task.

The hierarchal relations among higher-level and lower-level kurakas continued during the colonial era; however, under Spanish rule, more power became concentrated at the topmost position, to the detriment of the low-er kuraka positions. Among the Chankas during the Inka period, for exam-ple, the head kuraka of the upper moiety, Hanansaya, functioned as a "first among equals" over all the Chankas, while the lower-level kurakas still held considerable power. Under Spanish rule, more power and privilege was con-centrated in the hands of the apu (head) kuraka or governor of the entire ethnic group, at the expense of the privileges enjoyed by the lower-ranking kurakas.

As the next chapter will reveal, the leading Chanka kurakas faced many pressures—the threat of imprisonment for nonpayment of tribute, the need to exercise legal vigilance to protect the community's rights, and the possi-ble retribution carried out against kurakas who complained about abusive priests or officials. One might wonder why ayllu members accepted the po-sition. In fact, in the region around Cusco, by the late seventeenth century, it occasionally became difficult to locate anyone willing assume the burdens of the kurakazgo.[32] Nonetheless, among the Chankas, the benefits of the of-fice outweighed its disadvantages, and competition among families for the kurakazgo remained high until the end of the colonial period. Kuraka fam-ilies at all levels, from a minor kuraka in a small village to the governor of all the Chankas, were exempt from tribute payments, including *mita* labor.

They also received a large share of communal lands and were paid a salary. The kuraka salaries derived, in part, from the Cusco rents; because the Chankas' rents were significantly higher than those of neighboring ethnic groups, their kuraka salaries were higher as well.[33]

Kurakas also enjoyed the benefit of labor tribute on their own farms and in their workshops. The government routinely granted kurakas the use of a certain number of mit'a laborers to assist in the kurakas' fields and other enterprises. Numerous scholars have described the use of the native workforce by kurakas, focusing on the frequent accusations of abuse and overwork lodged against the Andean chiefs.[34] Complaints by the "common Indians" about the kurakas' excessive demands for labor have often been seen as evidence of a growing class conflict within rural society, as ever more powerful indigenous elites exploited the Indian peasantry. Throughout the seventeenth century, one encounters such cases in Chanka territory, in which ayllu members accused their kurakas of illegally forcing them to work excessively, well beyond the limits of the chiefs' mit'a privileges.[35] Generally, however, such complaints were enmeshed in a complex struggle between two or more parties over the kuraka office. Although the responsibilities of the kurakazgo were daunting, its rewards were great enough throughout most of the colonial period for the Chanka leaders to struggle fiercely for the position.

Don León Apu Guasco

While we know little about Don León's personal life, we can form an idea of how he may have lived by examining the lives of his contemporaries. His paternal uncle Diego Condorguacho served as the leading Chanka kuraka during the 1560s, after the death of Don León's grandfather.[36] Diego Condorguacho was a man of property, as Don León must have been. Condorguacho had four houses—one very large house in Andahuaylas and three smaller ones in different communities. Sixteen *yanaconas*—unpaid retainers—formed a personal retinue of assistants. His clothing was a mixture of Andean and Spanish garments. He wore cloaks and shirts of the finest-quality woven Andean cloth, known as cumbi; wearing cumbi cloth had been a mark of high status during the days of the Inkas.[37] Yet he also possessed five Spanish-style shirts made of colorful French cotton, two pairs of leather boots (one black pair and one white pair), and eleven Spanish handkerchiefs. Guaman Poma depicted a kuraka sitting next to his wife and wearing Castilian garments, including a shirt made of Andean cumbi cloth. The chronicler's drawing shows how

FIG. 22 Provincial lord
and lady. From Guaman
Poma, *Nueva corónica y
buen gobierno* (1615), p. 761,
no. 289. The Royal Library,
Copenhagen, GKS 2232
quarto.

Don León may have dressed; it should be noted that the lady's attire is more traditionally Andean than that of her husband (fig. 22).

Condorguacho was quite prolific, fathering ten illegitimate children and three legitimate children. Don León would not be so fruitful. His two marriages to native women did not yield any children; however, his mistress Doña Magdalena Pusachilla did give birth to a daughter, Doña Ana Guasco, who was "respected and loved by all the Indians of the said ayllu [of Hanansaya] as the daughter of the said governor [Don León Guasco]."[38] Don León was never able to speak Spanish fluently and had to rely on translators and bilingual scribes in order to carry out his affairs.

Don León's administrative activities included dealing directly with the corregidors who administered the Chanka repartimiento, collecting rents, and gathering and auctioning tribute, which was collected in the form of goods such as maize, wheat, potatoes, and clothing. For example, on January 25, 1603, in the city of Andahuaylas, Don León and Don Luis Tomay Guaraca, the head of Urinsaya, presented 989 pesos to the corregidor.[39] This sum represented the additional tribute that the Chanka Indians owed to the government after the auctioning of tribute goods on June 24 of the previous year. Yet by far the most difficult task faced by the head kuraka was gathering Chanka men to provide the yearly labor tribute that the native people owed to the colonial government. The Chankas suffered from the misfortune of owing labor tribute—known as the mit'a—in the deadly mercury mines of Huancavelica. Throughout the colonial period, many Chankas fled to sugar plantations and cities such as Cusco to avoid the dreaded mercury mines. While all parts of the Andes experienced internal migration and depopulation as people fled from their obligation to provide labor tribute to the state, regions with the most oppressive mit'a burdens—which included work in the silver mines of Potosí and in the mercury mines of Huancavelica—had the highest rates of internal migration.[40] Throughout the colonial period, the Andahuaylas region experienced a degree of migration that would eventually leave many traditional Chanka settlements virtually devoid of able-bodied adults (see chapter 8).

Mercury, extracted from the royal mines in Huancavelica, was essential to the refinement of silver ore in the seventeenth century.[41] Miners working in the long underground tunnels of the mines breathed in the mercury vapors and trudged, often barefoot, through mercury-filled slag.[42] Most toxic to humans when inhaled, the metal harms the central nervous system, the kidneys, and other organs, causing brain damage and eventual death. Men who survived the mit'a in Huancavelica returned to their villages in broken health, weakened, without teeth, and coughing blood; they suffered from uncontrollable trembling, irritability, loss of memory, and, in some cases, insanity. Pregnant women exposed to mercury vapors frequently give birth to infants with severe birth defects. Fernando de Montesinos, a Spanish priest who was an expert on mining in colonial Peru, described the effects of mercury thus: "the mineral is of such a malignant nature that within fifteen days [of working the mines] men become pale, and soon open sores appear all over their bodies, and they become paralytic, or they lose their lives."[43] In a tract written toward the end of his life, Montesinos referred to the mines of Huancavelica as "the greatest known devourer of Indians."[44]

Miners laboring in Huancavelica were not devoid of medical care. Royal officials maintained a hospital near the mines that, in addition to Spanish medical treatments, offered the care of indigenous shamans. In 1679, for example, two convicted Indian "witches" from the city of Andahuaylas, Lorenza Sisa and Magdalena Tucuman, were sent to this hospital to provide treatment to patients for ten years.[45] One wonders how these two native healers treated the horrifying ailments they encountered; the outlook must have been grim for most of their patients.

The number of able-bodied Chanka men who were forced to work in the mines was determined by censuses, known as *visitas*, carried out on the orders of the viceroy. In 1594, the visita conducted by Rodrigo Delgadillo determined that there were 4,520 tributaries, or able-bodied men, in the Chanka nation; approximately one-seventh of this number were sent to the mercury mines or to perform other forms of forced labor.[46] However, in 1603, Don León Apu Guasco traveled to Lima to petition Viceroy Luis de Velasco for another census. Due to deaths in the mines, disease, and internal migration as Chanka tributaries fled the horrors of the mercury mines, the total number of tributaries had fallen, he argued. In later testimony, Don León would complain that the Chankas could not fulfill their tribute requirements "because of the lack of Indians who have fled, who number more than one thousand, and do not show up." Don León's petition was successful, and the viceroy ordered Agustín Arce de Quiroz to carry out a new visita in order to determine whether there truly were fewer Chanka tributaries.

In 1604, Arce de Quiroz journeyed through greater Andahuaylas with his retinue of scribes and assistants, assiduously gathering information for the census. From June to August 1604, he visited every priest and curate in the region, collecting the census data that the priests were obliged to keep about all the births and deaths in their doctrinas.[47] Albadán was unusual in having ignored his responsibility to record this information. After collecting these preliminary results, Arce de Quiroga, Don León, and Don Luis Tomay Guaraca gathered together all the residents of the town of Talavera (today a suburb of Andahuaylas) and announced in Spanish and in Quechua that if anyone had knowledge of Indians who had been hidden from the census, they must come forward privately to inform the visitor. They repeated this announcement to the crowd in the city of Andahuaylas a week later, on August 22. The visitation officially concluded on September 9, when Don León and Don Luis, with the sacerdotal census ledgers about them, ratified the results and swore that no Indians had been hidden from the census.

The results of the 1604 census were a personal triumph for Don León. Arce de Quiroz found that the total number of able-bodied Chanka men had declined by 1,243.[48] That meant that the Chankas owed fewer annual tributaries; approximately 170 Chanka men would be saved from either death or mental incapacity in the mercury mines every year. One can imagine the rejoicing that must have taken place in Don León's household when the results of the census were ratified in September!

Sometime late in the following year, on the heels of this victory, Don León submitted his complaint against Albadán. As described in chapter 2, Guaman Poma recorded that Don León protested the priest's habitual sexual abuse of the young women of Pampachiri. By March 1606, the wheels of Albadán's retaliation were set in motion. By this time, the viceroy had received Albadán's intelligence that Indians had been purposefully hidden during Arce de Quiroz's 1604 census.[49] On June 1, 1606, the Audiencia in Lima therefore dispatched a lawyer, Licenciado Francisco Rodríguez Plata, to perform another visitation of the Chankas to investigate and to determine the true tributary population. His orders stated explicitly, "caciques and other persons found guilty will be punished by being removed from the *cacicazgo* and other offices."[50] Rodríguez Plata seems to have performed his visita quickly, with relatively little pomp and ceremony. By June 1, 1606, he presented his findings to the Audiencia, and the results were not good news for Don León. The visitor found that 641 able-bodied men had been hidden from Arce de Quiroga's census. An additional 89 Chanka men would now be liable to perform labor in the mercury mines and provide other forms of compulsory tribute.

Given the slow pace of colonial justice, the results were not made known immediately. Later that year, Don León and Don Luis Tomay Guaraca faced another demand upon their people. In Andahuaylas on October 26, 1606, the Jesuit brother Gonzalo Ruíz[51] presented the corregidor with a royal petition that granted fifteen Chanka workers to the Jesuits for two years to build the Jesuits' residence in Guamanga.[52] Don León and Don Luis fought this order for many months, claiming that because their tributary population had declined so significantly, they already provided too many workers for mit'a service. However, their efforts were for naught. Between May and October 1607, Don León was found guilty of hiding Indians from the 1604 census and removed from office. His nephew Don Juan Topa Guasco replaced him as the head kuraka of the upper moiety, Hanansaya. On October 12, 1607, the corregidor, Don Miguel Gerónimo de Cabrera, threatened Don Juan Topa Guasco and Don Luis with jail unless they turned over the fifteen workers to the Jesuits. The two Chanka leaders spent the next day in prison, where they finally agreed to provide the additional workers.

In an unusual move, the Audiencia also demoted the Guasco ayllu and promoted the head of the lower moiety, Urinsaya, to be the governor and supreme head of the Chanka nation. The seasoned leader Don Luis Tomay Guaraca was now governor and apu kuraka. This suggests that all of the men whom Don León had hidden from the census were from the ayllus of the upper moiety, many of them men whom Don León had grown up with and known since childhood. If men from the lower moiety had been concealed during the census, Don Luis Tomay Guaraca would have been punished, not promoted. According to Guaman Poma, Don León was exiled from Chanka territory and died of grief.[53] The former lord had faced the ignominy of a trial and conviction along with the loss of his power, office, and wealth; moreover, he found himself powerless to save his followers from the terrors of the quicksilver mines and from the horrific abuses committed by Albadán in Pampachiri. It is not surprising that he did not live long after his conviction. Challenging Albadán had led to his downfall.

8. THE RIVALRY

Following the promotion of Don Luis Tomay Guaraca as governor of all the Chankas, this position remained with the leaders of the lower moiety for two hundred years. This move deeply intensified the rivalry between the most prominent Urinsaya ayllus—the Guachacas and the Tomay Guaracas—for the headship of their moiety, since the headship now included the governorship over all the Chankas. This competition would dominate elite Chanka politics for the next 123 years. The Tomay Guaraca ayllu would eventually win this contest; it would do so by adopting a profoundly non-Andean institution—the dowry—for the very Andean practice of making strategic marriage alliances. In Satire VI, Juvenal bemoaned the power of the dowry to inflame men with the desire to marry, just as it gave married women a measure of independence. As he wrote, "Censennia's husband swears she's the perfect wife: why so? Because she brought him three million; in exchange he calls her chaste. The shafts that waste him, the fires that burn him up have nothing to do with desire. That torch was lit by cash; it was her dowry that fired those arrows and purchased her freedom. She can make come-hitherish signs, or write billets-doux in front of her husband; your wealthy woman who marries a miser has a widow's privileges."[1] Dowries would enable noblewomen from the Tomay Guaraca ayllu to marry powerful creole landowners. We do not know whether these Chanka noblewomen were as flirtatious and unchaste as Juvenal suggests; however, they were able to persuade their husbands to protect the interests of their ayllu.

Don Diego Quino Guaraca

One of the most powerful kurakas to emerge in the colonial period was Don Diego Quino Guaraca, who became the governor and apu kuraka of all the Chankas in 1647.[2] Don Diego spoke Spanish fluently,[3] having attended the Colegio de San Borja in Cusco in his youth. The Jesuits founded San Borja in 1621 to educate the oldest sons of the head kurakas from various ethnic groups in the dioceses of Cusco, Arequipa, and Guamanga.[4] No more than twenty young men attended at any one time. The viceroyalty fully supported the students, providing free room, board, and instruction, except in the case of the Chanka students. Because the Chankas enjoyed such high rents from their properties, these students were expected to pay the Jesuits yearly for the privilege of a Spanish education in Cusco.[5] During Don Diego's lifetime, Cusco was home to the great flowering of Andean baroque art known as the "Cusco school,"[6] in which indigenous artists combined Andean elements within European visual norms. In the churches of Cusco, the young heir to the kurakaship had the opportunity to see, firsthand, evocative works similar to an anonymous image of the Virgin of the Rosary of Guápulo painted in Cusco in the seventeenth century (fig 23). At San Borja, the teenaged Don Diego received the humanistic education promoted by the Jesuits, while also becoming conversant in the Spanish language and Hispanic culture. Fluency in Spanish and urban customs would have given Don Diego a significant advantage in promoting his political interests.

Such cultural capital may have also facilitated his marriage to a creole woman of Spanish descent, Doña Elvira Martínez. Through Doña Elvira, Don Diego was linked by marriage to "many Spaniards . . . and hacienda owners,"[7] as Pedro Alca, the head of the Guachaca ayllu, would later testify bitterly. Don Diego's union with Doña Elvira in the 1640s is the first recorded wedding between someone from a Chanka kuraka lineage and someone of primarily European descent. Doña Elvira later inherited the Moyomoyo ranch, along with its sheep and cattle, from her relative Cristina Reynoso,[8] but it is unlikely that she possessed a large dowry, if she had a dowry at all. As David Garrett has noted, when native noblemen married Spanish women in the later colonial period, "the women tended to bring less wealth to the marriage."[9] In fact, Don Diego probably gave Doña Elvira a large marriage gift—the *arras*, which the groom presented to the bride upon their marriage. Certainly, Don Diego and his children benefitted from Doña Elvira's kinship with other powerful Spanish creoles in the area, regardless of whether she brought a dowry.

FIG. 23 Virgin of the Rosary of Guápulo, seventeenth century, Cusco school. Metropolitan Museum of Art, 64.164.385. Gift of Loretta Hines Howard, 1964. http://www.metmuseum.org.

It is likely that Don Diego's influential creole in-laws helped secure his position as head kuraka of Urinsaya and over all the Chankas, although we do not have concrete evidence of this. After 1607, when the head kuraka of the lower moiety was made governor over the entire Chanka nation, there was a constant fluctuation between the Guachaca ayllu and the Tomay Guaraca ayllu in the governorship. The Guasco ayllu maintained its ascendancy over the upper moiety throughout the entire colonial era, but the office of head kuraka of the lower moiety shifted across this period. The following chart demonstrates how the headship of Chanka Urinsaya fluctuated between the rival ayllus throughout the colonial era, from 1553 to 1775:[10]

Juan Guaman *Guachaca* (Lurinchangas), 1553, 1570
Luis Tomay *Guaraca*, 1587, 1607
Francisco Guaman *Guachaca* de Ayala, 1615
Diego Quino *Guaraca*, 1647–68
Juan Quino Tomay *Guaraca*, 1668–69
Andrés Haparco (*Guachaca*), 1669
Juan Quino Tomay *Guaraca*, 1669–87
Juan Bautista Haparco (*Guachaca*), 1687–1706
Gregorio Haparco (*Guachaca*), 1706 (interim)
Cayetano Alca de la Cruz (*Guachaca*), 1706–12
Juan Basilio Quino *Guaraca*, 1712–30
Thomas Quino *Guaraca*, 1730–47
Francisco Tomay *Guaraca*, 1747–75 (and beyond)

Guaman Poma informs us that Juan Guaman Guachaca (also known as Juan Guaman Lurinchangas), the head of the Guachaca ayllu, was the Chanka leader of Urinsaya in 1553;[11] he was still listed as the ruler of Urinsaya twenty years later, in the 1570s.[12] In 1607, rulership over the lower moiety had shifted to Don Luis Tomay Guaraca, but his ayllu was unable to maintain control over the office of governor after his death. By 1615, the next head of the Chankas was a member of the Guachaca ayllu—Francisco Guaman Guachaca de Ayala, grandson of Juan Guaman Guachaca.[13] Don Diego Quino Guaraca subsequently regained control of the headship of the Tomay Guaraca ayllu, presumably through the influence of his wife's relatives. The political rivalry between these two ayllus dates to the time of the Inka conquest, when the Tomay Guaracas were demoted from their position as head of Urinsaya and the Guachacas were put in their place. However, their competition was greatly exacerbated by the flipping of moiety power in 1607, when the head of the lower moiety suddenly became the beneficiary of the authority and wealth of the governorship.

Competition for power and a high position within the kuraka ranks was common among Chanka ayllus during Spanish colonial rule. Garrett has demonstrated the existence of bitter competition among families for the kurakaship in the towns surrounding Cusco in the eighteenth century.[14] In communities such as Anta, San Sebastián, and Maras, the position of kuraka moved among various families, who aggressively claimed their rights to the office. In 1614, the Crown imposed male hereditary succession on the Andean kurakazgo; however, the appointment of kurakas was not based merely on hereditary succession.[15] In reality, the selection of kurakas, particularly those of the highest level, revolved around a combination of factors, including election by one's peers, recognition by Spanish authorities, and the aggressive assertion of legitimacy by the aspirant. Corregidors played a key role in confirming kuraka candidates, frequently intervening to choose kurakas who were amenable to Spanish authority and able to maintain the tribute payments. Nonetheless, the corregidor's power was itself limited by the need to appoint kurakas who were recognized as legitimate by their ayllus, so that they could effectively command the native labor force.

Don Diego's tenure as governor and apu kuraka was far from peaceful. Beset by three forces—a dwindling labor force due to internal migration, the rise of sugar plantations in the area, and problems receiving the rental income from the Cusco properties—he found it difficult to meet the tribute payments required of the Chankas, payments for which he was personally liable. In fact, he was eventually sent to jail for three months because he could not pay the required tribute.

Internal migration, in which men and/or entire families fled their ancestral ayllu lands, was a major concern for Chanka leaders, including Don Diego.[16] Having abandoned their ancestral homes, migrants, known as *forasteros*, were no longer required to perform the mit'a or to fulfill the tribute payments. Given the harsh realities of life in the mercury mines, many natives of the Andahuaylas region chose to leave their lands and ayllus, and escape either to the high, desolate regions or to Spanish haciendas. In 1625, Francisco de Verdugo, bishop of Guamanga, described the problem in a letter to the king. Verdugo had recently completed a visitation of his diocese, which included the city of Andahuaylas and the surrounding territory. The bishop complained that so many had fled the Huancavelica mit'a that "the doctrinas that used to have four very full, good towns today are reduced to only one or two towns without people and the other towns and churches are ruined and without anyone."[17] Those who remained in the towns were "weak and ill and poor," comprising "women, widows, or Indians handicapped by nature or sickness."[18] The bishop explained that the natives had moved to the most remote areas of the diocese, the "hollows, and high plains, and eastern mountains."[19] Because of the lack of tributaries, he continued, "it is impossible to fulfill the Huancavelica mit'a . . . and the poor few Indians remaining are made to return to carry out a second mit'a."[20]

Verdugo's impressions about the impact of internal migration within his territory are confirmed by the available census figures. In 1573, the repartimiento of Andahuaylas boasted a total native population of 28,840;[21] by 1607, the number had declined to 16,406.[22] In May 1620, the Chanka kurakas requested a new census since the number of tributaries had fallen since 1606; the Indians, they stated, were suffering terribly "because the living have paid for the dead."[23] The problem was particularly urgent, it was claimed, because the indigenous communities had consumed all of their food and were starving. In 1660, Don Diego petitioned for a new census because, he stated, "the pueblos have become depopulated"[24] and he could not find able-bodied men to work in the Huancavelica mines.

Some of this depopulation was due to disease and deaths in the mines,[25] but much of it came from the fact that numerous Chankas had fled their traditional communities to avoid the mit'a. Many of the Indians who left their ancestral lands went to work on Spanish sugar plantations and haciendas. As Bishop Verdugo wrote, "[the *hacendados*] gather together those Indians and promise them mountains of gold, and that they will defend them from the mit'as and from the priests and corregidors, and as the Indians do not wish for anything other than being free of the mit'as, they contract themselves for little."[26]

Before the arrival of the Spaniards, there was little or no private land in the Andes; instead, communities or ayllus controlled large areas of the countryside. During the seventeenth century, as Indian land became alienated from the communities and fell into Spanish and creole hands, private haciendas and ranches developed throughout the Andahuaylas region.[27] The economy of the haciendas in this area was mixed, many farms being either subsistence operations or devoted to cattle ranching. The largest and wealthiest holdings, however, were sugar plantations, and these were the haciendas that required the greatest number of native workers. Nonetheless, even the sugar plantations, or *cañaverals*, as they were called, varied in size. A modest cañaveral, such as Yaramay in Huancarama, was auctioned off in 1694 to pay the dowry of the owner's daughter.[28] It consisted of a house containing three oil paintings on canvas (one of them a portrait of the owner), two sugar fields, a building with two cauldrons for processing sugar, a mill, a potter's workshop, eighteen horses, and ten mules.

The Chacabamba cañaveral and hacienda in Ongoy was a more impressive operation. When it was inventoried in the eighteenth century, its goods included a large house with an inner courtyard, an outdoor oven and kitchen, a flour mill, a building with cauldrons for processing sugar, a "purging" house for whitening the sugar, a storehouse, and eight sugar fields; it also comprised the Toruro farm—with a farmhouse, 45 mules, 52 pairs of oxen, 189 cows, 110 bulls, 198 sheep, more than 400 mares, and fields planted with wheat, maize, and barley—and the Pumachuco ranch. Among the decorations in the big house in Chacabamba was "an old, large canvas on which was painted the series of Inka kings . . . and another [canvas] two meters long with a portrait of King Philip V . . . and another picture in the hallway titled *The Four Parts of the World*." Most impressive was its chapel, which contained a gilded altarpiece; a statue of Our Lady of the Immaculate Conception adorned with 144 pearls and a silver crown garnished with gold; 12 large oil paintings of angels; a three-meter-high canvas of the Last Judgment; side altars dedicated to Our Lady of Dolour, Our Lady of Carmel, Saint Joseph, Saint Anthony, and Saint Michael the Archangel (including images of the Angel Raphael and the Guardian Angel); statues and images of many other saints, with their accompanying mantles and robes; silver vases for flowers; and silver candlesticks. Attached to the church was a tower with five bronze bells (two large and three medium sized) to call the faithful to church.[29]

In most cases, forasteros left their ayllus for the sugar plantations without the knowledge or consent of their kurakas, who badly needed the forasteros' labor to fulfill their mit'a quotas. The kurakas' traditional power base was eroded as their population of subjects dwindled away. Forasteros, on the other hand, endured the loss of both their land and their community identity, which included proximity to ancestor mummies and other sacred beings. The forasteros also suffered because, as they fled from their ayllus, they could no longer count on the protection of their kurakas. Despite the promises made by hacienda owners in order to lure Indian workers onto their lands, the peons' well-being on the sugar plantations was precarious, at best, without their kurakas to serve as potential advocates. The sugar plantations of the Andahuaylas region were often centers of injustice until their dissolution in the twentieth century.[30] In the novel *Deep Rivers*, written by Andahuaylas native José María Arguedas, the protagonist visits the Patibamba sugar plantation outside of Abancay. There, as he smells the sour scent of rotting cane trash, he listens to a priest weep with the peons over the sorrows of their lives: "'Who has suffered more than [Our Lady]? You perhaps, Patibamba peasant, whose heart is as beautiful as that of the bird who sings in the *pisonay*? Do you suffer more?' . . . 'Weep, weep,' he cried, 'the world is a vale of tears for the poor little children, the Indians of Patibamba.'"[31]

In addition to depopulation, internal migration, and the growth of sugar plantations, Don Diego had to contend with administrators in Cusco who did not collect the rents that were owed to the Chankas. He had to exercise constant vigilance to recover the monies that were due to his people. For example, in 1656, Captain Fernando de Castillo, the royal defender of the Indian rents in Cusco, finally agreed to auction off the goods of a citizen of the city who had died owing the Chankas hundreds of pesos in rent for many years. The following year, Don Diego recovered 272 pesos in delinquent rents for the Chankas' house and grounds in Lichacancha, but only after he had initiated an expensive court case.[32] However, even when the Chankas received their rents, some of their property had declined dramatically in value. For example, tenants had allowed the Chankas' houses in the Cabracancha neighborhood to fall into ruin. By 1659, the property had become so dilapidated that the buildings served as gambling dens for "mule drivers" and Indian and mestiza prostitutes. When these buildings were rented to new tenants, the value of the rents had decreased.[33]

Don Diego's inability to deliver the required tribute payments reached a climax in 1656. On November 14, 1656, soldiers burst into Don Diego's home in Andahuaylas, capturing him and hauling him off to jail.[34] The corregidor also seized Don Diego's goods, including his residence, with its parlor, bedrooms, and kitchens; his farm, called Rumi-Rumi, with its straw shed containing eight loads of maize and six loads of wheat; and his house and cornfields, known as Curibamba. Three months later, on February 28, 1657, Don Diego was released from prison, but only so that he could collect mit'a workers for the Huancavelica mines. Don Diego claimed that he was unable to pay the tribute because the Chankas had not received their rents from their Cusco property; only when these rents were finally paid in 1658, after a lengthy court battle initiated by Don Diego, was the kuraka able to settle this matter. Garrett has noted that kurakas who failed to collect the required tribute payments were often jailed,[35] and Don Diego was no exception.

In 1659, Don Diego accompanied Cabrera Lartaún, the new *visitador de tierras*, on his inspection of land titles throughout the Andahuaylas region.[36] The following year, in response to the dwindling population of tributary Indians under his authority, Don Diego sold communal lands to pay the legal costs of securing a new census.[37] Don Diego was still alive in July 1660; however, by 1668, he had died and been succeeded by his oldest son, Juan Quino Tomay Guaraca.

In arranging the marriages of his children, Don Diego followed the same strategy of building ties to creole elites that had guided his own marriage. His oldest son, Juan Quino Tomay Guaraca, wed a "Spanish" woman, Doña Isabel Entonadillo.[38] Three of Don Diego's four daughters married creole landowners—unions that required large dowries for each of the young women. For example, when Don Diego's daughter Isabel Quino Guaraca wed Juan Antonio de Velasco, a major landowner and sugar planter, her dowry consisted of several houses, the estate of Miscabamba, the cattle ranch of Guancabamba,

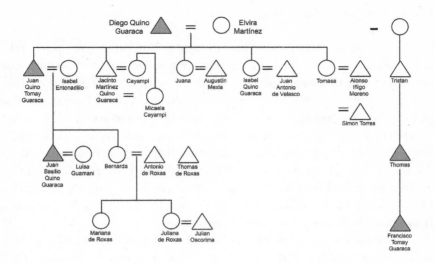

FIG. 24 Kinship chart of the Tomay Guaraca family (kurakas shown in gray), ca. 1640–1775. Chart prepared by Eleanor Hyland.

and thirty-six mules.[39] Isabel and her sisters Juana and Tomasa were of mixed Spanish and Indian descent and were fluent in both Spanish and Quechua. Their "Spanish" mother, Doña Isabel, would have raised them to be at home in the highest circles of creole society in Andahuaylas and Cusco, in addition to functioning as highborn members of the Chanka elite. One wonders what Isabel Quino Guaraca must have felt as she became the mistress of her husband Juan's household and large sugar plantations.

Don Diego's youngest daughter was sent to the convent of Santa Clara in Guamanga, "where she might grow up civilized and Christian."[40] Only Don Diego's other surviving son, Jacinto Martínez Quino Guaraca, took an indigenous spouse. Don Jacinto allied himself with another ruling native dynasty by marrying the daughter of Huancarama's head kuraka, Francisco Cayampi. After his wife's untimely death, Don Jacinto continued his alliance with the Cayampis in 1676 by marrying his wife's sister, Doña Micaela Cayampi.[41] The marriage alliances that Don Diego and Doña Isabel made for their children, and particularly for their daughters, which required large outlays of capital for their dowries during Don Diego's lifetime, would bear fruit for the succeeding generations, and especially for the oldest son, Don Juan Quino (see fig. 24).[42]

The Succession Crisis of 1669

Don Juan Quino Tomay Guaraca succeeded his father as apu kuraka and governor of all the Chankas. A literate mestizo fluent in Spanish and Quechua—and wed to a "Spanish" woman, Doña Isabel Entonadillo—Don Juan Quino was well placed to serve as a mediator between the corregidor and the Chanka people. As a boy, Don Juan Quino had attended the Jesuit Colegio de Caciques in Cusco for two years, 1655 and 1656,[43] and thus partook of the same basic humanistic education that his father had enjoyed. By the age of twenty-four, he had been named governor over all the Chankas by the corregidor Juan Luis de Resa. However, as soon as a new corregidor, Thomas Básquez de Velasco, came into office, the leaders of the Guachaca ayllu moved to depose Don Juan Quino permanently.

On January 3, 1669, the kuraka Don Pedro Alca of the Guachaca ayllu, son of Sebastián Alca, Don Diego Quino Guaraca's second-in-command,[44] brought a case against Don Juan Quino before the new corregidor.[45] Don Pedro was accompanied by other members of his ayllu, as well as by the head of the Yañic ayllu (Urinsaya) and a lower-ranking kuraka from the Guaraca ayllu. To support his demand that Don Juan Quino be removed from office, Don Pedro argued first that the head kuraka's appointment had been illegal. Under colonial law, mestizos were not allowed to serve as kurakas, and Don Juan Quino was a mestizo. Don Pedro brought forth the priest of Andahuaylas to read Don Juan Quino's birth record from the baptismal books, proving that Don Juan Quino was of mixed Indian and European descent.

Additionally, Don Pedro and others testified at length that Don Juan Quino routinely mistreated and exploited the native Chankas under his care, and therefore was unfit to rule. One of those to testify on Don Pedro's behalf was Pascual Coyca, the head kuraka of Andarapa, who would himself be accused of cruelly abusing Indians eighteen years later.[46] Don Pascual stated that he had known Don Juan Quino since his birth and also knew his late father, Don Diego, and his widowed mother, Elvira Martínez, who still lived in the city of Andahuaylas. Don Juan Quino and all of his relatives, Don Pascual continued, "treat the Indians very badly, using violence to make [the Indians] serve them without paying them, and giving them blows to the face, as this witness has seen on many occasions."[47] Don Juan Quino allegedly made the Indians pay more in tribute than they owed and, Don Pascual concluded, was hated by "all the Indians of quality" (todos los indios de calidad) in the region. Following Don Pascual's presentation of evidence, members of the Guachaca ayllu testified for days, repeatedly accusing Don Juan Quino of abusive exploitation of Indian commoners. In particular, witnesses described how Don Juan Quino had forced Indian women to weave cloth for him, but had never paid them.

The corregidor reacted harshly to this testimony. In sentences given on January 12 and 18, he officially removed Don Juan Quino from office and ordered that he be imprisoned indefinitely. Furthermore, he added that Don Juan Quino was *never* to serve again as kuraka and would be exiled if he even attempted to retake the office. In Don Juan Quino's place, a member of the Guachaca ayllu, Andrés Haparco, was installed as the head kuraka and governor over all the Chankas. The Guachacas' victory over the Tomay Guaracas seemed complete.

However, the next day, on January 19, Don Juan Quino's brother-in-law, the powerful sugar plantation owner Juan Antonio de Velasco, appeared in court on the prisoner's behalf.[48] Don Juan Antonio requested that Don Juan Quino be released and that there be a further investigation of the charges against him. Furthermore, Don Juan Antonio pledged his own goods as surety for any money that Don Juan Quino might be found to owe. This intervention was successful; the next time Don Juan Quino is mentioned in the historical record, he not only had been released from prison, but was once again the leader of Urinsaya and of all the Chankas.[49] Don Juan Quino's sister Isabel had apparently persuaded her influential creole husband to intervene on behalf of her brother, restoring him to power. The word of Don Juan Antonio sufficed to stave off this succession crisis for the Tomay Guaracas.

During the years of Don Juan Quino's tenure, he maintained a "Spanish" mistress, Doña María Mella, with whom he fathered at least one son.[50] Don Juan Quino continued to rule the Chankas until his untimely death in 1687, during his yearly trip to take mit'a workers to Huancavelica.[51] Interestingly, after his death, his legitimate daughter Bernarda described both of her parents as governors of the Chankas, perhaps reflecting an Andean view that the wife of a kuraka was an important leader in her own right.[52]

The Succession Crisis of 1712

By the time of the next succession crisis for the Tomay Guaracas, Peru had entered the eighteenth century. The cities of Lima and Cusco had developed a distinguished and aristocratic culture, and their centers of learning were in touch with intellectual and artistic developments in Europe. The ideas of the Catholic Enlightenment would deeply influence Peruvian theology and

Habit of a Lady of Lima in Peru.

FIG. 25 *Habit of a Lady of Lima in Peru*, 1779. From Carver, *New Universal Traveller*, 580. Collection of the author.

science during this century,[53] while neoclassicism would reign in the arts. We can see the differences between the seventeenth and eighteenth centuries, for example, even in depictions of women and women's fashions. The stiff and elaborate dress of the Virgin Mary (fig. 23) in Peruvian paintings from the early 1600s gave way to the loose and elegant gowns worn by Peruvian ladies in the late 1700s (fig. 25).

Throughout Don Juan Quino's tenure as head kuraka, his Guachaca enemy Don Pedro Alca served as his second-in-command (*segunda persona*). When Don Juan Quino died at the age of forty-three, his oldest son and heir,

Don Juan Basilio Quino Guaraca, was too young to assume the position of kuraka. The Guachacas used this opportunity to press their own candidate, and Don Juan Bautista Haparco of the Guachaca ayllu was chosen to succeed Don Juan Quino. Don Juan Bautista, who spoke fluent Spanish,[54] governed as the leading Chanka kuraka from 1687 until his death in an epidemic in 1706. He repeatedly sold communal lands, ostensibly to meet the tribute payments,[55] although it was later claimed that he kept the profits for himself.[56] After Don Juan Bautista's death in 1706, another member of the Guachaca ayllu, Don Gregorio Haparco, was selected as the interim governor.[57] Finally, the corregidor appointed Don Cayetano Alca de la Cruz, a member of the Alca family from the Guachaca ayllu, to be the apu kuraka and governor of the Chankas. Seemingly, the Guachacas' ascendancy over the Tomay Guaracas had been assured.

However, Don Juan Basilio Quino Guaraca, the son of Don Juan Quino, had not given up his hopes of becoming head kuraka. As the child of a mestizo man and a Spanish creole woman, Don Juan Basilio's racial heritage was primarily European, not Indian. He married an Indian noblewoman, Doña Luisa Guamani, from the Aymaraes tribe, located directly to the east of the Chankas.[58] Although Doña Luisa did not possess a dowry, her noble indigenous ancestry helped legitimate Don Juan Basilio's claim to the kurakaship. Most importantly, Don Juan Basilio provided a large dowry so that his sister Bernarda could marry Antonio de Roxas, who came from an important Spanish creole family in Andahuaylas.

Early in 1712, when the corregidor Don Alonso García Ciudad had left office and his successor, Don Luis de la Fuente, had just arrived to assume his new position, Don Juan Basilio conspired with a leading vecino, Juan de Osorio, to imprison Don Cayetano. Don Cayetano was thrown into jail without charges, where he remained for at least fourteen years, while Don Juan Basilio claimed the rank of head kuraka and governor.[59] Don Juan Basilio and his supporters might have argued that their actions against Don Cayetano were justified because, under Spanish law at the time, the kurakaship should have been passed from father to son, from Don Juan Quino to Don Juan Basilio. During Don Juan Basilio's rule, which lasted until his death in 1730, his brother-in-law Antonio de Roxas acted on at least one occasion as the leading kuraka for Urinsaya, revealing the close ties between the two men.[60]

Supporters of the illegally imprisoned Don Cayetano repeatedly appealed to the corregidor to release the Guachaca leader. However, their petitions fell on deaf ears, particularly once Don Gregorio Ortíz de Landaeta came to power as corregidor. Ortíz de Landaeta conspired with Antonio de Roxas to defraud the Chankas in the upper moiety of their lands; he would later admit that Don Juan Basilio was deeply involved in these dishonest transactions, which were greatly profitable for him, for his sister and brother-in-law, and for the corregidor.

Under Ortíz de Landaeta, Don Thomas de Roxas, a relative of Don Juan Basilio's brother-in-law Don Antonio de Roxas, was named inspector of land titles in 1721. As inspector of land titles, Don Thomas was supposed to ratify existing land titles and reassign vacant lands. In a court case fourteen years later, numerous Indians testified that Don Thomas kept their land titles— which they had turned over to him for confirmation of their land rights—and illegally sold the lands for his own profit. The lands that were sold fraudulently all came from the ayllus of Hanansaya, not from the Urinsaya moiety, to which Don Thomas was related through marriage. In every single case, Don Thomas sold these indigenous lands to one man: Don Juan Iñigo de Ortíz de Landaeta, a close relative of the corregidor.[61] It is not surprising, then, that the corregidor Ortíz de Landaeta supported the Tomay Guaraca claim to the kurakaship and kept Don Cayetano in prison; the family of Don Juan Basilio's brother-in-law was helping the corregidor's family acquire the Indian lands of Hanansaya. The brother-in-law relationship between Antonio de Roxas and Don Juan Basilio was a crucial link in this unholy alliance; the Tomay Guaracas' strategy of marrying their daughters/sisters to leading creole elites in the region allowed the ayllu to retain the head kurakaship over all the Chankas yet again.

The Uprising of 1726

During the years when the Tomay Guaracas and Guachacas competed for supreme leadership of the Chankas, the Guasco ayllu maintained its authority over Hanansaya. Back in the 1650s, when Don Diego Quino Guaraca had served as the primary Chanka leader, Sebastián Topa Guasco had enjoyed the leadership of Hanansaya.[62] The Guasco dynasty would continue to rule Hanansaya into the eighteenth century. By the 1720s, the rule of Hanansaya went to Don Bernardo Minaya, the illegitimate son of Esteban Minaya, the most powerful creole landowner in Cachi.[63] Don Bernardo claimed the kurakaship on the basis of his marriage to a noblewoman of the Guasco ayllu, Doña Juana Apu Guasco, who was the sister of his father's legitimate wife, Doña Fabiana Apu Guasco. In other words, the illegitimate Don Bernardo married his stepmother's sister, Doña Juana Apu Guasco, in order to claim the position of head kuraka of the upper moiety.

In 1726, Don Bernardo led an uprising against the corregidor, Ortíz de Landaeta, in which the kuraka was accompanied by all the Hanansaya Indians of Talavera, San Jerónimo, and Andahuaylas, as well as by the Catholic vicar of San Jerónimo, Don Gaspar de Grado y Mancilla.[64] Few of the details of the rebellion against Ortíz de Landaeta were recorded; however, this uprising seems to have been inspired by Don Thomas de Roxas's illegal theft of Hanansaya land for the benefit of Ortíz de Landaeta's family. Apparently, the goal of the revolt was to recover the Hanansaya properties and fields that were stolen by Don Thomas and the corregidor's family with the complicity of Don Juan Basilio. Significantly, none of the Tomay Guaracas participated in this revolt, which was unsuccessful. Don Bernardo's punishment included imprisonment and the royal confiscation of numerous properties in Talavera, some of which were communal Hanansaya lands.[65]

The rebellion created a long-standing enmity between two powerful landowning creole families: the Minayas and the Ortíz de Landaetas. In 1729, for example, Ortíz de Landaeta gave a ranch belonging to Estevan de Minaya, Don Bernardo's father, to an Indian family.[66] This was an extraordinary decision for a corregidor who virtually always ruled against native interests, even if he had to defy a direct order from the Audiencia in Lima to do so.[67] The intermarriages of high-ranking Spanish and Chanka families created a situation in which the politics of the two groups in Apurimac—the "colonizers" and the "colonized"—became intertwined, such that there was no simple separation of "Spanish" and "Indian" interests. Moreover, the rebellion reveals the strength of loyalty to one's moiety into the eighteenth century, along with the power of moiety politics to shape creole alliances and feuds resulting from intermarriages between creole men and women from specific Chanka ayllus.

An unexpected twist of fate occurred five years after Don Bernardo Minaya's Indian uprising against the corregidor. In 1730, Don Juan Basilio, the principal kuraka of Urinsaya and all the Chankas, passed away from illness. From his deathbed, Don Juan Basilio dictated an unusual will, lamenting his unjust treatment of the Indians during his government. Lacking any children to inherit his goods, the dying kuraka instructed his executors to call forth the Indians of the region, "having them declare the abuses that I have done to them, and . . . compensating them in some manner." Don Juan Basilio admitted that he had taken much from the Indians "in bad faith," and he begged his executors to ask the Indians "with all affection and love" to pardon him. In the absence of heirs, he willed that the kurakaship pass to his cousin, Don Thomas Quino Guaraca, the legitimate son of his paternal uncle Don

Tristan Quino Guaraca (an illegitimate son of Don Diego Quino Guaraca). He explained that Don Thomas was highly capable and, moreover, had listened to the kuraka "communicate many things concerning the discharge of my conscience."[68]

Based on Don Juan Basilio's last will and testament, Don Thomas assumed the head kurakaship of Urinsaya and the governorship of the Chankas without opposition. In 1731, during his first year in office, he was forced to sell property—specifically, a house and orchard in Andahuaylas—to pay the tribute, which, he explained, the Chankas could not afford because so many Indians were either dead or absent, having fled the mercury mines.[69] Two years later, he began working with Bernardo Minaya, who had been reinstated as the principal kuraka of Hanansaya, to recover the Indian lands stolen by Thomas de Roxas.[70] The two men put forth extraordinary effort to regain these lands and were successful in some cases. After Don Bernardo's death, however, frequent tensions over land rights continued between the two moieties. Eventually, Don Thomas's son Francisco Tomay Guaraca succeeded his father, again without any evidence of opposition from other ayllus or families. Apparently, the Tomay Guaracas had secured their rights to the rank of principal kuraka; however, it may have been the case that no one wanted the position any longer.

In 1749, beset by poverty, Don Francisco Tomay Guaraca went to court to claim the lands of Pachapuquio near San Jerónimo. His petition proudly stated that "all the said lands belong to me as a noble Indian from the time of the Inkas."[71] Twenty-six years later, in 1775, embittered by his experiences, Don Francisco provided grim testimony about how penurious and difficult the life of the head kuraka had become. Writing to the viceroy, Don Francisco explained that the reason he had accepted the role of kuraka was to obtain access to the extra land that was attached to the post; presumably, the mit'a exemptions for himself and his three sons were also incentives. He had faithfully collected the tributes, and his people had carried out their mit'a responsibilities. Yet because there were so few Indians left to fulfill these obligations, Don Francisco frequently suffered imprisonment and was forced to pay the tributes out of his own property in order to be released from the public jail. Left "totally poor and in debt without any relief," he lacked the resources to prevent "Spaniards and mestizos" from taking over his fields.[72] Previous kurakas had sold communal lands to cover the shortfall in tribute payments, but by 1775 very little extra land remained that could be alienated from the native community. Moreover, by the late eighteenth century, the indigenous population of the central Andes experienced a demographic recovery, putting increased pressure on the lands still retained by the communities. Once one of the wealthiest and most powerful indigenous lords in the Andes, the governor and apu kuraka of the Chankas had now sunk into relative penury.

Dowries and Inheritance

Central to the ayllus' success in their efforts to gain power in the Spanish colonial period were carefully chosen marriages with elite creole families in the Andahuaylas region. Don Diego Quino Guaraca's marriage to Elvira Martínez in the 1640s not only provided him with links to the Martínez family, but also ensured that his legitimate children would be mestizos. Given the colonial racial politics of the seventeenth century, girls of mixed racial descent were more acceptable as potential brides to creole landowning elites than were young women of a purely Indian heritage. In the 1640s, indigenous-creole intermarriages were still fairly uncommon in much of the rural Andes. Marital unions between Inka elites and Spaniards had been frequent in urban Cusco from the beginning of Spanish colonialism; however, in Upper Peru (now Bolivia), as well as in the provinces around Cusco, kuraka-creole unions did not become common until the eighteenth century.[73] After the success of Don Juan Quino, Don Diego's son, in retaining the kurakaship through the intercession of his powerful creole brother-in-law in 1669, other leading families, such as the Guascos and Guachacas, eventually followed suit and married into creole families. The case of the Chankas reveals that kuraka-creole intermarriages did not occur by happenstance. Rather, these unions were the result of deliberate decisions in which parents planned for their children, sacrificing current resources for the benefit of future generations.

Such intermarriage was possible only because of the Spanish custom of providing dowries to daughters. Large dowries gave the sons of creole landowning families an incentive to marry women of acknowledged Indian descent. There is evidence of an economic crisis throughout the Andahuaylas region in the 1650s, which would have fueled the interest of creole families in marrying the heiresses of kuraka lineages.[74] As noble Indian families within the Chanka ayllus adopted the practice of providing dowries for their daughters in order to gain access to creole power and influence, the inheritance practices of native Andean society were altered profoundly.

According to Spanish practices of the time, each legitimate child was supposed to inherit equally from the father's estate.[75] The dowry was considered the daughter's portion of the inheritance, one that was usually alienated from her father's property before his death. The dowry remained the woman's property throughout her life. Often, an elite woman received a generous *arras*, or marriage gift (dower), from her husband, ostensibly at the time of the wedding, although the actual arras might not be handed over to the wife until years later. This arras, once given, belonged to the wife throughout her life and could not be seized to pay her husband's debts. The husband managed his wife's dowry, although supposedly he could not sell it without her permission. Upon the husband's death, the principal of the dowry was returned to his widow, who could only then administer it as she wished. Frequently, when determining the size of a daughter's dowry, the mother's assets, including her own dowry, were incorporated into the calculations, so that the dowry was derived from the estates of both parents. For example, when Doña Tomasa Quino Guaraca, the youngest daughter of Don Diego Quino Guaraca and Doña Elvira Martínez, married her first husband, Don Alonso Iñigo Moreno, her dowry agreement was witnessed by all of her brothers and her sister's husband. These witnesses signed an agreement that the value of Doña Tomasa's dowry—one thousand pesos—was her equal share in the paternal and maternal inheritance.[76] Her dowry was to be paid in goods—the fields of Moyomoyo, 20 cows, 140 sheep, 4 mules, and 50 arrobas of sugar. Eight years later, in 1689, her husband, Don Alonso, recalled bitterly on his deathbed that, although he had received the land and the sheep, the cows were very old and the mules and sugar were never given to him.[77] The fields, as well as the value of the cows and sheep, were returned to Doña Tomasa to serve as the dowry for her next marriage, to Simon Torres. Finally, in 1693, she sold her Moyomoyo fields, her main security for her future, giving the money to her husband so that "he can begin to work and take on the responsibilities of marriage."[78] One hopes that she did not eventually come to regret her generosity to her spouse.

These Spanish inheritance practices, which took such firm root among the Chanka elites, were distinct from Inka custom. Under Inka colonial rule, most rights to land, irrigation, and livestock were held communally by the ayllus.[79] Therefore, individuals primarily passed usufruct rights on to their heirs. For commoners, who generally married endogamously within their ayllu, the only tangible inheritable property consisted of a house, yard, and personal effects. Members of the provincial nobility, however, often owned livestock, lands, and important sumptuary goods, such as garments or jewelry granted by the Inka emperor. Neither bridewealth nor dowries were given upon marriage, although in some places a short period of bride service—in which the groom performed labor for the bride's parents—was required. Throughout the central Andes, both usufruct rights and tangible goods were divided among heirs on the basis of "parallel transmission," with boys inheriting from their fathers, and girls from their mothers.[80] As Irene Silverblatt notes, "Accordingly, women perceived that it was through relations with women that they could make use of their environment's riches. We cannot estimate what portion of the ayllu's resources were in the hands of women, but we can note that parallel transmission rights ensured that women, independently of their kinsmen, enjoyed access to society's means of subsistence."[81]

When high-ranking Chanka families adopted the Spanish dowry, and the inheritance system implicit in this custom, they abandoned the earlier practice of parallel transmission. Elite Chanka women no longer received goods through an unbroken line of women, and the property that they did inherit—their dowries—remained under the husband's control during his lifetime. In the archives, one can occasionally find a will in which a Chanka noblewoman left her inheritance to daughters and nieces only, following the older Andean tradition. For example, in 1768, Doña Francisca Minaya y Apu Guasco dictated a will that left nothing to her son, whom she named as executor and with whom she apparently had good relations. Doña Francisca, the legitimate daughter of Esteban Minaya and Doña Fabiana Apu Guasco, descended from the Guasco kuraka family. Her half brother, Bernardo Minaya, had succeeded to the kurakaship of Hanansaya through his marriage to Doña Francisca's aunt Doña Juana Apu Guasco. Doña Francisca excluded not only her son but also her nephews (Don Bernardo's sons) from any inheritance. All of her numerous properties and other goods were willed to her niece, María, and her five granddaughters, Ubalda, Panchita, Pepilla, Melchorita, and Fernanda. Although Doña Francisca stated clearly that her father's goods had been divided equally among his nine legitimate children (four boys and five girls), she chose to follow the more ancient Andean custom of parallel transmission, passing her property exclusively to her female kin.[82]

However, wills such as Doña Francisa's were quite rare. By the eighteenth century, most Chanka elites divided their inheritance according to Spanish norms, providing dowries for daughters and inheritances for sons. While Spanish law offered some basic protections of a woman's dowry, this was a far cry from the freedom to manage her own property, which Chanka women had enjoyed under Inka rule. Yet their generous dowries enabled Chanka aristocrats such as Doña Isabel Quino Guaraca and Doña Bernarda Quino Guaraca to garner their husbands' support for their brothers, the apu kurakas Don Juan Quino Tomay Guaraca and Don Juan Basilio Quino Guaraca. By

1730, the Tomay Guaracas had secured the governorship of all the Chankas, in part through careful marriages, defeating their Guachaca rivals. How unfortunate for them that by 1775, when Don Francisco Tomay Guaraca penned his complaint to the viceroy, it seemed to have become a Pyrrhic triumph.

CONCLUSION: THE AFTERMATH

The warm highland sun shines on the wooden scaffolding erected over the facade of the Pampachiri church. Noisy schoolgirls spill out of the village school on the square, curious about the North American visitors resting on a bench in front of the church. They shyly ask us questions, wanting to know the English words for "backpack," "jacket," and "scarf." Our crew has come to see Pampachiri on a spring afternoon, and we have tramped all through the town, looking for evidence of Albadán's existence there. We can find no trace of him, other than the curious life-size statues of naked women created by his artists on the church portal, under his direction. The unusual exterior statues are now a local tourist attraction and are undergoing repair; their novelty is a source of pride to the people of Pampachiri. The previous Sunday was Easter, and faded carpets of flowers, scuffed and wilting in the mountain air, cover the central plaza. The wind picks up a handful of limp roses and blows pinkish-brown petals along the stony dirt road that runs through the village. Similar flower images must have decorated the village square in the days after Albadán's death in 1611, right before Holy Week and the Paucar Huaray festival.

Father Alonso de Sigura did not last long as Albadán's replacement in Pampachiri; he soon left the doctrina and a local creole priest, Father Francisco de Aldana from Guamanga, took his place.[1] Father Francisco, son of the "noble" Baltasar Rodríguez and Isabel Aldana of Guamanga, had studied Latin, rhetoric, arts, and theology in Lima; as he testified in court, he had been a student since his childhood. Moreover, he was fluent in Quechua and preached diligently to the natives of Pampachiri in their own tongue. The great Quechua scholar and Peruvian churchman Fernando de Avendaño even testified on Father Francisco's behalf, stating that he had known him for over sixteen years and that he was a fine linguist. Yet Father Francisco was unhappy in Pampachiri and anxious to leave. One suspects that the villagers were deeply wary of him and his attempted evangelization. Father Francisco petitioned for a position as a cathedral canon in any city of the realm; however, he would have to content himself with removal to another doctrina, Quinua, closer to his family in Guamanga.[2] It would be a long time before the parishioners of Pampachiri would trust another Catholic priest. Nonetheless, years later, the kurakas of Pampachiri would find an advocate in their new vicar Don Carlos López de Rivera. In 1727, the corregidor Ortíz de Landaeta (see chapter 8) threatened the kurakas with imprisonment over their failure to pay a 325-peso fine for the natives who had fled from compulsory labor in the mercury mines. Father Carlos gave the necessary sum to the Pampachiri kurakas to keep them from prison.[3] The priest then presented a strongly worded memorial before the court, decrying the injustice of making the kurakas pay for men who had fled rather than serve in the mines.[4] Through Father Carlos's efforts, Don Marcos Sivi Paucar and the other kurakas in the doctrina were freed from the obligation of paying for those tributaries who absented themselves from mine duty.[5] Father Carlos left behind a very different sort of legacy in Pampachiri than Albadán did.

Guaman Poma provides us with the most complete description of Albadán's atrocities; however, the chronicler's assertions about the priest's activities are supported by other documentation. The size of Albadán's estate speaks to his thefts and the fear that he inspired among the local populace. The extraordinary efforts of the corregidor Mendoza Ponce de León and the royal judge Arias de Ugarte to distribute the estate among the people of Pampachiri in compensation for the suffering the priest had caused suggest a level of crime far beyond the ordinary forms of rural corruption. The personal letters to Albadán from his brother and uncle refer to the priest's evil deeds and his need for redemption. Many of the details of Guaman Poma's story about Albadán, such as how Albadán hid the natives during López de Quintanilla's inspection or how the priest's accusations against Don León led to the latter's downfall, are confirmed in official, unpublished reports from the time. In other instances, Guaman Poma's accusations of corruption have been found to be completely reliable, underscoring his credibility.[6]

Even the way in which Albadán strictly refused to allow his relatives to visit him in the doctrina, despite their pleas, is consistent with his crimes. By the time of his death, Albadán was on good terms with his brothers and uncles—albeit only from a distance—giving them large amounts of money and silver. Yet he stringently kept them from his private lair in Pampachiri, while he simultaneously begged to be allowed to return to Spain to see them.

Mario Aguilar, a Chilean anthropologist who was tortured by Pinochet's forces, has called for modern academics to seriously consider the "indecent" subject of torture, rather than sweeping it under a rug of silence. In his work, he has argued that the physical arena where torture is performed merits analysis. As he writes, "torture camps become liminal spaces not known by citizens";[7] great efforts are usually made to keep the zone of torture secret and hidden, in part because the secrecy helps strip the inhabitants of their humanity. Not only did Albadán keep his family away, but he also arranged for the natives to be working elsewhere when a royal official arrived, further isolating the area from outside influence as best he could. For Albadán, the Pampachiri plaza and his home in the town became his personal dungeon where he tortured and sexually abused the population of "barbarians" at will. Other priests in colonial Peru were corrupt in a variety of ways: they forced natives to work for them without pay; they coerced indigenous women into sexual liaisons; and they stole goods from the local peoples.[8] Yet the character of Albadán's abuse is qualitatively different, as observers such as Guaman Poma noted. Albadán apparently enjoyed torturing naked men at the stake, burning their genitals and anuses with candles for hours, along with a host of other "games" that Guaman Poma felt unable to describe. Albadán's actions may have been colored by the legal forms of violence that he witnessed around him, such as the disciplining of slaves; however, as argued in chapter 6, Albadán's profile fits that of a psychopath, a form of mental illness that can leave great suffering in its wake. Neither colonial Peru nor Western society today has found ways to prevent psychopaths from harming others. In Peru, nonetheless, Albadán was able to manipulate colonial institutions and attitudes in order to escape official retribution for his crimes. It is highly unlikely that he would have been able to commit such atrocities against his parishioners had he been in Spain itself, and not in the colonies.

As described in chapter 2, Albadán retaliated against Don León Apu Guasco by engineering his downfall. When Albadán's accusation that Don León had hidden natives from the census was shown to be true, the kuraka was deposed and exiled, and he died of grief. It is not known whether Albadán played a role in choosing a kuraka from the lower moiety as Don León's successor; nonetheless, when the leader of the lower moiety became the head of the entire ethnic group, the rivalry between the lower-moiety Tomay Guaracas and Guachacas deepened dramatically, becoming one of the primary features of Chanka political life in the seventeenth and eighteenth centuries.

The rivalry between the two ayllus had its beginnings when the Inkas made the Guachacas the head of the lower moiety (Urinsaya), displacing the Guaracas. This rivalry was still evident in 1712, when the Guaraca heir to the headship of all the Chankas, Don Juan Basilio Quino Guaraca, conspired with a leading creole resident of Andahuaylas to oust the Guachaca ruler of the Chankas, Don Cayetano Alca de la Cruz. Similarly, forty-three years earlier, the Guachacas had tried to depose the Tomay Guaraca kuraka Don Juan Quino Tomay Guaraca as head of all the Chankas. In 1669, a leading member of the Guachuaca ayllu, Don Pedro Alca, brought charges against Don Juan Quino, accusing him of abusing the native Chanka peoples. As described in chapter 8, all of the witnesses who testified against Don Juan Quino were from the Guachaca ayllu (with only two exceptions). Whatever degree of truth may have existed in the accusations, the case clearly followed the divisions of political rivalries among the Tomay Guaraca and Guachaca ayllus. In fact, when the new corregidor sentenced Don Juan Quino to be deposed, he replaced the former head kuraka with a member of the Guachaca ayllu, Andrés Haparco. Only the intervention of Don Juan Quino's wealthy creole brother-in-law Juan Antonio de Velasco restored the Tomay Guaraca leader to power.

Had we not traced the ayllu affiliations of the Chanka kurakas over many generations, we would not be aware of how important ayllu politics were in Don Juan Quino's 1669 abuse trial. Trials in which indigenous commoners accused their kurakas of abuse occurred throughout the Andes in the late seventeenth and eighteenth centuries. Historians have analyzed these trials in terms of a growing class division between a newly emerging Andean peasantry and its kuraka lords.[9] Sinclair Thomson has even argued that the abuse trials in the eighteenth century are evidence of a growing democratization of the Andean peasantry.[10] While these arguments about class and democratization certainly have merit, it may be worthwhile to explore whether the other late colonial Andean abuse trials were also motivated by the kinds of bitter ayllu rivalries that appear in the Chanka case.

Not only ayllu membership, but moiety affiliation as well, continued to play an important political role for the colonial Chankas; this can be seen in the Hanansaya land thefts in the 1720s and the subsequent 1726 uprising of the leader of Hanansaya moiety, Don Bernardo Minaya. In his work *Subverting Colonial Authority* (2003), Sergio Serulnikov argues that the great Andean revolts of the 1780s had their roots in the smaller uprisings that began in the 1740s. Serulnikov, whose research focused on the Chayanta province in Alto Peru, found that between the 1740s and 1780s there was a gradual process of social unrest as Andeans confronted their rural overlords over unjust taxes, church fees, labor obligations, and land distribution. Yet, in the case of the Bernardo Minaya and Hanansaya Chanka uprising of 1726, we see a similar protest occurring decades earlier than the "prerebellion" era studied by Serulnikov. Moreover, tracing the moiety and ayllu affiliations of the actors in this conflict reveals that this uprising can be understood as a violent incident within a long-standing moiety rivalry stretching back to when the Tomay Guaracas displaced the Guascos as the supreme Chanka kurakas. The uprising began when the kuraka of the lower moiety, Don Juan Basilio Quino Guaraca, conspired with his brother-in-law's relative and the corregidor to defraud the upper moiety of its land, culminating in the violent protest of this injustice by members of the upper moiety. Both the Minayas (the upper-moiety representatives of the Guasco ayllu) and the Tomay Guaracas (from the lower moiety) furthered their moiety and ayllu interests through marriage alliances with leading creole and landowning families. Until now, it has been assumed that ayllu and moiety affiliation no longer mattered to the ruling indigenous elites by the eighteenth century because of their high rates of intermarriage with creole landowners. In the case of the Chankas, not only did moiety affiliation continue to be important, but the creole landowners were also drawn into moiety rivalries through their intermarriages. The enmity between the Ortíz de Landaeta landowners and the landowning Minaya family that ensued after the 1726 uprising reveals how the *hacendados'* internal politics could be influenced by moiety rivalries on the eve of the "Age of Andean Insurrection." This study of the Chankas in the colonial Andes has demonstrated that the native institutions of ayllu and moiety were able to respond in a dynamic way to the political and social forces that impinged on them as the kurakas adapted their marriage and inheritance patterns; consequently, ayllu and moiety affiliation continued to motivate political action at the highest levels of the Chanka leadership well into the eighteenth century.

Yet, while moiety and ayllu politics continued to be important for the Chanka elites in the eighteenth century, the membership of the local village-level ayllus shifted over time. Spanish resettlement programs in the sixteenth century had moved Chanka ayllus away from the huacas of their ancestors, whose worship underwrote the ayllu system in a politico-religious whole.[11] Through migration to work on haciendas or in the cities, Chanka commoners were further dislocated; those men and women who moved to the plantations and cities often abandoned their loyalties to their kurakas and their ayllus. By the latter half of the seventeenth century, kurakas increasingly accepted forasteros from other regions as ayllu members in order to swell the ranks of their diminishing communities. Children of forasteros, faced with the unpleasant realities of hacienda or urban life, might aspire to join an ayllu, accepting mit'a service in return for land and a place in the community. One such individual was Juan Bautista Flores Aroní del Castillo, a forastero from Yanaca in Aymaraes territory. In the late 1670s, Aroní and his wife, Christina Choque, were allowed to settle in the indigenous pueblo of Cachi, in return for agreeing to pay all tributes and perform mit'as—including work in the Huancavelica mines—and free labor in the priest's household.[12] The couple was granted fields and a house, where they lived for over forty years. Unfortunately, in 1718, as the indigenous population was growing larger, the kurakas of Cachi wanted Aroní and Choque removed from the community as forasteros, and their land given to the descendants of an original ayllu member. The corregidor, however, accepted Aroní's claim, and use of the land was granted to the forastero's son. This case exemplifies the tensions that developed between forasteros and the land's original inhabitants as local populations became increasingly mixed, with many ayllu members fleeing their pueblos to the punas, the haciendas, or the cities, while other indigenous Andeans settled in ayllus far from their native lands.[13] By the eighteenth century, in some cases, ayllus were composed almost entirely of forasteros.[14] These shifts occurred within the context of traditional kurakas, such as Don Francisco Tomay Guaraca, losing economic and political power to alcaldes and other indigenous officials, such as *mayordomos*.[15]

The latter half of the eighteenth century was far from peaceful for the Chankas. After the death of Bernardo Minaya, the head kuraka of Hanansaya, bitter tensions resurfaced among the native leadership over land rights. For example, in 1753, Minaya's heirs, along with the native alcaldes of Talavera, traveled to Lima to petition for the return of fields that had been stolen from them in the early 1720s; the case dragged on for over five years without resolution.[16] By the late 1760s, riots against local viceregal authorities had become commonplace at the largest yearly public gathering in the Andahuaylas zone—the September feast of Our Lady of Cocharcas, held at the shrine of Cocharcas.[17] In a report written in 1771, the corregidor Joseph Ordóñez described a rock-throwing riot at the shrine, known as the Sanctuary of Our Lady of Cocharcas; at least one person was killed. He explained that such "uprisings" had occurred every year at the sanctuary in recent memory.

However, neither the Chanka leadership nor the Chanka commoners are known to have joined in Tupac Amaru II's violent rebellion in 1780 against the viceregal government centered in Cusco and the southern Andes.[18] It is likely that the reasons for this are similar to those proposed by historian Steve

Stern for the failure of the rebellion to spread in the central sierra: intranobility rivalries that made the native leadership unable to direct a concerted military stance, combined with local military and political conditions.[19] We see such long-standing rivalries among the Chanka elites in the Andahuaylas region, although the fierce struggle over the governorship seems to have died down by 1730. Moreover, intermarriage between Chanka elites and Spanish creole landowners had become so prevalent by the late eighteenth century that the interests of both groups were truly intertwined; the Chanka kurakas in 1780–82 apparently had no interest in a rebellion that would have been carried out against their brothers-in-law, nephews, nieces, and cousins. Further research will clarify the attitudes toward the rebellion among the Chankas during this period.

Walter Mignolo has noted that the "colonization of time and space and the universalization of Western history" since the sixteenth century have relegated colonized peoples to the margins of history: "By confusing the European narrative of global history with the history of Europe, the self-fashioning narrative of Western Civilization left at the margins of history the regions and people that Europe colonized."[20] Ethnohistory, for the most part, attempts to "decolonize" the past by turning its focus to the civilizations and peoples colonized by Europeans. Moreover, it often does so by trying to use indigenous concepts of kinship and historical action, such as ayllu and moiety, rather than by utilizing only Western categories of analysis, valuable as such categories may be.[21] Understanding Chanka colonial history in terms of how ayllu and moiety politics played out in the changing circumstances of the seventeenth and eighteenth centuries is part of this effort to "decolonize" Andean history. Too often in the past, the complexities of indigenous political structures have been dismissed as mere "native infighting." Hopefully this present study will demonstrate to readers how the Chanka elite families responded with ingenuity and political acumen to the changing forces of colonial society.

One of the most unexpected surprises of researching Albadán's life in Pampachiri was discovering how closely he was linked to notables in Spain, such as his uncle Fray Francisco de Prado, his uncle's confrere Tirso de Molina, and other members of the Mercedarian order. Through their associations, Albadán and the Chankas were very much part of the world of elegant dinner parties at Doña Ana's home and of the Mercedarians' magnificent baroque library in Seville. The glittering wealth enjoyed by the elites in Seville at this time was due, in part, to the exploitation of native Peruvians in the mercury and silver mines of the Andes. While the suffering of the native peoples was at a comfortable remove from the fashionable neighborhood of La Magdalena in Seville, the misery of indigenous workers in places like the quicksilver mines of Huancavelica underwrote the lifestyles available to the Spanish elites. Does this suggest that European colonialism itself can be viewed as a form of social and political psychopathology?

It is extraordinary to see how Albadán tried to emulate his relatives' dinners and library in the rural Andes. What a tragedy for the people of Pampachiri that Albadán's family exiled him to Peru. Anthropologists often claim that traveling abroad to experience other cultures broadens one's outlook, creating a more humane person. In many ways, the antecedents for the anthropological belief that exposure to another culture brings about positive personal transformation can be found in medieval writings on spiritual pilgrimages. Strenuous journeys to the Holy Land and other distant sacred sites were intended to enlarge the soul, leading the pilgrim closer to God. Yet Albadán's anguished exile in Pampachiri was no holy pilgrimage; it seems only to have increased his sadistic tendencies, while his status as a priest in a colonized village allowed him to indulge his most psychopathic fantasies. Medieval monks often cautioned would-be pilgrims against falling into corruption on their journey by quoting the words of Horace, one of the classical authors found in Albadán's library. This famous passage—"Caelum non animum mutant qui trans mare currunt"—forms a fitting epitaph for this evil priest: "Those who rush across the sea merely change their skies, not their souls."[22]

Ultimately, the story of Albadán, the mad priest of Pampachiri, is a tale about the Chanka people in the Spanish colonial world—their sufferings, struggles, and triumphs. It is a pity that we do not possess personal letters from any of the main Chanka protagonists, such as Don León Apu Guasco or Don Diego Quino Guaraca, or their sisters and wives, such as Doña Isabel Quino Guaraca or Doña Bernarda Quino Guaraca. However, the wills, trial records, dowry settlements, property sales, and other documents generated by the Tomay Guaracas over the centuries have allowed us to witness the ayllu- and moiety-based competition that characterized elite Chanka life under Spanish rule. Economic, demographic, and episcopal reports have also enabled us to explore the changes experienced by ordinary Chanka people throughout the sixteenth and seventeenth centuries. The twin pressures of forced labor in the mercury mines and abusive conditions on many of the sugar plantations led to a high level of internal migration and exile, as people moved to haciendas to avoid service in the mercury mines, but then, in some cases, returned to the ayllus to flee abusive hacendados. During

FIG. 26 The Sanctuary of
Our Lady of Cocharcas.
Photo by Brian S. Bauer.

the warfare and violence in the 1980s and 1990s, families again splintered, with some people fleeing to Lima and other cities for safety, and others remaining behind in Apurimac. Today, internal migration continues to be an ever-present theme, as family members move to Lima for economic opportunities, while maintaining strong ties to their natal communities in the highlands.

This theme of traveling and impermanence is expressed every year in the songs sung by Andean pilgrims when walking to the most important Chanka religious shrine, the Sanctuary of Our Lady of Cocharcas (fig. 26). Every September since the 1620s, indigenous Chankas have walked long distances to the Virgin's shine to express their devotion to the "Mamacha Cocharcas," or "Beloved Mother Cocharcas."[23] The Quechua laments sung during the pilgrimage speak of journeys and of the tenuousness of life. A typical song in honor of Our Lady of Cocharcas runs,

> Oh, Mother of mine, you are with God.
> Until my return,
> Whether in life or in death, ay!
> Please do not forget me.

Next year, like today,
Perhaps we shall meet each other, or perhaps not;
Or maybe you will see me, your child, beneath the earth.

In my journeying over mountains and valleys,
My Mother, give me strength.
Free me, my Mother, ay! from all my sorrows.

Mother of God, you are with God.
Beautiful Mother, you are with God.
Leave me in my pueblo, ay!
With God alone, with God alone.

Mother without stain, listen to me.
To me, your sinful child, give me your hand,
Ay! until the day I return.[24]

In his novel *Deep Rivers*, José María Arguedas recorded a similar Quechua song from a traveling Chanka minstrel, known as a *kimichu*.[25] Arguedas was born and raised in Andahuaylas and spent his formative years living with his family's Quechua-speaking servants there. One of the foremost writers of the twentieth century, Arguedas desired to find new ways to express Andean reality, while exploring the impact of centuries of colonialism on the indigenous peoples of Apurimac. As Monica Barnes once wrote, "Like the wisest of his characters, Arguedas had 'an acute sensitivity to human corruption or degradation' and saw the struggle between good and evil as a permanent one."[26] In this passage from his most famous novel, he provided the Chanka singer with lyrics reflecting the same themes of wandering, love, and uncertainty that run through Chanka life; this song serves as a fitting tribute to the ever-unfolding history of the Chanka people:

River Paraisancos,
strong-flowing stream,
you must not fork
until I return,
until I come back.
Because if you divide,
if you branch out,
someone will prey upon

the little fish I have bred
and they will die, scattered on the shore
. . . .
When it is the traveler who returns to you
you will fork, you will branch out.
Then I myself will care for the little fish,
and raise them.
And if they need more of the water
and the sand you have given them
I shall care for them
with my tears alone,
with the pools of my eyes.

Who is capable of setting the bounds between the heroism and the iciness of a great sorrow? With music such as this a man could weep until he was completely consumed, until he vanished, or could just as easily do battle with a legion of condors and pumas, or with the monsters that are said to inhabit the depths of the highland lakes and the shadowy mountain slopes.[27]

APPENDIX: THE CHANKAS PRIOR TO THE

SPANISH INVASION

The Chanka War

According to Inka legend, the Chankas burst into the Inkas' consciousness in the early fifteenth century, during the rule of Inka Viracocha, the eighth Inka ruler.[1] Viracocha had enjoyed a successful reign: he could boast of victorious conquests in the region surrounding Cusco, the Inka capital; he was credited as the inventor of a special type of fine embroidered textile design known as the *Viracocha-tocapu*; and he delighted in many healthy sons and daughters from his wives and concubines. His wife, Queen Runtucaya, had given birth to four sons, including the oldest, Inka Roca, an able military leader, as well as the ultra-capable and popular prince Inka Yupanqui, the third son. However, when it came time for the elderly ruler to name his successor, he chose another son, Inka Urqon, whose beautiful mother, Churi-Chulpa, was Viracocha's favorite concubine. As Inka historians would later tell the tale, Viracocha's choice of crown prince caused consternation among the emperor's advisors and relatives, but there was little that could be done to alter his decision. In Inka society, the emperor had the right to pick his successor from among all of his children, selecting his most capable son and daughter to marry and rule together as king and queen, or, as the Inkas called their rulers, "Sapa Inka" (Unique Inka) and "Mama Coya" (Lady Queen). The royal brother/sister incest was, the Inkas believed, modeled upon the sun and the moon themselves, the magnificent brother/sister, husband/wife pair who ruled over the heavens and determined the fates of men and women.

Inka Viracocha lived in an elegant palace in the capital of Cusco, a city revered as "the navel of the universe."[2] Yet meanwhile, in the territory of the Chanka confederacy to the northwest of Cusco, two self-styled brothers—Astoy Guaraca and Tomay Guaraca—were preparing a massive siege of Cusco. The Guaracas had amassed a superior army composed of troops from many smaller groups, such as the Uranmarca kingdom; they were convinced that they would crush any military force that the Inkas mustered against them and take the Inka kingdom for themselves. Carrying the mummified body of their ancestor Ancoallo into battle as a pledge of victory, the Chankas were "proud and insolent"[3] and felt assured of success. Setting out from their capital of Andahuaylas, the brothers and their troops marched to a place called Ichu-pampa (Grassy Plain), five leagues west of Cusco. There "they remained for some days, terrorizing the region and preparing to enter Cusco."[4]

Upon observing the overwhelming size of the Chanka forces, Inka Viracocha's advisors urged the elderly emperor to retreat from the city with his heir, Inka Urqon, leaving its defense in the hands of his sons by Queen Runtucaya. Amazingly, Viracocha did just that. The very next day, he—along with his wives and concubines, Inka Urqon, and his young children—traveled in palanquins, each borne by four servants and covered in elaborately woven cloths (perhaps with the famous Viracocha *tocapu* designs), to safety in the town of Chita. Accompanying the emperor was a long, winding train of llamas loaded with his treasures and daily necessities.

Despite the overwhelming size of the Chanka army, the Inka troops, led by Prince Inka Yupanqui, inflicted a grievous defeat upon the Chankas, scattering their forces and toppling the mummy of their ancestor Ancoallo. Undaunted, the Chankas regrouped and attacked the Inkas again. Once more, Prince Inka Yupanqui seized victory; this time, however, both Chanka leaders were decapitated in the vicious fighting. While the battle was still raging, the Inka prince commanded that Astoy Guaraca's and Tomay Guaraca's heads were to be placed on stakes; these were displayed to the now terrified Chanka troops, who fled at the sight of their leaders' sightless and blood-soaked heads atop the Inka lances. Later, the prince would make drinking cups out of the Guaracas' flayed skulls, ensuring that the two brothers would be forced to toast Inka victories even in death.

Inka Yupanqui would claim that his triumphs over the Chankas' overwhelming forces had been granted to him by none other than the Sun God. When the Spanish writer Sarmiento de Gamboa interviewed Inka historians in Cusco in the 1570s, they told him that the Sun God appeared to the prince before the first battle:

One day when [Inka Yupanqui] was in Susurpuquio in great pain, reflecting upon how he would face his enemies, a being like the Sun appeared to him in the air, consoling him and calling him to battle. He showed Inca Yupanqui a mirror in which he pointed out the provinces he would conquer, noting that he would be the greatest of all his ancestors, and that he should not doubt, and should return to Cuzco, because he would defeat the Chancas who were advancing on the town. Inca Yupanqui was inspired by these words and vision. Taking the mirror, which he ever after carried with him in war and in peace, he returned to the city and began to encourage those who had remained, and some who were coming from afar to watch.[5]

After the first victory over the Chanka forces, Inka Yupanqui sent to his father the choicest spoils of war, asking Inka Virachocha to accept the triumph as his own. However, Viracocha refused, saying that the victory rightfully belonged to Inka Urqon, since the latter was the legitimate heir to the Inka kingship. The messenger whom Inka Yupanqui had sent with the war trophies "rose and with angry words said that he had not come so that cowards could triumph from the deeds of Pachacuti [Yupanqui]. So if he did not want to receive this service from such a valiant son of his, it would be best that he who had earned the glory should enjoy it." The messenger then departed abruptly and returned to Inka Yupanqui in Cusco.[6]

After the second and final defeat of the Chankas, Inka Viracocha reluctantly accepted the spoils, yet refused to join in the victory celebrations in Cusco, upset at the upstaging of his favorite son, Urqon. Inka historians and poets recounted that the ensuing parties in Cusco were particularly rowdy—the inhabitants were relieved that they had not fallen to the Chankas and been forced to accept servitude to the Guaraca brothers and their people. During the victory festivities, Inka Yupanki crowned himself emperor and took the name Pachakuti, translated as "He Who Overturns the World." As Emperor Pachakuti, he reorganized the government, rebuilt the capital of Cusco, and began a campaign of conquest that would greatly enlarge the boundaries of the Inka state. Inka historians later told the Spanish that it was Pachakuti who transformed the Inka state from a local Cusco kingdom to a juggernaut that would eventually be the largest Native American empire ever to exist. In commemoration of these pivotal events in Inka history, Pachakuti and his successors often harked back to the first two triumphs over the Chankas and the war that marked the beginning of the Inkas' imperial aspirations.

Chanka Views of Their Relations with the Inkas

Not surprisingly, perhaps, the Chankas' own early versions of their relations with the Inkas differ from the standard account of the Inka historians in Cusco.[7] In the village of Uranmarca, once the seat of the small Uranmarca kingdom that was part of the Chanka confederacy, Brian Bauer and I found a copy of a 455-year-old manuscript that told the history of Inka rule in the region. This version of the Chankas' relations with the Inka victors leaves out the Chanka War entirely, presenting a vision of peaceful rule in which the Chankas were incorporated into the Inka Empire in 1218, about 200 years before the Chanka War!

The document was originally signed on June 22, 1558, and recounted a ceremony held atop the Muyu Muyu (Round-Round), a large man-made ritual mound in the village that still commands a stunning view of the Uranmarca Valley and the Pampas River down below (fig. 27). On that day in 1558, a Spanish Dominican friar from Lima named Juan Pedro de Balboa and his companions gathered with village leaders to witness the 340th anniversary of the founding of the village. During this assembly, the principal village leader, Cusipacha, displayed 340 small stones, stating that each one represented a year in the village's history, and then proceeded to speak the names of the four Inka leaders who had governed the region since its foundation.

It is intriguing that the document suggests that small stones were involved in recording the passing of years since the founding of the village. Although the Inkas are best known for using a system of knots on strings, called *khipu*, to record important events, they also used pebbles, seeds, and other objects to help recall past events and important information. As one Spanish Jesuit wrote in 1590, "Apart from these string khipus, they have others composed of pebbles, from which they accurately learn the words they want to commit to memory."[8] These objects were often considered sacred and passed down from one religious specialist to another, as described in this passage by a Spanish Jesuit, Bernabé Cobo, who refers to the Andean ritualists as "sorcerers": "They practiced this task with different types of instruments and contrivances. The most common way was with maize, beans, and black pebbles and other pebbles of different colors. The sorcerers and their successors were very careful to keep these things when the one who used them died, and when they got old, they used the same things."[9]

As Cusipacha read the Uranmarca stones, he revealed that the community's first Inka regent, Inka Apu Kuraka Cusi Ccoyllur, founded Uranmarca on June 22, 1218. In describing the territorial holdings of the village, Cusipacha

FIG. 27 The Uranmarca Muyu Muyu. Photo by Brian S. Bauer.

mentioned various toponyms that are still used today; in fact, the area seems to have changed little since the recording of the document. Cusipacha also noted that the first regent, Cusi Ccoyllur, built a number of installations in the area, including the mound and plaza of Muyu Muyu.

After defining the boundaries of the community and the major Inka works within it, Cusipacha recorded a four-generation-long dynastic line of men who ruled the region. He indicated that Cusi Ccoyllur ruled for eighty years and was followed by his son Ccori Ccoyllur, who likewise ruled for eighty years. This regent governed not only Uranmarca but also the neighboring communities of Uripa, Ocobamba, Cayara, and Ccascabamba. Ccori Ccoyllur was followed by Ccondor Ccoyllur, who ruled for seventy-eight years, and then by Inka Mascaypacha, who ruled for eighty years. Cusipacha, the current Inka regent in 1558, had governed for thirty-two years. Thus, he had come to power in 1526, on the eve of the Spanish invasion and at the height of the dynastic war between two rivals for the Inka throne, Huascar and Atahualpa. The ceremony ended with Cusipacha asking Pedro de Balboa for protection in the name of the then-ruling Spanish viceroy, Hurtado de

Mendoza, who governed Peru from 1556 to 1561. Balboa signed the document, and his companions signed as the four native witnesses.[10]

Why would this local account of Chanka/Inka history claim that these Chanka kingdoms had peacefully been part of the Inka Empire for centuries before the Chanka War, and not even mention the Chanka War once? This is exactly the sort of contradiction that bedevils any investigator of Inka history. The early historical chronicles contradict each other; with patience one can suss out the most likely version of events, but there is never certainty and experts often disagree. It is possible that Cusipacha, the Inka regent, exaggerated the length of Inka rule in the area in an effort to bolster his own position with the Spanish colonial authorities. That is, he might have wanted to demonstrate that the Inkas were the legitimate leaders in the region due to the length and peacefulness of their reign in Uranmarca. As the representative of the Inka Empire there for thirty-two years, Cusipacha probably wanted to make it clear that he should remain in charge, and that authority should not be handed to a local, non-Inka Uranmarca lord.

There exists yet another early account of the Chanka War, as seen from the perspective of the Chanka people. In this version of the hostilities, the Inkas are clearly the aggressors, marching into Chanka territory and demanding the submission of the various kingdoms of the Chanka confederacy. In April 1640, a Spanish priest and chronicler, Fernando de Montesinos, passed through Chanka territory in the region of Andahuaylas. Following the old Inka road from the town of Andahuaylas to Cusco, he went through Huancarama, the seat of one of the Chanka kingdoms. In Huancarama, he questioned the local Indians about the history of the idol they had worshipped and was told how the idol had been destroyed by the Inkas. As Montesinos narrated the story, the emperor Inka Roca, who ruled before Pachakuti, amassed an army and set out to conquer the territories to the west of Cusco. Upon reaching Huancarama, the emperor demanded the submission of the local peoples. However, the king of Huancarama opposed the Inkas, declaring that his most holy idol, or *huaca*, had revealed to the king's mystics and diviners that the Inka emperor was not the rightful lord. This idol, in conformity with Andean traditions that continue today, would have been an unusually shaped stone that embodied the spirit of the local Huancarama deity. Given the deity's message, the armies of Huancarama established themselves in a defensible spot, preparing to withstand an Inka attack. However, they were no match for the Inka troops. As Montesinos wrote, "there was a very bloody battle in which the King of Huancarama was left defeated and killed."[11] After his victory, Inka Roca grabbed the huaca that had denied his authority and threw it down the hill on which it had stood. As the huaca hurtled through the air, a brightly colored parrot soared out of the rock and entered another stone, which the Indians subsequently venerated.

Before setting out against the Chanka lords in Andahuaylas, Inka Roca spent some time at the "fort" of Curamba outside of Huancarama. Sir Clements Markham, who passed by the site in the 1850s, described it thus:

> Leaving the vale of Pincos, we had to skirt for two leagues along the sides of the mountains in the midst of magnificent scenery. There is a small plateau beyond, on which is situated the ancient fortress of Curamba. Though small, it has some interest connected with Inca history, having been originally a stronghold of the Chancas. Curamba is a square fort of solid masonry in three terraces, one above the other, the wall of the outer terrace being thirty feet on each side. The upper terrace is approached by a ramp from the plain, with a slope sufficient to enable a mule to ride up to the summit. There are extensive ruins near the fort, the whole overgrown with bushes.[12]

Curamba contains a large area with several furnaces, which, until recently, were thought to have been used in Inka times for smelting silver. In 2012, a team of scientists carried out mineralogical studies at the site and discovered that the furnaces were producing lead, not silver. Moreover, they suggested that the lead was used in the production of lead "bullets" for ammunition in slingshots, the Inkas' preferred weapon.[13] If this was the case, then it certainly made sense for Inka Roca to spend time at Curamba resupplying his armory before moving on to the next attack. Finally, he was ready to confront the Chankas in Andahuaylas:

> [the Inka] went forward with his army; and before arriving in Andahuaylas, he discovered many troops impeding him in the bottom of a ravine. Inka Roca had foreseen this, being aware that the king of Andahuaylas [was opposed to him] because of the reply given by the huaca of Huancarama. Therefore, Inka Roca sent a third of his army in complete silence and speed along the mountain ridge that guarded the entrance to the ravine, so that their enemies could not take it, with the order that if the Chankas were to enter the ridge, the Inka rearguard would attack them. . . . Thus it happened, and the people of Andahuaylas were caught in the middle [of the Inka troops]. The Inkas inflicted huge losses on those from Andahuaylas,

until they begged for peace. The Inka received those who were still alive with great benignity, and they affirmed that they believed him to be the true child of the sun.[14]

This version, related to Montesinos by the local Chanka natives in 1640, presents the Inkas as the aggressors against an innocent Chanka population. A Jesuit priest, Luis de Teruel, collected a similar history in the first decades of the seventeenth century from the same local people.[15] Several other chroniclers, including the seventeenth-century Jesuit writer Bernabe Cobo, stated that the enmity between the Inkas and the Chankas began before the reign of Emperor Viracocha. Cobo, for example, wrote that the Inka/Chanka aggression emerged during the time of the earlier emperor Inka Roca, but that the Chankas were only fully pacified during the later reign of Pachakuti, who finally subdued them.[16]

Again we are faced with a contradiction in the historical sources—one that is not easy to resolve. Did the Inkas invade Chanka territory with a powerful army, initiating the conflict between the two peoples? Or did the Chankas march on Cusco with overwhelming forces without there having been any earlier hostility between the two groups? From this vantage point in time, it is impossible to say definitively. However, Bauer's archaeological survey of the Chanka heartland in the Andahuaylas valley can give some insights into the relative strengths of the two peoples. On the eve of Inka expansion, the Inka region in the Cusco Valley possessed more large settlements with a higher level of development than did the Chanka region in the Andahuaylas valley. If the Chankas did try to invade Cusco, it was probably in response to the growing expansion and consolidation of Inka power within the Cusco Valley.[17] Personally, I suspect that the local Indians who told Montesinos about the earlier invasion of Chanka territory by the Inkas were correct, and that the later Chanka attack on Cusco in the time of Prince Yupanqui was carried out as an act of vengeance. In any event, rather than being a divinely ordained gift from the Sun God, the Inka victory over the Chankas was more likely the inevitable result of superior Inka power and organization.

The Chankas Under Inka Colonial Rule

What happened to the Chankas once the Inkas had conquered them? As part of the Inka Empire, the Chankas would have been forced to set aside up to a third of their farmland for the state. That is, Chanka farmers might have continued to farm this land, but the proceeds would belong to state officials, who would distribute the crops and other goods as the emperor wished—perhaps to the army, perhaps to the Inka priests, or perhaps to be stored for times of scarcity. Within the Inka Empire, citizens owed labor tax to the government, which they would fulfill in a variety of ways, such as farming the Inka fields, working on building projects, serving in the army, and so forth. An elite group of Chanka warriors served the Inka emperor as select bodyguards, dedicated to preserving the life of their ruler at all costs. Within the empire, the Chankas were noted for their distinctive style of headgear: "They had long hair, delicately braided, and arranged with some wool cords that come to fall below their chins."[18] They wore wool shirts and mantles and lived in round stone houses quite distinct from the square and rectilinear buildings of the Inkas.

Archaeological evidence suggests that life for the Chanka people, on the whole, was much easier and healthier as part of the Inka Empire (A.D. 1400–1532) than during the preceding period of Chanka independence (A.D. 1100–1400). From around A.D. 700 to 1050, the peoples of Andahuaylas were under the rule of an Andean empire known as the Wari, whose capital was located near the modern-day city of Ayacucho, to the northwest of Andahuaylas. While under Wari influence, the Chankas built their communities at lower elevations, close to their fields and to their sources of water. Mortuary remains from burials in Andahuaylas during this period reveal that Wari rule was a relatively peaceful time for the Chankas. Danielle Kurin's examination of the skeletal remains from an ancient mortuary near the community of Turpo, for example, showed that only 8 percent of the teenage and adult population from the Wari period (the tenth century) sustained traumatic injuries, possibly caused by warfare. So there is evidence of some violence, but not a high level.[19]

Yet, in this same site near Turpo, the skeletons from the Chanka period—that is, from the time between the Wari and Inka Empires, often referred to as the Late Intermediate Period (LIP) by archaeologists—showed that 58 percent of teenage and adult individuals had at least one traumatic cranial wound. Kurin's forensic analysis demonstrated that these were, by and large, wounds caused by violence. For example, the Chanka skeletons with traumatic head wounds often exhibited defensive wounds on the arms and hands, indicating that the wounds were caused by violence, not accidents. Overall, Kurin's research revealed that during the period prior to Inka rule, one out of five, or 20 percent of all Chanka individuals—both men and women—died from violent injuries. Many of these fatalities occurred when the victims were helpless, probably with their hands tied behind their backs; they were struck about the head and face until they died. This dramatic upsurge in signs of intentional trauma on Chanka skeletons suggests an increase in warfare among Chanka communities in the LIP (A.D. 1100–1400), prior to the Chankas' incorporation into the Inka Empire.

We can also observe a major shift in where the Chankas built their settlements during the LIP. In the more peaceful Wari era, the Chankas built their main villages lower down on the mountain slopes, near their fields and water sources. But with the collapse of the Wari Empire throughout the area, the Chankas retreated to highly defensible hilltop locations. Between A.D. 1000 and 1100, the Chankas abandoned most of their towns for high-altitude ridge and mountaintop settlements at between 12,000 and 13,000 feet.[20] These very high Chanka cities, whose stone ruins sit today along ridge-tops wreathed in clouds, were often ringed by walls and defensive moats to hinder attack. Most of these settlements lacked sources of fresh water, and many had precipices on three sides. It must have been a difficult life for women, hours away from any spring or river; rainwater must have been conserved, reused, and guarded as a precious thing. Disease and infections would have been common in these densely packed cities in the clouds. It is no surprise that Kurin discovered that the Chanka people in the pre-Inka period had poorer health than those in Wari times due to more parasites and bacterial infections. As she wrote,

> Survey data demonstrates that the post-imperial era in Andahuaylas was characterized by a major shift to amalgamated, high elevation, defensible ridge- and hilltop settlements. Agglutinated, defensive habitation sites . . . would have been crowded, with the living, the dead, animals, and their waste all located in close quarters. Because hilltop sites in Andahuaylas have no immediate water sources, inhabitants would have had to leave the safety of the settlement for refills (leaving them vulnerable to attack), and water may have been stored for long periods of time. Brackish water, or water contaminated by human and/or animal waste, could have spawned a host of infections (viral, protozoal, bacterial, and parasitic). Vectors like fleas and bats, and zoonotic diseases could have also easily fluoresced [sic] in unsanitary and unhygienic living conditions, while crowded settlements could have eased the spread of communicable pathogens from human to human.[21]

As soon as the Chankas became incorporated into the Inka Empire, their settlements moved back down to the riverbeds at the foot of the mountains.[22] Clearly, the Chankas were no longer fighting endemically among themselves and could enjoy the luxury of living close to their fields and sources of fresh water.

NOTES

Chapter 1

1. Archivo Departamental del Cusco (ADC), Protocolo notarial de Andahuaylas del siglo XVIII, Registro de Gregorio Antonio Pacheco, Testamento de Núñez de Guevara, 1705.
2. Unfortunately, Gutiérrez later had the native farmers violently thrown off the land, which he claimed for the sugar plantation of Caruayaco. In May 1656, the case went before the local corregidor, who decided in favor of the Indians of Ocobamba. Gutiérrez then petitioned the Audiencia in Lima for title to the land, and by July 26, 1656, he was once again its legal owner (Archivo General de la Nacion [AGN], Real Audiencia, Causas criminales, legajo 154, cuaderno 579, Autos seguidos por D. José Gutierres contra los indios de Ocobamba, 1656, fol. 61). Gutiérrez subsequently used his influence to move Aponte out of the Indian parish of Ocobamba.
3. For the study of crime with particular reference to race, gender, and age in colonial Latin America, see Premo, *Children of the Father King*; Uribe-Uran, "Innocent Infants or Abusive Patriarchs?"
4. See, for example, Wardle, "Cosmopolitan Anthropology?"
5. McCall, "American Woman Discovers an Ancient Empire." For more on Monica's project, see Barnes, "Chicha Project"; Meddens, "Chicha/Soras Valley."
6. McCall, "American Woman Discovers an Ancient Empire."
7. Ibid.
8. At Cornell, Monica and I took seminars on the Andes taught by Craig Morris, Billie Jean Isbell, Tom Abercrombie, and Don Solá. Later, at Yale, I studied with Richard Burger, Mike Coe, Noble David Cook, Floyd Lounsbury, Hal Conklin, and Emilia Da Costa, among others.
9. See Barnes, "Yawar Fiesta of Pampachiri."
10. Archivo General de las Indias (AGI), Contratación 305B, no. 1, ramo 6, Bienes del difuncto del Padre Juan Bautista Albadán, 1612.
11. This account of the famous Chanka War is taken from the writings of Sarmiento de Gamboa. Sarmiento's narrative came from the mouths of Inka historians in Cusco and has long been considered one of the most reliable Spanish chronicles of the Inkas (Sarmiento de Gamboa, *History of the Incas*). Bauer argues that, based on the chronologies of Spanish chroniclers who drew on the accounts of Inka informants, the Chanka War probably occurred between 1400 and 1438. For a more detailed account of early Chanka history, see the appendix, where I present local variations of the Chanka War myth, which differ markedly from the Cusco-centered version provided here.
12. Kurin, "Bioarchaeology of Collapse," 46.
13. Cook, *Demographic Collapse*, 227; Monzón, "Descripción de la tierra."
14. See Isbell, *To Defend Ourselves*; Salomon and Grosboll, "Names and Peoples in Incaic Quito"; Godoy, "Fiscal Role of the Andean Ayllu"; Zuidema, *Inca Civilization in Cuzco*; Decoster,

"La dualidad andina revisitada." In a recent article, Weismantel describes how, even as the role of ayllus in rural Andean life has diminished in the twenty-first century, the idea of the ayllu has emerged as a central symbol in current indigenous activism in the Andes (Weismantel, "Ayllu").

15. AGN, Derecho indígena, legajo 3, cuaderno 17, Visita de Juan de Palomares, ca. 1570.

16. Cieza de León, *Obras completas*, 246. "Apu kuraka" means leading kuraka or head kuraka; in Quechua, "apu" means lord.

17. Visita de Juan de Palomares, ca. 1570.

18. In Monzón's 1586 description of the *reducciones* in this region, Pampachiri is listed among the other Chanka settlements; it does not appear among the towns of Hatun Soras (Monzón, "Descripción de la tierra"). Meddens and Vivanco Pomacanchari have argued that the Soras were allies of the Chankas and formed part of the Chanka confederacy (Meddens and Vivanco Pomacanchari, "The Chanca Confederation"). Further archaeological research is needed in the Chicha Valley to delineate the relations between the Soras and Chanka peoples.

19. When Brian, myself, and our crew prepared for our trip to Pampachiri from our base in Andahuaylas, our local neighbors in Andahuaylas refused to believe that we were going there to study the archaeological remains. In the previous weeks, the rumor had spread in Andahuaylas that we were actually a Hollywood film crew, intent on finding an Andean location for our next movie project. Someone thought that they had recognized me as a Hollywood actress, and Brian as a film director. When we bought supplies for the trip, our neighbors winked and smiled knowingly—they didn't believe for a minute that we were going to look at ruins!

20. Meddens, "Chicha/Soras Valley."

21. In December 2000, Ann Kendall and the nonprofit Cusichaca Trust initiated a project to revive ancient irrigation canals in the Andahuaylas and Ayacucho region; Pampachiri was one of four communities included in this project. Information about the Cusichaca Trust can be found at http://www.cusichaca.org.

22. Ethnographic studies about the impact of the Shining Path in rural Ayacucho and Apurimac include González, *Unveiling Secrets of War*; Theidon, *Intimate Enemies*; and Cecconi, "Dreams, Memory, and War."

23. Castillo, "Guzmán ordenó asesinar."

Chapter 2

1. On Guaman Poma, see Adorno, *Guaman Poma: Writing and Resistance* and *Guaman Poma and His Illustrated Chronicle*; Puente, "Felipe Guaman Poma de Ayala." As I have discussed elsewhere, Guaman Poma clearly authored the *Nueva corónica y buen gobierno*, despite assertions in the Miccinelli documents that the Jesuit Blas Valera wrote most of the chronicle. The Miccinelli documents appear to be colonial-era forgeries; see Hyland, *The Jesuit and the Incas* and *Gods of the Andes*.

2. Stern, *Peru's Indian Peoples*, 86n18, 96n51, 230, 232.

3. Guaman Poma de Ayala, *Nueva corónica*, 3:1176–77.

4. Ibid., 2:748–49.

5. Ibid., 2:672: "¡O Cristiano padre Uendaño, treynta años estar en la doctrina cin pesadumbre y murir seruiendo a Dios y a los pobres yndios! . . . Y no quería uer soltera en su casa in lo mandaua ajuntar a los donzellas. A las biejas y enfermos le seruía y a los foresteros le confesaua y bautisaua de limosna . . . murió y muy cristianamente y muy pobre que no se le halló en su poder cosa de plata ni hazienda alguna, cino todo pobresa. Y sus pobres yndios están llorando y toda la prouincia del padre."

6. Ibid., 2:598: "El padre Juan Buatista Aluadan . . . fue muy apsoluto, cruel

padre, las cosas que este hombre hazía no se puede escriuir."

7. Ibid., 2:734: "Ues aquí, soberbioso padre, ci castiga a los rrebeles soberbiosos señores apsolutos, se quexan después del jues. Y ací meresen grandes castigos."

8. Ibid., 2:598: "que el padre Albadan le desnudaua y le miraua el culo y el coño y le metía los dedos y en el culo le daua quatro asoticos; cada mañana le hacía a todas las solteras." The English translation of this passage is true to Guaman Poma's use of Spanish slang.

9. Ibid., 2:598.

10. AGI, Contratación 305B, no. 1, ramo 6, Bienes del difunto, del Padre Juan Bautista Albadán, 1612, fol. 29r. All of the folio citations in this chapter, in the text and notes, refer to this document, unless otherwise noted.

11. Wealthier churches in colonial Peru used beeswax candles, which burned more cleanly and had a pleasant odor. The Roman Missal specified that the candles used during Mass should be made of beeswax. However, in rural doctrinas such as Pampachiri, tallow candles were common at the altar for Mass.

12. Guaman Poma de Ayala, *Nueva corónica*, 2:598: "Y dizen que hizo otras muchas más, que no se puede escriuir, cino que Dios lo sepa y otros muy muchos daños y males hacía."

13. Hagen and Yohani, "Nature and Psychosocial Consequences," 16.

14. Weingarten, *Common Shock.*

15. Fol. 85v: "[Yo] hubiera entrado en algunos vicios"; fol. 88v: "en que de más de dos años a esta parte estoy tan trocado en mugeres y otras cossas al que sse espantará a Vuestra Merced." Fols. 87v–88r: "Que prometo a Vuestra Merced Sseñor hermano, que quissiera que Vuestra Merced esperimentará mi voluntad en cossas muy difficultosas y de su gusto."

16. Fol. 86r: "Vuestra Merced está rrico e me podrá hacer vien, y Vuestra Merced lo hace por estraños y por quienquijano; se lo agradecerá mucho favoreciendome pues."

17. It is notoriously difficult to calculate the equivalences between currencies today and those of many centuries ago. In the seventeenth century, 1 Spanish peso was worth 2 Dutch guilders. In terms of labor equivalence, 2 Dutch guilders equaled approximately 370 U.S. dollars in the 1600s; in other words, 1 peso was roughly equivalent to 185 U.S. dollars today. See McCusker, *How Much Is That in Real Money?*; Turner, "Money and Exchange Rates in 1632."

18. This discussion of the Inka legal system is informed by Brundage, *Empire of the Inca*, 222–26; Mirow, *Latin American Law*, 6–7; and McEwan, *Incas*, 107–12.

19. It was decided at this time that the diocese of Guamanga would include the *corregimientos* of Guamanga, Huancavelica, Castro Virreina, Choclococho, Vilcasguaman, Sangaro, Soras, Lucanas, Andamarcas, Los Chocorvos y Angaraes, Parinacocha, Pomatambos y Guayca, and, finally, "Andahuaylas and the Chankas." The Audiencia allocated eleven priests for the corregimiento of Andahuaylas. Four were to serve in the towns of Andahuaylas, San Jerónimo, Talavera, and Mayomarca, while the remaining seven were divided among the following doctrinas: Huancaray and Turpo; Kula and Chullisana; Huayana, Ulcay, and Curamba; Pampachiri, Umamarca, and Pomacocha; Huancarama and Cotarma; Ongoy, Piscobamba, Omaca, and Ocobamba; and Uripa, Cayara, Cocharcas, Mollepampa, and Uchupampa. These areas were quite large to be administered by individual priests, each of whom exercised a high degree of autonomy within his doctrina. AGI, Escribanía de Cámara 503B, 1613–16, Pleytos de Audiencia, Recibimiento del Obispo Fray Agustín de Carvajal, January 23, 1614, fol. 87.

20. AGI, Lima 211, no. 12, Información del Padre Alonso Martínes, 1596.

21. For example, in one of the visitations of the Cusco diocese (including Andahuaylas and Pampachiri) called by the cathedral chapter, the *visitador* simply took the money given to him to

perform the visitation and vacationed in Lima for a year. When he returned to Cusco, he never submitted a visitation report. AGI, Lima 305, no. 17a, Información de los excesos que se hacen en las de vacantes en este obispado, 1598.

22. Bishop Antonio de Raya Narvarrete, who was bishop of Cusco from 1594 until his death on July 28, 1606, was primarily concerned with the construction of an elaborate seminary in Cusco during his episcopacy. He was succeeded by Bishop Fernando de Mendoza González, who was consecrated as bishop in January 1609 and arrived in Peru later that year.

23. See Peters, *Inquisition*.

24. Chuchiak, "Sins of the Fathers."

25. Hyland, *The Jesuit and the Incas*, 62.

26. Avendaño, *Sermones de los misterios*, Book I, fols. 1, 6, 60, and Book II, fols. 14, 15, 46; also Mills, *Idolatry and Its Enemies*, 170–210.

27. AGI, Lima 238, no. 11, Información de Antonio Calderon de la Barca, 1646; AGI, Lima 224, no. 12, Información de Francisco de Aldana, 1622.

28. Guaman Poma de Ayala, *Nueva corónica*, 2:653–55.

29. This indifference is comparable, perhaps, to that of the white settlers in nineteenth-century California who looked the other way when bounty hunters scalped and beheaded the Yahi Indians, decimating the Yahi population. See Kroeber, *Ishi in Two Worlds*.

30. AGI, Lima 226, no. 1, Información del Licenciado Garcia Ortiz Cervantes, 1622–26. During his visitation, Quintanilla condemned Father Garcia Ortiz Cervantes, who had served in the doctrinas of Pampamarca and Turpo, for abuse on September 26, 1607, in San Gerónimo in greater Andahuaylas. Juan Peres Bocanegra, the famous musician and author, was involved in the investigation of Ortiz Cervantes.

31. Guaman Poma de Ayala, *Nueva corónica*, 2:734–35: "en el dicho pueblo no hallo ánima beuiente y serrado la dicha iglesia, todos los yndios escondidos en la puna, ni halló un jarro de agua."

32. Ibid., 2:598–99.

33. Ibid.: "deziendo que escondía yndios de la uecita."

34. AGN, Derecho indígena, legajo 4, cuaderno 50, Autos que promovió Arce de Quiroz, 1606, fol. 51.

35. Biblioteca Nacional del Perú (BNP), Ms. B-28, Relación de la visita . . . al repartimiento de los indios chancas, 1606–1697, fols. 3v–5v.

Chapter 3

1. AGI, Contratación 305B, no. 1, ramo 6, Bienes del difuncto del Padre Juan Bautista Albadán, 1612, fol. 78r–v. All of the folio citations in this chapter, in the text and notes, refer to this document, unless otherwise noted.

2. Fol. 81r–v: "aunque es mi hermana muerta, mi obligación no se murió ni mi voluntad que tengo como de padre."

3. Ibid.: "perdido" and "condenado."

4. Fol. 82r: "viviendo entre bárbaros."

5. Fol. 81r–v: "por la sangre de Dios le suplico que pues ya no ay para que venir a España, que Vuestra Merced no es niño; aqui lo procure hacer asiento en la virtud e trate de ganar de comer como tantos lo saben ganar. . . . Qué no aya más juegos sino que Vuestra Merced sepa guardar acordándose que es hijo de buenos padres y que debe aplicarse de suerte de su persona no se pierda nada."

6. Harrison, *Sin and Confession*, 128–29.

7. Fol. 82r: "la large relación que Vuestra Merced me da de sus trabajos e destierros que los siento en el alma."

8. Fol. 82v: "vivir muy descansado en España."

9. Fol. 77v: "y si hasta aqui escribía con aspereza, era solo por despertar a Vuestra Merced del sueño en que estaba . . . y aunque pudiera ahora decir mucho de lo que siento, quedará en ese rincón sin tratar de venir a gozar a este cielo y patria y ver la grandeza deste ciudad."

10. See Taylor, *Structures of Reform*; also Hughes, *Religious Imagery*.

11. Téllez, *Historia general*; Taylor, *Structures of Reform*, 338.
12. Téllez, *Historia general*, 284–86: "solicitud y buena maña."
13. Ibid., 419.
14. Doña Ana and her husband, Diego de Albadán, were buried in the chancel of the Iglesia del Carmen in Seville; Diego had been given this tomb as a gift by his fellow confraternity member Alonso de Roderos (fol. 57r–v). In her will, Doña Ana described exactly where their tomb was: "que entierren mi cuerpo en la iglesia del monasterio de Nuestra Señora del Carmen desta ciudad, en la capilla mayor en el entierro que alli tengo, que es en el altar de Nuestra Señora de la Cabeza, que está en la dicha capilla mayor." Fol. 162v.
15. Téllez, *Historia general*, 481.
16. The family lineage can be found in the documents granting Gerónimo permission to voyage to Peru: AGI, Contratación 5235, no. 2, ramo 47, Licencia de pasajero a indias de Jerónimo de Albadán, 1592.
17. Pike, "Seville in the Sixteenth Century"; Perry, *Gender and Disorder*; Nash, *Seville, Córdoba, and Granada*.
18. Fol. 77r: "Viendo que la flota está, andaba a prisa, me vine aquí a Sevilla por escribir a Vuestra Merced con mejor comodidad e responder a tres que recibí."
19. Fols. 60v–61r: "En los galeones que ahora vinieron . . . recibí la de Vuestra Merced y con esto toda la merced que me hace."
20. Fol. 180v: "corredor de lonja."
21. Fol. 67r: "nuestro apellido honorosso con hacerle estimar en esta ciudad por muy noble y honorado . . . sea muy aventajado por ser Albadán . . . está en ojos de hijodalgo notorio Christianos Viejos." For an excellent analysis of concepts of Old Christian status and honor in colonial Latin America, see Martínez, *Genealogical Fictions*.
22. Fol. 50r: "digno de buena memoria . . . su buena nobleza e papeles."
23. Fols. 156v–157r: "me ha servido muchos años con mucha amor e voluntad, diligencia y cuidado."
24. Ibid.: "esclavas cautibas . . . de color negra"; "las quales les tengo grande amor y voluntad por el buen servicio que me an hecho."
25. Martín Casares and García Barranco, *Esclavitud negroafricana*.
26. Fracchia, "Constructing the Black Slave," 186.
27. Ibid.
28. Fol. 52v: "es para mi de mucho sentimiento y pena e tenido y tender por lo mucho que le amaba por su noble e principal proceder e antigua e buena amistad que nos teníamos."
29. Fol. 82r: "el estar desterrado casi desde nació, fuera de su patria y de los suyos."
30. Fol. 51r: "que año queda atrás año, yo en este lugar y de los tres que fuimos, quedé solo"; "siento mucho que digan todos los que tratan a Vuestra Merced que sienten tanto para ellos y para sí tan poco perdón."
31. Her total estate was valued at 606,872 maravedís, which is equal to 1,618.36 ducats of gold (fol. 171r).
32. Fol. 164v: "el mucho amor que tengo a Francisco."
33. AGI, Indiferente 2090, no. 163, Licencia de pasajeros a indias de Juan de Albadán, 1576; the license read, "pasa por via de Andrés Núñez de Prado."
34. Other seminaries in Peru, such as the Seminario de San Antonio Abad (1598) in Cusco, were founded too late for Albadán to have attended them; see Burkholder, *Spaniards in the Colonial Empire*. There is no evidence that Albadán ever completed a degree at San Marcos.
35. AGI, Contaduria 1827, 1591–1629, Caja del Cuzco, 1591, fol. 54.
36. Licencia de pasajero a indias de Jerónimo de Albadán, 1592.
37. Fol. 85v: "y acuerdome que cuando vine chapetón a Lima, le escribía a Vuestra Merced, me quería subir al Cuzco a ganar de comer si Vuestra Merced me daba licencia para ello y me respondió no hiciese tal porque Vuestra Merced estaba pobre y no tenía con que remediarme porque si vaya, sería donde gente no me viesen. E cumplí su gusto."
38. Fols. 85v–86r: "vicios de la tierra."

39. Taylor, *Structures of Reform*, 370.
40. Téllez, *Historia general*, 283.
41. AGN, Derecho indígena, legajo 4, cuaderno 50, Autos que promovió Arce de Quiroz, 1606.
42. Ibid., fol. 51.
43. Acosta Rodríguez, "Los doctrineros y la extirpación"; see also Powers, "Battle for Bodies and Souls."
44. AGI, Escribanía de Cámara 503B, 1613–16, Pleytos de Audiencia, Salarios de doctrineros—Corregimiento de Andahuaylas, 1614, fols. 49–52.
45. AGN, Derecho indígena, legajo 3, cuaderno 17, Los tributos de los Chancas, 1552.
46. AGI, Contratación 253, no. 3, Testamento de Bachiller Fausto Lopez, June 18, 1591, fol. 19r.
47. AGI, Escribanía de Cámara 503B, Pleytos de Audiencia, Diezmos de Andahuaylas, 1608–12, November 16, 1613.
48. AGI, Lima 308, Remate de los diezmos, obispado de Guamanga, April 8, 1633.
49. Guerra, *Ensayo de un padrón histórico*, 353–54.
50. Fol. 112v: "un librillo de quentas que tiene de su mano e letra."
51. See chapter 2, note 17, for a discussion of the equivalence between current and historical currencies.
52. Testamento de Bachiller Fausto Lopez, June 18, 1591, fol. 19r.
53. AGN, Lima, Titulos de propiedad, 1596, legajo 2, cuaderno 28, Venta de tierras, July 6, 1596, fol. 3.
54. ADC, Protocolo notarial de Andahuaylas del siglo XVII, Notarial Pedro de Ojeda, Venta de tierras, July 25, 1660.
55. AGI, Contratación 486, no. 1, Autos de bienes de difuntos, Testamento de Diego Sánchez Gordillo, June 22, 1591.
56. ADC, Protocolo notarial de Andahuaylas del siglo XVII, Notarial Pedro de Ojeda, Testamento de Don Lope de Mendoza, June 9, 1660.
57. ADC, Protocolo notarial de Andahuaylas del siglo XVII, Registro de Joseph Cardenas y Paredes, Renta de Cotaguacho, October 20, 1691.

58. ADC, Protocolo notarial de Andahuaylas del siglo XVII, Notarial Joseph de Cordoba, Donación de Francisco de Peroza, May 5, 1639.
59. ADC, Protocolo notarial de Andahuaylas del siglo XVIII, Registro de Juan Thomas Rojas, Venta de tierras, March 14, 1712.
60. ADC, Protocolo notarial de Andahuaylas del siglo XVIII, Registro de Joseph Antonio de Castro, Venta de la hacienda de Tancaillo, September 17, 1726.
61. ADC, Protocolo notarial de Andahuaylas del siglo XVIII, Cuaderno de Joseph Antonio de Castro, Venta de tierras, April 10, 1756.
62. ADC, Protocolo notarial de Andahuaylas del siglo XVIII, Cuaderno de Joseph Antonio de Castro, Arrendamiento, April 15, 1784.
63. ADC, Protocolo notarial de Andahuaylas del siglo XVIII, Registro de Gregorio Antonio Pacheco, Venta de tierras, May 9, 1788, fol. 2.
64. Mestizos were allowed to be ordained as Catholic priests in colonial Peru, but could only be ordained to serve in native doctrinas (Hyland, "Illegitimacy and Racial Hierarchy"). In 1624, Bishop Verdugo of Guamanga prepared a report on the priests of his diocese, which revealed that two of the nine doctrina priests in the corregimiento of Andahuaylas were mestizos (AGI, Lima 308, no. 71, Memorial de las doctrinas del Obispado de Guamanga, ca. 1624, fols. 2v–3r).
65. AGI, Patronato 135, no. 2, ramo 7, Información de méritos y servicios de Alonso Mendoza Ponce de León, 1594.
66. Fol. 54r: "muchas calamidades . . . cargado de mil obligaciones forzosas que a mi me an vuelto viejo . . . que en la casa donde se padece todo es guerra."
67. Documents concerning the settlement of Don Andrés's estate can be found in AGI, Contratación 941B, no. 18, Autos sobre los bienes de Andrés Núñez de Prado, 1608/1610.
68. Fol. 6or–v: "es tan galeanda de cuerpo"; "los mejores ojos que hay en esta

tierra"; "está en tiempo de multiplicarse porque es moza."

69. Fol. 68v: "la vida que se pasa en este lugar es con mayor quietud del alma, aunque hacienda es poca."

70. Fol. 69r: "quería me hiciesse Dios tan dichosa que viese a Vuestra Merced en este lugar que yo pienso que es Vuestra Merced tan discreto y buen christiano."

71. Fol. 69v: "le parece en tener el oficio de escribano tiene todo el mundo."

72. Fol. 70r: "le tengo muy grande su valor e christianidad y asi le pido se acuerde de nosotros e no nos olvide siquiera por estos hijos que son muchos."

73. Fol. 85r: "algunas personas que conocen a Vuestra Merced." This statement must refer to José de Billela, who was the corregidor of Andahuaylas until 1601, when his position was taken over by Captain Juan de Marzano.

74. Fol. 87r: "algunas malas ynformaciones."

75. Fol. 85v: "Quando he podido, no ha querido que yo le sirve; que lo haré mejor que los estraños, a quien Vuestra Merced siempre hace bien."

76. Fol. 87v: "Señor hermano, no creerá Vuestra Merced el gusto y content que recibí con una de Vuestra Merced que me vino por mano de Alonso Herrera y por la merced que en ella Vuestra Merced me hace."

77. AGI, Audiencia de Charcas 64, no. 10, Confirmación de oficio por Alonso Nieto de Herrera, March 22, 1610.

78. Fols. 87v–88r: "Vuestra Merced esperimentará mi voluntad en cosas muy difficultosas y de su gusto."

79. Fol. 88v: "solo me contentará estar con Vuestra Merced"; "mejor amigo."

80. Ibid.: "a esta parte estoy tan trocado en mujeres y otras cosas al que se espantará Vuestra Merced."

81. Fol. 82v: "pero no quiero decir más porque no diga a Vuestra Merced que le reprehendo e escripto a Vuestra Merced como se llevó Dios al Señor Andrés Núñez de Prado, su tío."

82. Fol. 83v: "será para mi un gran regalo saber de Vuestra Merced . . . y pues está Vuestra Merced en parte donde le sobra el tiempo y escribir cartas."

83. Lynch, *Spain Under the Hapsburgs*, 47.

84. Cited in Said, "Reflections on Exile," 146.

85. Ibid., 137, 141–44, 146.

Chapter 4

1. González Sánchez (*New World Literacy*) provides a comparison of many private libraries in the Americas from 1500 to 1700, including Albadán's collection.

2. García Bernal, "Biblioteca del Convento."

3. See Dadson, "Private Libraries"; Gilbert Santamaría, *Writers on the Market*.

4. Leonard, *Books of the Brave*, 212–25.

5. Dadson, "Private Libraries," 58: "y no se maraville alguno que tanta diligencia pongo en mis libros, porque segun mi affection, más valen que todo el resto de mi mueble."

6. Hampe Martínez, *Cultura barroca y extirpación*.

7. See Hyland, *Quito Manuscript*, 22–25.

8. Burns, *Into the Archive*, 3.

9. Salomon and Niño-Murcia, *Lettered Mountain*, 1–69.

10. For an analysis of how a nineteenth-century herder's khipu recorded information, see Hyland, "Ply, Markedness, and Redundancy"; for a hybrid khipu/alphabetic text, see Hyland, Ware, and Clark, "Knot Direction."

11. ADC, Cabildo justicia ordinaria, legajo 2, 1601–26, cuaderno 5, Proceso de Juan Francisco Arias Maldonado contra Juan de San Pedro, 1614. I am currently preparing an analysis of the khipu testimony in this case, comparing the khipu texts with the Spanish ledger records kept for the same hacienda over the same ten-year period. I hope that this will illuminate the contrasting manner in which information was stored on hacienda khipus and in Spanish account ledgers.

12. See Urton, "From Knots to Narratives"; Pärssinen, *Textos andinos*.

13. Curatola Petrocchi and Puente Luna, "Estudios y materiales."

14. ADC, Corregimiento de Andahuaylas, Causas ordinarias, legajo 2, 1680–99, Remate de Yaramay, March 18, 1694.

15. ADC, Protocolo notarial de Andahuaylas del siglo XVIII, Notarial Gregorio Antonio Pacheco, Inventorio de Pincos, November 28, 1700.

16. ADC, Corregimiento de Andahuaylas, Causas ordinarias, legajo 2, 1680–99, Inventario de los bienes de Francisco Lopez, 1680.

17. ADC, Corregimiento de Andahuaylas, Pedimientos y intendencia, legajo 13, 1668–1891, Testamento de Don Fernando de Naucayalli, July 16, 1725.

18. AGI, Contratación 253, no. 3, Testamento de Bachiller Fausto Lopez, June 18, 1591, fol. 19r.

19. ADC, Corregimiento de Andahuaylas, Causas ordinarias, legajo 2, 1680–99, Inventario de los bienes de Don Pedro Berrocal y Valenzuela, April 21, 1687. Father Berrocal y Valenzuela regularly transported sugar from Apurimac by mule train to Potosí, where he sold it for a considerable profit. ADC, Corregimiento de Andahuaylas, Causas ordinarias, legajo 2, 1680–99, Causa ordinaria seguida por Francisco del Castillo, April 28, 1687.

20. ADC, Corregimiento de Andahuaylas, Pedimientos y intendencia, legajo 1, 1626–72, expediente 3, Testamento del Maestro Joseph de Vargas, 1677.

21. According to his will, the church and furnishings cost 1,700 pesos.

22. Calepino's dictionary was originally published in 1502 and went through innumerable editions in the sixteenth and seventeenth centuries.

23. *Concilium Limense* (Madrid, 1591).

24. *Vita Sanctae Rosae* by P. Hansen, OP (Rome, 1664–68).

25. Prado, *Directorio espiritual.*

26. See Hyland, *The Jesuit and the Incas,* 170–81.

27. Hampe Martínez, *Santidad e identidad criolla.*

28. Durston, "Apuntes para una historia."

29. *Apologia ad monachos hispanos* (Basel, 1527).

30. Albadán's books were inventoried with his other belongings. AGI,

Contratación 305B, no. 1, ramo 6, Bienes del difuncto del Padre Juan Bautista Albadán, 1612.

31. Ibid.: "diccionario de boperio"; "diccionario de Estefano"; *Vocabulario eclesiastico* by Rodrigo Fernandez de Santaella (1499); "un calendario viejo."

32. Barr, "Influence of Saint Jerome"; Martin, "Anti-feminism."

33. Cited in Silverblatt, "Family Values," 71.

34. Santana Perez, "Sobre el encierro."

35. Covarrubias Orozco, *Emblemas morales.*

36. Zavala, "Emblemas Morales."

37. Covarrubias Orozco, *Emblemas morales,* emblem 18: "La verdad no tiene mas de una cara, siempre es una, y está firme, aunque padezca mil adversidades, que le acarrean la calumnia, y la mentira. Los Filosofos Gentiles, anduuieron a buscar esta verdad, y no pudieron atinar a ella, por no auer conocido el verdadero Dios que es suma verdad. Y ansi se divieron en diferentes sectas y opiniones."

38. Zavala, "Emblemas Morales."

39. Donahue Wallace, *Art and Architecture,* 180–81; Bailey, *Andean Hybrid Baroque,* 15–18.

40. The original stone sculptures on the church portal were created during Albadán's tenure in Pampachiri. In the 1730s, the roof and interior sections of the church were rebuilt under the supervision of licenciado Don Toribio Gutiérrez, the priest of Pampachiri at that time. As Father Gutiérrez wrote in his will, "it must be understood that the said community of Indians from the said doctrina has carefully and promptly attended to the construction of this church, personally making the roof tiles, [and] handling the wood and other necessary materials by ayllus" (se ha de entender que dicho comun de yndios de esta dicha doctrina an de asistir presisa y puntualmente a la refacción de esta yglesia con sus personas haciendo las texas por sus ayllos en la conducción de la madera y demás materiales que fueren necesario). ADC, Protocolo notarial de Andahuaylas del siglo XVIII, Registro de Joseph Antonio

de Castro, Testamento de Don Toribio Gutierrez, January 1, 1735.

41. For an additional explanation of the significance of the façade of the Pampachiri church, see Barnes, "Análisis de la iconografía."

42. Gibbs, *Aesop's Fables.*

43. Juvenal, *Sixteen Satires*, 263.

44. Carrillo Cázares, "Tratados novohispanos."

45. Boone, "Pictorial Documents."

46. Mitchell and Jaye, "Pictographs in the Andes."

47. Durston, *Pastoral Quechua*; Hyland, *Gods of the Andes*; Harrison, *Sin and Confession.*

48. The last line of Albadán's sermon lacks a topic marker and evidence marker: "Suc garrotillauan padre canca. Alli oyariuay."

49. Guaman Poma de Ayala, *Nueva corónica*, 2:653–55.

50. Peters, *Inquisition.*

51. Valderrama also applauds the persecution of Moriscos (individuals of Moorish descent) in Spain and links the expulsion of the Moriscos and the beatification of Saint Ignatius Loyola in the same year as simultaneous acts of God's grace.

Chapter 5

1. Juvenal, *Sixteen Satires*, 117.

2. Ibid., 122.

3. Ibid.

4. Guaman Poma de Ayala, *Nueva corónica*, 2:644.

5. Cheese and butter production were introduced to South America by the Spanish colonizers. Although Andean peoples could have consumed milk products from llamas and alpacas prior to the European invasion, they did not do so (Hastorf, "Steamed or Boiled"), holding milk consumption from animals in low regard.

6. AGI, Contratación 305B, no. 1, ramo 6, Bienes del difuncto del Padre Juan Bautista Albadán, 1612, fol. 130r–v. All of the folio citations in this chapter, in the text and notes, refer to this document, unless otherwise noted.

7. Earle, "'If You Eat Their Food,'" 688.

8. Cited in ibid.

9. Cited in ibid., 693.

10. Ibid., 699.

11. Huertas Vallejos, "Historia de la producción."

12. Sempat Assadourian, "Sobre un elemento," 145–48.

13. Cited in Soldi, "La vid y el vino": "lo mejor del reino."

14. Allen, "'Let's Drink Together, My Dear!'"

15. Ibid.

16. AGN, Derecho indígena, legajo 4, cuaderno 50, Autos que promovió Arce de Quiroz, 1606, fol. 51.

17. The Sivi Paucars remained in power in Pampachiri after Albadán's death. In 1694, for example, Don Gabriel Sivi Paucar, the kuraka of Pampachiri, and his second, Don Miguel Ticlla Guaman, petitioned the corregidor for a new visitation (ADC, Corregimiento de Andahuaylas, Causas ordinarias, legajo 2, 1680–99, Petición de Don Gabriel Sivi Paucar, August 1694). Albadán had not been able to depose the Sivi Paucar family in Pampachiri, despite the fact that its kuraka refused to work openly with him. Perhaps this refusal was mitigated by the fact that a member of a lower-ranking branch of the family— Don Alonso—was willing to help the priest cheat his parishioners. According to a document from 1539, the Sivi Paucars were Inka administrators in Umamarca—*orejones*—not autochthonous Chanka rulers (Julien, "Diego Maldonado y los chancas").

18. Charles, *Allies at Odds*, 115.

19. Goñi Gaztambide, *Historia de la bula.*

20. For an excellent discussion of indulgences and their importance in urban confraternities in late colonial South America, see Fogelman, "Economía espiritual de la salvación."

21. Hernández Méndez, "Acercamiento histórico," 2–6.

22. Reina Maldonado, *Norte claro*, 80–81.

23. Ibid., 80.

24. Ibid., 246: "recibiendola con procession solemne, repique de campañas, chirimias, y trompetas concurso de la justicia, Españoles, y demás gente que en cada doctrina hallare, con todos los Indios, Cofrades y pendones."

25. For the text of such a sermon, see Itier, "Sermón desconocido."

26. Hernández Méndez, "Acercamiento histórico," 8–9.

27. ADC, Corregimiento de Andahuaylas, Causas ordinarias, legajo 3, 1701–29, Testamento del Doctor Bartolomé Lodeña y Espinoza, March 14, 1709.

28. ADC, Corregimiento de Andahuaylas, Causas ordinarias, legajo 2, 1680–99, Inventario de los bienes de Don Pedro Berrocal y Valenzuela, April 21, 1687.

29. Hernández Méndez, "Acercamiento histórico," 25.

30. Fol. 126v: "atento que el dicho Corregidor no puede acudir a hacer diligencias porque muy breve entrara en este corregimiento."

31. Weismantel, *Food, Gender, and Poverty*; Bray, "Commensal Politics"; Hastorf, "Steamed or Boiled."

32. Hastorf, "Steamed or Boiled"; Burger and van der Merwe, "Maize and the Origin"; Burger and Salazar, *1912 Yale Peruvian Scientific Expedition Collections*. For an overview of maize in the ancient Americas, see Staller, *Maize Cobs and Cultures*.

33. Juvenal, *Sixteen Satires*, 205–6.

34. Barroso, "Bezoar Stones."

35. Stephenson, "From Marvelous Antidote"; Millones Figueroa, "Bezoar Stone."

36. Stephenson, "From Marvelous Antidote."

37. Barroso, "Bezoar Stones."

Chapter 6

1. The details of Albadán's funeral Mass are derived from the list of funeral expenses prepared by the corregidor and reimbursed from the priest's estate. The description of the vestments in which he was buried come from Don Juan Topa Guasco's request for repayment for these garments; AGI, Contratación 305B, no. 1, ramo 6, Bienes del difuncto del Padre Juan Bautista Albadán, 1612, fols. 104v–108v. All of the folio citations in this chapter, in the text and notes, refer to this document, unless otherwise noted.

2. For an excellent analysis of the Catholic Church's attempts to inculcate Christian ideas of death and burial in the Andes, see Ramos, *Death and Conversion*; Martiarena, "Social Life of Death." These studies reveal that while natives in the cities complied with Spanish Christian norms for burials (Ramos), those living in the countryside continued indigenous burial practices well into the eighteenth century (Martiarena).

3. Fathers Pérez Ramírez and Núñes de Ilescas both said that they had been on friendly terms with Albadán; however, they both provided the wrong name for Albadán's brother Francisco when questioned about the dead priest's relatives.

4. See, for example, Montesinos, *Anales del Perú*, 144.

5. Fol. 9v: "alló el dicho padre Juan Bautista de Albadán en su cama acostado muy enfermo e casi fuera de su sentido porque apenas hablaba e conocía."

6. Elferink, "Use of Poison."

7. Garcilaso de la Vega, cited in ibid., 351.

8. Elferink, "Use of Poison."

9. Part of the loan—250 pesos—was personal, while the rest was intended to pay the corregidor's administrative expenses. Most of the loan, therefore, was due to a shortfall in the coffers of the corregimiento, but the corregidor was nonetheless personally responsible and could be sent to jail for nonpayment.

10. The mark (*marco*) was a standard measurement developed in the Middle Ages. The weight of the mark varied considerably over time and location.

11. For an outstanding discussion of private art collecting in the colonial Andes, see Stanfield-Mazzi, "Possessor's Agency."

12. On the caja de comunidad, see Salomon, "Collca y sapçi."
13. Nébias Barreto, "Legal Culture and Argumentation."
14. Hernando Arias de Ugarte was a creole born in 1561, the son of Don Hernando Arias Torero, an *encomendero* in Bogotá, and Doña Juana de Ugarte. He studied law in Salamanca, Spain, graduating from the University of Lérida. He was already a judge in the Lima Audiencia when he became a priest. In 1613 he was made bishop of Quito, and in 1628 he became archbishop of Lima. Egaña, *Historia de la Iglesia*, 289; see also Burns, *Into the Archive*.
15. Fol. 194v: "en misas e obras pías por su anima."
16. To appreciate the irony that Gerónimo de Valera was chosen to say masses for Albadán's soul, see Hyland, *The Jesuit and the Incas*.
17. For the concept of restitution to native Andeans, see Harrison, *Sin and Confession*, 220–36.
18. At the *juicio de residencia* held after the Marquess of Montesclaros left office, he was accused of intervening in the provincial elections of the Mercedarians in Peru in favor of Fray Paredes.
19. See Murphy, "Psychiatric Labeling"; Regeser López and Guarnaccia, "Cultural Psychopathology."
20. Cleckley, *Mask of Sanity*; Hirstein, "What Is a Psychopath?"
21. The PCL-R and the PPI are the most commonly used measures of psychopathy in the United States. Elsewhere, clinicians are more likely to use the criteria of the World Health Organization for a dissocial personality disorder. Clear evidence of at least three of the following six traits indicates the disorder: (1) callous unconcern for the feelings of others; (2) a gross and persistent attitude of disregard for social norms; (3) an incapacity to maintain enduring relationships; (4) a low tolerance for frustration and a low threshold for violence; (5) an incapacity to experience guilt; and (6) a marked proneness to blame others. Lee, *Treatment*.
22. Hirstein, "What Is a Psychopath?"
23. Martens, "Hidden Suffering."
24. Fols. 12v–13r: "su amigo e vecino de muchos años"; "esto lo trató muchas y diversas veces . . . deseaba a hir a los reinos de Castilla y él passarse con una capellania."
25. Williamson, Harpur, and Hare, "Abnormal Processing"; Brinkley, Schmitt, and Newman, "Semantic Processing."
26. Blair, "Neurobiological Basis"; van Goozen et al., "Evidence for a Neurobiological Model."
27. Lee, *Treatment*.
28. For the treatment of mental illness in colonial Mexico and Peru, see Viqueira, "Hospitales para locos."
29. See Tirso de Molina, *Condenado por desconfiado*.
30. Hughes, *Religious Imagery*.
31. Tirso de Molina, *Condenado por desconfiado*: "pero fui desconfiado de la gran piedad de Dios, que hoy a su juicio desconfiado, me dijo: 'Baja maldito de mi Padre, al centro airado de los oscuros abismos, adonde has de estar penando.' Malditos mis padres sean mil veces, pues me engendraron!"

Chapter 7

1. In 1659, Don León's daughter Doña Ana Guasco brought a case against Juan Arenas for stealing the fields that she had inherited from her father. During the court case, Captain Álvaro Gil de Aragón testified that he knew Don León "and saw him govern for more than ten years" (y le vió gobernar más tiempo de diez años) (ADC, Corregimiento de Andahuaylas, Causas ordinarias, legajo 1, 1626–72, expediente 4, Expediente de deslinde y amojonamiento que hace Doña Ana Guasco, July 3–7, 1659.
2. After the victory of the royalist forces—which included the Chankas and Guaman Poma's father—at the Battle of Chuquinca, Hernández Girón and his troops retaliated against the Chankas. Garcilaso de la Vega wrote that the

rebel leader's troops burned Chanka villages and laid waste to their fields (Garcilaso de la Vega, *Primera parte*, pt. 2, bk. 7, ch. 21). This is confirmed by Juan de Palomares's investigation, which found that Hernández Girón and his men burned Chanka buildings near Talavera and stole Chanka cattle (AGN, Derecho indígena, legajo 3, cuaderno 17, Visita de Juan de Palomares, ca. 1570).

3. Guaman Poma de Ayala, *Nueva corónica*, 2:438–41.

4. After the death of Don León's grandfather Diego Guasco, the headship first passed to Diego Guasco's illegitimate son Diego Condorguacho (ADC, Protocolo notarial de Antonio Sánchez, protocolo 17, Testamento de Diego Condorguacho, May 8, 1568, fols. 612r–614v). After Diego Condorguacho's death in 1568, the headship passed to his brother (also illegitimate) Francisco Condorguacho (Visita de Juan de Palomares, ca. 1570). Diego Guasco's legitimate son Diego supplanted Francisco Condorguacho as governor of the Chankas by 1587 (ADC, Caja de censos, legajo 1, 1617–54, Poder que otorga Don Diego Guasco, April 3, 1587, fol. 5r–v), although Francisco Condorguacho would live until 1600 (Montesinos, *Anales del Perú*, 143).

5. Summarized in Bauer, Kellet, and Aráoz Silva, *Chanka*, 25–46.

6. AGI, Patronato 93, no. 11, ramo 2, Información de los méritos y servicios de Diego Maldonado, 1561, fols. 186v–188v; Julien, "Diego Maldonado y los chancas"; Bauer, Kellet, and Aráoz Silva, *Chanka*, 29–37.

7. Lockhart, "Encomienda and Hacienda"; Stern, *Peru's Indian Peoples*; Puente Brunke, *Encomienda y encomenderos*.

8. ADC, Corregimiento de Andahuaylas, Causas ordinarias, legajo 2, 1680–99, Padrón de los indios tributarios de Andahuaylas, 1684.

9. Bauer, *Ancient Cuzco*.

10. ADC, Protocolo notarial de Antonio Sánchez, protocolo 19, 1570–72, Poder y testamento de Don Diego Maldonado, March 14, 1570, fols. 538r–558v.

11. Maldonado retained control over the communities of the highly populated Andahuaylas valley in the center of Chanka territory, but the eastern area of Curamba, which included the town of Huancarama, was given to Alonso de Alva. Uripa, to the north, was granted to Martín de Lezaña, while Ocobamba was granted to Pedro Ortiz. Cayara, including Cocharcas and Uranmarca, reverted to the Crown. After La Gasca's redistribution, the encomiendas were known as repartimientos. Bauer, Kellet, and Aráoz Silva, *Chanka*, 34–35.

12. Doña Francisca was the niece of Ortega de Briviesca, who arrived in Peru with the commissary Briviesca de Muñatones; this marriage allowed Maldonado to maintain favorable relations with the viceroy, the Count of Nieva. See Coello de la Rosa, *Espacios de exclusión*, 58n94.

13. For the identity of Juan Arias Maldonado's mother, see Alaperrine-Bouyer, "Cruzar el océano," 28. Doña Luisa's surname, "Palla," which means "noblewoman" in Quechua, indicates that she was an Inka aristocrat.

14. Poder y testamento de Don Diego Maldonado, March 14, 1570, fols. 546v–547r: "quiero y es mi voluntad que las restituciones que los dichos señores arzobispos y doña Francisca de Gúzman y Gaspar de Sotelo obieren de hazer y hizieren en descargo de mi anima e conciencia . . . y en los yndios que yo tengo en mi encomienda . . . en la cantidad y por la forma y horden que a ellos les paresciere."

15. See Harrison, *Sin and Confession*, 220–36.

16. Socolow, *Women of Colonial Latin America*, 84–96; Mannarelli, *Private Passions and Public Sins*.

17. In 1566, Juan Arias Maldonado led the so-called mestizo rebellion in Cusco; see López Martínez, *Rebeliones de mestizos*.

18. Visita de Juan de Palomares, ca. 1570.

19. Cited in Coello de la Rosa, *Espacios de exclusión*, 59n94.

20. Visita de Juan de Palomares, ca. 1570: "que todos los yndios generalmente

deste reyno son fáciles borrachos . . . sin honrra."

21. In a later court case, Don Diego Guasco, Don León's father, testified that Doña Francisca and canon Pedro de Quiroga left "certain houses and shops that the said encomendero owned in the city of Cusco" (ciertas casas e tiendas que el dicho encomendero tenía en la ciudad del Cuzco) to the Chanka Indians "as restitution" (por restituciones). Poder que otorga Don Diego Guasco, April 3, 1587, fol. 7r.

22. ADC, Caja de censos, legajo 1, 1617–54, Testimonio de P. Ximenes, September 24, 1587.

23. See for example, ADC, Caja de censos, legajo 3, 1683–84, Cuenta del repartimiento de Andahuaylas, 1683–84.

24. The Spanish also referred to kurakas as *caciques*, a native Caribbean word for "chief."

25. Among the many excellent studies of kurakas in the Inka and Spanish colonial worlds, see Villanueva Urteaga, *Cajamarca*, 1–22; Ramírez, *World Upside Down*; Spalding, "Crisis and Transformation"; Ramírez, *To Feed and Be Fed*.

26. Información de los méritos y servicios de Diego Maldonado, 1561, fols. 186v–188v; Julien, "Diego Maldonado y los chancas."

27. Salomon, introduction to *The Huarochirí Manuscript*, 16. See also Mannheim and Salas Carreño, "Wak'as"; Bray, "Andean Wak'as."

28. For ten years, from roughly 1560 to 1570, belief in huacas played a major role in a millenarian movement known as the "Taqui Ongoy" (Dance of the Pleiades. This movement was led by Andean shamans who preached that the huacas would return and defeat the Christian god, thereby driving the Spanish out of the Andes. A hallmark of the movement was that its leaders, claiming to be possessed by the spirits of powerful huacas, would dance frenziedly until exhausted; this dance was known as the "Taki Onqoy." See Duviols, *Lutte contre les religions autochtones*; Mumford, "Taki Onqoy." The

need to crush this movement inspired the first Spanish ecclesiastical campaign to destroy indigenous idols, of which Albornoz was a part. From the 1560s onward, Spanish priests attempted to eradicate all traces of pre-Christian religion in the Andes. Thousands of huacas were burned, smashed, thrown into rivers, or otherwise demolished in their sporadic yet destructive campaigns. For analyses of the episcopal visitation campaigns to extirpate idolatry throughout the sixteenth, seventeenth, and eighteenth centuries, see Mills, *Idolatry and Its Enemies*; Griffiths, *The Cross and the Serpent*.

29. Llahapalla, or Yapapalla, can also be translated as "Extra Gift Lady."

30. Albornóz, "Instrucción para descubrir," 172: "es guaca de los indios ananchancas; es una piedra a manera de indio bestido. Tenía casa en el pueblo de Andaguailas"; "era guaca de los indios hurinchangas; era una piedra que traían consigo donde quiera que iban y tenía casa"; "era una piedra bestida y tenía un agujero en el hombre y tenía casa."

31. See Mills, *Idolatry and Its Enemies*; Griffiths, *The Cross and the Serpent*; and Duviols, *Lutte contre les religions autochtones*.

32. Garrett, *Shadows of Empire*, 49–50.

33. For example, see ADC, Corregimiento de Andahuaylas, Causas ordinarias, legajo 5, 1612–14, cuaderno 1, Autos contra José de Billela, corregidor de Andahuaylas, 1604; Cuenta del repartimiento de Andahuaylas, 1683–84; ADC, Caja de censos, legajo 3, 1683–84, Censos de los indios de Andahuaylas, 1684.

34. Stern, *Peru's Indian Peoples*; Powers, *Andean Journeys*; Spalding, *Huarochirí*; Stavig, *World of Túpac Amaru*; Rasnake, *Domination and Cultural Resistance*; Glave, *Vida, símbolos y batallas*; Burga, *Nacimiento de una utopia*.

35. An example of a legal case involving accusations against a kuraka by lower-ranking Indians occurred in Andarapa in 1687 (ADC, Corregimiento de Andahuaylas, Causas criminales,

legajo 10, 1595–1695, Causa contra
D. Pascual Coica, March 13–July 15,
1687). In a trial over whether a kuraka,
Don Pascual Coica, had illegally kept
buried Inka treasure (such treasure
was supposed to be turned over to the
corregidor), several witnesses testified
that Don Pascual whipped them unjustly. Other witnesses, however, claimed
to have overheard Don Pascual's
second-in-command, Don Gregorio
Haparco, encourage false testimony against Don Pascual so that Don
Gregorio could become the kuraka.

36. Testamento de Diego Condorguacho,
May 8, 1568.

37. For cloth in the Inka state, see Murra,
"Cloth and Its Functions." For an
analysis of colonial Andean clothing,
see Zuidema, "Guaman Poma"; Phipps,
"Garments and Identity"; Presta,
"Undressing the Coya."

38. Expediente de deslinde y amojonamiento que hace Doña Ana Guasco, July
3–7, 1659: "los indios del dicho ayllo lo
respeta y quieren como a hija del dicho
gobernador."

39. Autos contra José de Billela, corregidor
de Andahuaylas, 1604, fols. 355v–356r.

40. Wightman, *Indigenous Migration*.

41. For mercury extraction in Andean
prehistory, see Cooke et al., "Use and
Legacy of Mercury"; for the colonial
mercury trade, see Platt, "Container
Transport."

42. For plans of the mines, see Lohmann
Villena, *Minas de Huancavelica*; for
an outstanding investigation into the
impact of colonial mercury mining in
Peru, see Robins, *Mercury, Mining, and
Empire*.

43. New York Public Library, Rich 75,
Fernando de Montesinos, "Memorias
antiguas historiales del Perú," ca. 1780
(copy of lost Merced manuscript, ca.
1645), fol. 39r–v: "el mineral es de tan
maligno temple que a los 15 días pone
a los hombres pálidos, y de repente le
salen unas berrugas por todo el cuerpo
que . . . los pone gafos, o les acaba la
vida."

44. Yale University Library, Manuscripts
and Archives, Latin American

Manuscript Collection, series 1, box
2, folder 23, Fernando de Montesinos,
"Memorial sobre las minas de indias," [1645]: "el mayor consumidero de
Indios que se conoce."

45. ADC, Corregimiento de Andahuaylas,
Causas criminales, legajo 10, 1595–1695,
Sentencia contra Lorenza Sisa y
Magdalena Tucuman, August 21, 1679.

46. AGN, Derecho indígena, legajo 4,
cuaderno 50, Autos que promovió Arce
de Quiroz, 1606, fols. 79r–107v; and
BNP, Ms. B-28, "Relación de la Visita
practicada al repartimiento de los indios chancas de andahuaylas," 1606–1607.

47. Autos que promovió Arce de Quiroz,
1606, fols. 79r–91v. For an analysis of
the ceremony that accompanied such
visitas, see Salomon and Guevara-Gil,
"'Personal Visit.'"

48. BNP, Ms. B-28, "Relación de la Visita
practicada al repartimiento de los indios chancas de andahuaylas."

49. Autos que promovió Arce de Quiroz,
1606, fol. 51.

50. Autos que promovió Arce de Quiroz,
1606, fol. 88r–v: "a los caciques y otras
personas que hallasen culpados los cas-
tigase hasta privarlos de su cacicazgo y
oficios."

51. See Hyland, *The Jesuit and the Incas*.

52. BNP, Ms. B-28, "Relación de la Visita
practicada al repartimiento de los indios chancas de andahuaylas"; see Stern,
Peru's Indian Peoples, 118.

53. Guaman Poma de Ayala, *Nueva corónica*, 2:599.

Chapter 8

1. Juvenal, *Sixteen Satires*, 132.

2. According to a list of rents received
by Don Diego as head kuraka, the
first year that he received the *censos*
was 1647, his first year in office. ADC,
Corregimiento de Andahuaylas, Causas
ordinarias, legajo 16, 1657–63, cuaderno
2, Autos seguidos por el Capitan Don
Francisco Flores de Montoya, corregidor, contra Don Diego Quino Guaraca,
1656–57.

3. In a court document from 1668, Don Diego is described as "ladino en la lengua Española." ADC, Corregimiento de Andahuaylas, Causas ordinarias, legajo 16, 1657–63, cuaderno 2, Poder que ortorga Don Diego Quino Guaraca, 1658, fol. 14r.

4. Angles Vargas, *Historia del Cusco*, 657–60; Alaperrine-Bouyer, "Saber y poder" and *Educación de las elites*.

5. ADC, Colegio ciencias, legajo 45, 1816–34, cuaderno 2, Colegio de Hijos de Caciques, Carta del Conde de Chinchón, January 13, 1631.

6. See Fane, *Converging Cultures*.

7. ADC, Corregimiento de Andahuaylas, Causas ordinarias, legajo 1, 1626–79, Proceso contra Juan Quino Tomay Guaraca, January 5–18, 1669: "muchos españoles . . . y hacendados."

8. ADC, Protocolo notarial de Andahuaylas del siglo XVII, Escritura de Pedro de Ojeda, 1659–63, Testamento del Capitán Alvaro Gil de Aragon, May 13, 1659.

9. Garrett, *Shadows of Empire*, 141.

10. The beginning and end dates of the kurakaship are unknown for the first three kurakas and the last kuraka in this list. Therefore, I have given the earliest and latest years in which they appear in the historical record. The documents on which this list is based are cited throughout the rest of chapter 8.

11. Guaman Poma de Ayala, *Nueva corónica*, 2:438.

12. AGN, Derecho indígena, legajo 3, cuaderno 17, Visita de Juan de Palomares, ca. 1570, fol. 178r.

13. Guaman Poma de Ayala, *Nueva corónica*, 2:868.

14. Garrett, *Shadows of Empire*, 88–96; 152–53. Thompson has also demonstrated that throughout the eighteenth century there existed considerable strife over kuraka succession within the leading Indian families of La Paz—conflicts that often revolved around the right of the firstborn son to rule (Thomson, *We Alone Will Rule*, 34; 70–105).

15. See Garrett, *Shadows of Empire*, 89.

16. See Wightman, *Indigenous Migration*; Cole, *Potosí Mita*; Sánchez-Albornoz,

Indios y tributos; Powers, *Andean Journeys*; Saignes, *Caciques, Tribute, and Migration*; Zulawski, "Migration and Labor."

17. AGI, Lima 308, no. 71, Carta del Obispo Verdugo de Guamanga, January 21, 1625: "las doctrinas que solían tener a quatro pueblos y buenos y muy llenos oy no son sino uno o dos pueblos y sin gente y los demás arruinados y las iglesias y sin ninguna." See Stern, *Peru's Indian Peoples*, 126.

18. Carta del Obispo Verdugo de Guamanga, January 21, 1625: "flacos y enfermos y pobres"; "mujeres y viudas y indios impedidos naturalmente o por enfermedad."

19. Ibid.: "huaycos, y punas, y andes."

20. Ibid.: "es imposible se pueda complir con la mita de Huancavelica . . . los pobres pocos indios que quedan a los quales los vuelven a llevar a la segunda mit'a."

21. AGI, Lima 464, Relación de los officios Visita de 1583, fol. 24.

22. AGN, Derecho indígena, legajo 4, cuaderno 50, Autos que promovió de Arce de Quiroz, 1606, fol. 88v.

23. Yale University Library, Manuscripts and Archives, Latin American Manuscript Collection, Libro de acuerdos tocante a la real hacienda, 1575–1624, fol. 137r–v: "por auer pagado los bibos por los muertos."

24. ADC, Protocolo notarial de Andahuaylas del siglo XVII, Notarial Pedro de Ojeda, Venta de tierras, March 31, 1660: "se an de despoblar los pueblos."

25. For the demographic collapse in Peru, see Cook, *Demographic Collapse*, 52.

26. Carta del Obispo de Guamanga, January 21, 1625: "recogen estos indios y les prometen montes de oro y que los defenderán de las mitas y de los curas y corregidores y como los indios no pretenden más de berse libres de las mitas se contratan con poco." See Stern, *Peru's Indian Peoples*, 144.

27. Numerous authors have examined the process by which communal ayllu lands became private in the colonial Andes. See Spalding, *Huarochirí*; Larson,

Cochabamba; Garrett, *Shadows of Empire*, 127–28. Royal *composiciónes de tierras*, in which the Crown reassigned communal Indian lands to creole and Spanish landowners, made land available for private haciendas. See Davies, *Landowners in Colonial Peru*, 117–58; Piel, *Capitalismo agrario*, 160–78.

28. ADC, Corregimiento de Andahuaylas, Causas ordinarias, legajo 2, 1680–99, Remate de Yaramay, March 18, 1694.

29. ADC, Protocolo notarial de Andahuaylas del siglo XVIII, legajo 3, 1700–1820, Registro de Gregorio Antonio Pacheco, Inventario de la hacienda Cañaveral de San Jacinto de Chacabamba, 1788: "un lienzo grande biejo donde está pintada la serie de los reyes incas . . . otro de dos varas de largo con el retrato del Señor Felipe Quinto . . . otro cuadro en el corridor entitulado los cuatro partes del mundo." Dr. Don Antonio Bosa Garces, a "vecino de la ciudad de los reyes," owned Chacabamba in 1788; his agent, the vicar of Andahuaylas, arranged for it to be leased to Lieutenant Colonel Don Joseph Carillo for the sum of 4,800 pesos a year, payable in white sugar.

30. See, for example, the abuses described in the testimony against Captain Joseph Gutiérrez de las Infantas: ADC, Corregimiento de Andahuaylas, Causas criminales, legajo 10, 1595–1695, Causa criminal contra el Capitán Joseph Gutiérrez de las Infantas, June 6–23, 1674. For a description of life on the haciendas of Apurimac and the struggle for justice, see Quintanilla, *Andahuaylas*.

31. Arguedas, *Deep Rivers*, 112.

32. ADC, Caja de censos, legajo 2, 1655–82, Censos de los indios de Andahuaylas, 1657.

33. ADC, Caja de censos, legajo 1, 1617–54, cuaderno 2, Petición de los indios de Andahuaylas, February 18, 1659.

34. Autos seguidos por el Capitan Don Francisco Flores de Montoya, corregidor, contra Don Diego Quino Guaraca, 1656–57.

35. Garrett, *Shadows of Empire*, 126.

36. ADC, Corregimiento de Andahuaylas, Causas ordinarias, legajo 6, 1750–63, Causa seguida por Don Thomas Intusca, Don Pedro Quipe, Lucas Antay, etc., 1751. For Cabrera Lartaún as a defender of Indian ayllu lands, see Seligmann, *Between Reform and Revolution*, 111–12.

37. Venta de tierras, March 31, 1660.

38. ADC, Protocolo notarial de Andahuaylas del siglo XVIII, Cuaderno de Joseph Antonio de Castro, Testamento de Don Juan Basilio Quino Guaraca, November 9, 1730.

39. ADC, Corregimiento de Andahuaylas, Causas ordinarias, legajo 1, 1626–72, cuaderno 10, Petición de Doña Isabel Quino Guaraca, January 18, 1672.

40. Cited in Stern, *Peru's Indian Peoples*, 169.

41. ADC, Corregimiento de Andahuaylas, Causas ordinarias, legajo 2, 1680–99, Causa seguida por Doña Micaela Cayanpi, 1693–94.

42. Fig. 24 is based on the following unpublished documents: ADC, Protocolo notarial de Andahuaylas del siglo XVIII, Cuaderno de Joseph Antonio de Castro, Testamento de Doña Bernarda Quino Guaraca, August 12, 1730, fol. 18r–v; (2) ADC, Protocolo notarial de Andahuaylas del siglo XVIII, Registro sixto de Gregorio Antonio Pacheco, Testamento de Juliana Rojas [daughter of Bernarda Quino Guaraca], 1796; (3) Petición de Doña Isabel Quino Guaraca [daughter of Don Diego Quino Guaraca and Doña Elvira Martínez], January 18, 1672; (4) ADC, Protocolo notarial de Andahuaylas del siglo XVII, Escritura de Joseph Cardenas y Paredes, Venta de tierras de Don Simón Torres y Doña Tomasa Guaraca, August 19, 1693, fol. 23; (5) ADC, Corregimiento de Andahuaylas, Causas ordinarias, legajo 3, 1701–29, Pleito que siguen entre los herederos de don Alonso Yñigo, January 1722; (6) ADC, Corregimiento de Andahuaylas, Causas ordinarias, legajo 9, 1775–89, Títulos de Argama, Memorial de Don Francisco Tomay Guaraca [son of Don Thomas Guaraca], November 14, 1775, fol. 152; (7) ADC,

Protocolo notarial de Andahuaylas del siglo XVII, Registro de Joseph Cardenas y Paredes, Dote de Doña Tomasa Quino Guaraca [daughter of Don Diego Guaraca], July 13, 1681; (8) Causa seguida por Doña Micaela Cayanpi, 1693–94; (9) ADC, Protocolo notarial de Andahuaylas del siglo XIX, Registro de Hilario Cusihuaman, 1850–52, División de la hacienda Tapaya [belonging to the deceased, Don Tomas Quino], 1850; (10) ADC, Corregimiento de Andahuaylas, Causas ordinarias, legajo 4, 1730–44, Causa de Don Andrés Machaca, Joseph Muños, etc., 1733; (11) Testamento de Don Juan Basilio Quino Guaraca, November 9, 1730; (12) ADC, Corregimiento de Andahuaylas, Causas ordinarias, legajo 4, 1730–44, Memorial de los indios ausentes de los Anansayas y Urinsayas del pueblos de Andahuaylas, 1737; (13) ADC, Colegio ciencias, legajo 45, 1816–34, cuaderno 2, Lista de estudiantes, 1650–56, 1656, fol. 52v; (14) Proceso contra Juan Quino Tomay Guaraca, January 5–18, 1669.

43. Lista de estudiantes, 1650–56, 1656, fol. 52v.

44. Venta de tierras, March 31, 1660.

45. Proceso contra Juan Quino Tomay Guaraca, January 5–18, 1669.

46. ADC, Corregimiento de Andahuaylas, Causas criminales, legajo 10, 1595–1695, Causa contra D. Pascual Coica, March 13–July 15, 1687; see chapter 7, note 36.

47. Proceso contra Juan Quino Tomay Guaraca, January 5–18, 1669: "hacen muy mal tratamientos a los indios obligándoles a que les sirvan forsada y violentamente sin pagarles y darles de moquetes como lo ha visto este testigo en muchas ocaciones."

48. Ibid., fols. 19r–21r.

49. ADC, Caja de censos, legajo 3, 1683–84, Censos de los indios de Andahuaylas, 1684; 1685.

50. ADC, Protocolo notarial de Andahuaylas del siglo XVIII, Cuaderno de Joseph Antonio de Castro, Testamento de Don Joseph Antonio Quino Tomay Guaraca, April 21, 1779: "hijo natural de Don Juan Quino Tomay Guaraca, Cacique Principal

y Gobernador que fue . . . y de Doña María Mella, española natural de la ciudad de Guamanga."

51. ADC, Caja de censos, legajo 3, 1683–84, Censos de los indios de Andahuaylas, 1687, fols. 30r–45.

52. Testamento de Doña Bernarda Quino Guaraca, August 12, 1730, fol. 18r–v: "gobernadores que fueron."

53. See Cañizares-Esguerra, *How to Write*; Berquist Soule, *Bishop's Utopia*; Lehner, *Catholic Enlightenment.*

54. In 1694, he was described as "ladino y capas en la lengua española." ADC, Corregimiento de Andahuaylas, Causas ordinarias, legajo 2, 1680–99, Expediente sobre el pedido de Don Juan Bautista Haparco, cacique y gobernador de Urinsaya y Don Felipe Tapaguasco de Hanasaya, February 13, 1694.

55. See, for example, ADC, Protocolo notarial de Andahuaylas del siglo XVII, Escritura de Joseph de Cardenas y Paredes, Venta de tierras, August 22, 1693; December 22, 1693.

56. ADC, Corregimiento de Andahuaylas, Causas ordinarias, legajo 2, 1680–99, Auto seguido por Pascuala Alca, July 1722.

57. ADC, Caja de censos, legajo 6, 1708–20, cuaderno 3, Cobro de censos, May 21, 1706.

58. Testamento de Don Juan Basilio Quino Guaraca, November 9, 1730.

59. ADC, Corregimiento de Andahuaylas, Causas criminales, legajo 11, 1702–66, Causa de Don Cayetano Alca de la Cruz, 1726.

60. ADC, Corregimiento de Andahuaylas, Causas ordinarias, legajo 3, 1701–29, Memorial de Gerónimo de los Reyes y Antonio de Roxas, April 7, 1718.

61. Causa de Don Andrés Machaca, Joseph Muños, etc., 1733. The stolen Hanansaya properties included maize fields and houses around the city of Andahuaylas. Native witnesses stated that they had possessed the following lands (and others) since the time of the Inkas: Argama, Molinopampa, Uscupuchac, Pariabamba, Moyabamba, Cantocpata, and Ancaypampa.

62. By 1684, Don Sebastián's son Felipe Topa Guasco had become the principal kuraka for their moiety. By 1698, the rule of Hanansaya had passed to Andrés Topa Guasco, who held power until at least 1706 and possibly beyond. Censos de los indios de Andahuaylas, 1684; Cobro de censos, May 21, 1706.

63. Ministry of Agriculture, Andahuaylas, Títulos de la comunidad, Cachi, Autos seguidos por Juan Bautista Flores de Castillo, October 31, 1729; ADC, Corregimiento de Andahuaylas, Causas ordinarias, legajo 6, 1750–63, Testamento de Doña Francisca de Minaya y Apoguasco, December 16, 1768. Don Bernardo and his wife/stepaunt had no children. Doña Juana Apu Guasco predeceased her husband; Don Bernardo went on to have five children with his second wife, Doña Juana Arenas from Andarapa.

64. BNP, C1925, 1727, Expediente sobre los autos seguidos contra Bernardo Minaya, 1727. The bishop of Guamanga, Alfonso López Roldán, supported his priests who backed the rebels, and unsuccessfully brought heresy charges against Ortíz de Landaeta and the viceroy for comments made in the course of this conflict. Archivo Histórico Nacional, Inquisición 1652, expediente 8, Competencias del Tribunal de la Inquisición de Lima y el Virrey del Perú, 1727.

65. Causa seguida por Don Thomas Intusca, Don Pedro Quipe, Lucas Antay, etc., 1751.

66. Autos seguidos por Juan Bautista Flores de Castillo, October 31, 1729.

67. See, for example, Ortíz de Landaeta's ruling that the Indians of Pampachiri had to go to the Huancavelica mines after the Audiencia decided that they did not owe this labor. ADC, Corregimiento de Andahuaylas, Causas ordinarias, legajo 2, 1680–99, Causa de Don Marcos Sibi Paucar, 1727–29.

68. Testamento de Don Juan Basilio Quino Guaraca, November 9, 1730, fol. 3: "llamandolos y acariciandoles que declaren los agravios que les tengo hecho y que se les compense en alguna manera de suerte que me consigan el que este cargo de restitucion me perdonen por amor de Dios y sea con todo afecto y amor"; "les ubiere llevado en mal fee"; "a quien le tengo comunicado muchas cosas tocantes al descargo de mi conciencia."

69. ADC, Protocolo notarial de Andahuaylas del siglo XVIII, Cuaderno de Joseph Antonio de Castro, Venta de tierras, April 4, 1731.

70. Causa de Don Andrés Machaca, Joseph Muños, etc., 1733. The last appearance of Don Thomas in the historical record is in 1647, when he granted the power of attorney to General Don Manuel de Arainda, a resident of Lima. ADC, Protocolo notarial de Andahuaylas del siglo XVIII, Registro suelto de Joseph Antonio de Castro, Poder de Don Thomas Quino Guaraca, December 20, 1747.

71. ADC, Corregimiento de Andahuaylas, Causas ordinarias, legajo 9, 1775–89, Títulos de Argama, Testimonio de Don Francisco Tomay Guaraca, April 29, 1749, fol. 153: "todas las dichas tierras me pertenecen como a yndio noble desde el tiempo del Ynga."

72. Títulos de Argama, Memorial de Don Francisco Tomay Guaraca, November 14, 1775, fol. 152: "totalmente pobre y atrasado sin alibio ninguno."

73. Garrett, Shadows of Empire, 100–111.

74. See "El Aprendiz de Rico" by the priest of Huancarama, Pedro Espinosa de los Monteros, [ca. 1654]; Carrión, Antología general, 89–94.

75. For dowries in the colonial Andes, see Gauderman, Women's Lives, 30–47; Burns, Into the Archive; Graubart, With Our Labor and Sweat. For recent anthropological discussions of marriage payments, see Raheja, "'Crying When She's Born'"; Anderson, "Economics of Dowry"; Jones, "Woman's Worth."

76. Dote de Doña Tomasa Quino Guaraca, July 13, 1681.

77. ADC, Corregimiento de Andahuaylas, Causas ordinarias, legajo 3, 1701–29, Los bienes de Don Alonso Yñigo Moreno, January 1722.

78. Venta de tierras de Don Simón Torres y Doña Tomasa Guaraca, August 19, 1693, fol. 23: "pueda empesar a trabajar y llevar la carga del matrimonio."
79. Moore, *Power and Property*, 89–98.
80. Silverblatt, *Moon, Sun, and Witches*, 5, 119–24, 219–20.
81. Ibid., 5.
82. Testamento de Doña Francisca de Minaya y Apoguasco, December 16, 1768.

Conclusion

1. AGI, Lima 224, no. 12, Información de Francisco de Aldana, 1622.
2. AGI, Lima 308, no. 71, Memorial de las doctrinas del Obispado de Guamanga, ca. 1624, fol. 3.
3. ADC, Corregimiento de Andahuaylas, Causas ordinarias, legajo 2, 1680–99, Expediente de autos que siguieron los indios de Pampachiri, 1727.
4. ADC, Corregimiento de Andahuaylas, Causas ordinarias, legajo 2, 1680–99, Memorial de Don Carlos López de Rivera, cura de la doctrina de Pampachiri, June 11, 1727.
5. By 1727, kurakas were no longer required to pay compensation for Indians who were absent from mine duty; the corregidor Ortíz de Landaeta apparently needed to be reminded of this fact.
6. Stern, *Peru's Indian Peoples*, 86n18, 96n51, 230, 232.
7. Aguilar, *Religion, Torture*, 26.
8. See Acosta Rodríguez, "Pleito de los indios"; Acosta Rodríguez, "Los doctrineros y la extirpación"; Taylor, "Santiago's Horse"; Charles, *Allies at Odds*.
9. See, for example, Rasnake, *Domination and Cultural Resistance*; Thomson, *We Alone Will Rule*.
10. Thomson, *We Alone Will Rule*.
11. On Spanish resettlements, see Mumford, *Vertical Empire*; Wernke, *Negotiated Settlements*.
12. Ministry of Agriculture, Andahuaylas, Títulos de la comunidad, Cachi, Autos

seguidos por Juan Bautista Flores de Castillo, October 31, 1729.
13. See Stern, *Peru's Indian Peoples*, 173–75.
14. See, for example, the testimony of Francisco Chipana in 1772 that the Indians of the Yunga ayllu of Andahuaylas were "forasteros agragados a la misma parcialidad." ADC, Corregimiento de Andahuaylas, Causas ordinarias, legajo 8, 1770–74, Causa seguida por el comun de yndios de los aillos Yunga, Cuncataca y Guaraca, 1770.
15. Carmen Arellano Hoffmann found similar results in Tarma with regard to the role of kurakas in the eighteenth century (Arellano Hoffmann, *Apuntes históricos*).
16. ADC, Corregimiento de Andahuaylas, Causas ordinarias, legajo 6, 1750–63, Causa seguida por Don Thomas Intusca, Don Pedro Quispe, Lucas Antay, etc., 1751.
17. BNP, C2478, 1772, Carta de Joseph Ordóñez, October 6, 1771. Although the largest crowds arrived for the Virgin's feast in September, native pilgrims visited the shrine throughout the year. In 1719, a wealthy Spanish priest, Juan Miguel Maldonado, who was in charge of the Confraternity of Our Lady of Cocharcas in the sanctuary, left an endowment to provide a Quechua-speaking chaplain to minister to the Indian pilgrims who visited the shrine. Maldonado explained that many natives came to the shrine throughout the year—not just in September—but often had difficulty finding a priest to hear their confessions and attend to them. ADC, Corregimiento de Andahuaylas, Causas ordinarias, legajo 3, 1701–29, Testamento del Licenciado Don Juan Miguel Maldonado, 1719. The shrine of Our Lady of Cocharcas is distinct from the colonial doctrina of Cocharcas; see Concha Pacheco and Villafuerte Acuña, "Espacios de inclusión y exclusión."
18. Walker, *Tupac Amaru Rebellion*. For divergent interpretations of this rebellion, see also Campbell, "Ideology and Factionalism"; Szeminski, "Why Kill the

Spaniard?"; Flores Galindo, *Buscando un Inca*; Cornblit, *Power and Violence*.

19. Stern, "Age of Andean Insurrection."
20. Mignolo, "Looking for the Meaning."
21. For in-depth considerations of what is meant by "ethnohistory," see Salomon, "Testimonies"; Abercrombie, *Pathways of Memory and Power*. On ayllus as political forces, see Platt, "Andean Experience" and *Estado boliviano*.
22. Horace, *Epistles*, book I, epistle xi, line 27. I am indebted to Dr. William Hyland for bringing the medieval use of this quote to my attention and for translating it from the Latin.
23. For an analysis of the artistic representations of the colonial-era pilgrimages to the Sanctuary of Our Lady of Cocharcas, see Engel, "Visualizing a Colonial Peruvian Community." For Marian pilgrimages in the Andes, see Salles-Reese, *From Viracocha*; Sallnow, *Pilgrims of the Andes*; Rostworowski, "Peregrinaciones y procesiones"; Núñez Zeballos, "Virgen Candelaria."
24. Translation by Edith Zavallos and Sabine Hyland.

Ay Mamallay Diosllawanña
　　—Kutirimunaykamaña
Kausaypipas wañuypipas ay!—Amayá
　　qonqawankichu.

Huk watapaq kunan hina—tinkusunchis
　　manañachus
icha allpa sonqonpichus ay!—wawaykita
　　tariwanki.

Urqun qasa purisqaypi—Mamallay
　　kallpanchawanki
Tukuy ima llakiymanta ay!—Mamallay
　　qespichiwanki.

Diosllawanña Diospa Maman—Sumaq
　　Mamay Diosllawanña
Llaqtallaypi saqepuway ay! —Diosllawanña
　　Diosllawanña.

Uyariway llumpaq Mama—Huchasapa
　　Wawaykita,
Haywariway makikita ay!—Kutimunay
　　Punchaukama.

25. The term *kimichu* is taken from the surname of the Cocharcas shrine's founder, Sebastián Quimichi. In 1625, the priest in charge of the shrine, Pedro Guillen de Mendoza, wrote a hagiographical account of Quimichi's life (published in Pélach y Feliu, *Nuestra Señora de Cocharcas*). In Cocharcas, the community members who run the Confraternity of Our Lady of Cocharcas are aware of Sebastián Quimichi's role in founding the shrine. However, many people within the Andahuaylas region, even those who have attended the celebrations at the shrine, do not know who Quimichi was. For example, in 2004, a *comunero* in Uranmarca told me that he was very devoted to the Virgin of Cocharcas and had visited her shrine. However, he had never heard of Quimichi; although he knew that wandering mendicants dedicated to honoring the virgin were called kimichus, he did not know the origin of the term. The story he had heard about the foundation of the shrine matched, in every particular, the history collected in the 1770s by Alonso Carrió de la Vandera (Concolorcorvo): "me dixo el Visitador, señalándome un elevado cerro, que a su falda estaba el memorable templo dedicado a la Sma. Virgen en su Soberana imagen, nombrada de Cocharcas, cuyo origen traía de que, pasando por allí un devoto peregrino con esta efigie, como tienen de costumbre muchos paisanos míos, se le hizo tan intolerable su peso que le agovió, y dando cuenta a los eclesiásticos y hacendados de la Provincia, se declaró por milagroso el excesivo peso, como que daba a entender el sagrado vulto que quería hacer allí su mansion. Desde luego que en aquella gente hizo una gran impresión el suceso, porque se labor en la planicie de el primer descenso una magnífica iglesia, que fuera impropia en un desierto." Concolorcorvo, *Lazarillo de ciegos caminantes*, 202.
26. Barnes, afterword to *José María Arguedas*, 253; her quotation is from Lastra, "Testimonial Portrait."
27. Arguedas, *Deep Rivers*, 171–72.

Appendix

1. This account of the famous Chanka War reflects the version found in the writings of Sarmiento de Gamboa. Sarmiento's narrative of the Chanka War came directly from the mouths of Inka historians in Cusco and has long been considered one of the most reliable Spanish chronicles of the Inkas. According to the chronologies of the Spanish chroniclers who recorded Andean history based on the accounts of their Inka informants, the Chanka War probably occurred between 1400 and 1438. Bauer's archaeological survey in the Cusco Valley puts Inka expansion at around A.D. 1400 (Sarmiento de Gamboa, *History of the Incas*).

2. For an alternate discussion of the indigenous etymology of the name "Cusco," see Hyland, *Quito Manuscript*. According to an anonymous seventeenth-century author, Topa Ayar Uchu decided to found the city "in these Cuscos" (en esos Cuzcos), which meant "in that site where there are those stones that seem to be riding [on top of each other]" (en esse sitio donde están esas piedras que parezen amontonamientos). Ibid., 107.

3. Sarmiento de Gamboa, *History of the Incas*, 105.

4. Ibid.

5. Ibid., 108.

6. Ibid., 111.

7. Hyland, Bauer, and Socualaya Dávila, "Acta de Uranmarca."

8. Acosta, *Historia natural y moral*, 108: "Fuera de estos quipos de hilo, tienen otros de pedrezuelas, por donde puntualmente aprenden las palabras que quieren tomar de memoria."

9. Cobo, *Historia del Nuevo Mundo*, 226: "Usaban este oficio con diferentes géneros de instrumentos y artificios, y lo más común era con maíz, con frísoles y con unas pedrezuelas negras y de otros colores diferentes; las cuales los hechiceros y sus sucesores guardaban con gran cuidado, cuando moría el que le usaba; y cuando ellos venían a ser viejos, con ellas mismas lo ejercitaban."

10. For the full text of the document and questions about authenticity, see Bauer, Kellet, and Aráoz Silva, *Chanka*.

11. Hyland, *Quito Manuscript*, 136: "ubo una vatalla muy sangrieta, en que quedó vençido y muerto él de Guancarrama."

12. Markham, *Markham in Peru*, 81.

13. Brooks et al., "Lead in Ancient Peru."

14. Hyland, *Quito Manuscript*, 136: "passó adelante con su exército; y antes de llegar a Andaguailas, halló mucha gente que le impedía el passo en la hangahora de una quebrada. Hauíase preuenido antes el *Inga Rroca*, porque, teniendo notiçia de que el rey de Andaguaylas estaua del mismo pareçer que el de Vilcas, por la rrespuesta que dió el ídolo de Guancarrama, imbió un terçio de su exérçito, para que por unos çerros, con todo silençio y presteça, ocupasen la entrada de la quebrada, para que los enemigos no la coxiessen, con horden de que si acaso ubiessen entrado, les convatiesen [/] por la rrectaguardia, avisando al *Inga* de lo que suçediesse para embestir él también. Así suçedió, y coxida en medio la gente de Andaguailas, hizo gran mortandad en ella el *Inga*, hasta que se dieron de paz; con que a los viuos reçiuió con toda venignidad, y ellos le confessauan por verdadero hijo del sol."

15. In Teruel's account, the Inka emperor who marched on the Chankas was the first emperor, Manco Capac. In Montesinos's history, Manco Capac was the first pre-Inka Andean king, not the first Inka emperor. Montesinos, who had read Teruel's tale, questioned the local people about the name of the Inka who had subjugated them. According to Montesinos, the people didn't know the name of the Inka; they merely referred to him as the "first Inka emperor." In their view, he could have been any of the Inka emperors, or maybe even a successful Inka prince. However, in Montesinos's lengthy and unorthodox narrative of indigenous Andean history, Inka Roca is identified as the first Inka emperor; therefore,

Montesinos considered him to be the Inka king who conquered the kingdoms of Andahuaylas.

16. Cobo, *Historia del Nuevo Mundo*. For other authors who have moved the Chanka War back chronologically, placing the decisive battle during the time of Inka Roca and Yawar Huaccac, see Gutiérrez de Santa Clara, *Historia de las guerras civiles*; Cabello de Balboa, *Miscelánea antártica*; Guaman Poma de Ayala, *Nueva corónica*.

17. Bauer, Kellet, and Aráoz Silva, *Chanka*, 2010.

18. Cieza de León, *Señorío de los Incas*, 211.

19. Kurin, "Bioarchaeology of Collapse," 156.

20. Bauer, Kellet, and Aráoz Silva, *Chanka*; Kellet, "Chanka Settlement Ecology." Kellet has argued that the Chanka relocation to the hilltops between A.D. 1000 and 1100 was due to increasing aridity in the environment, which favored a shift to camelid pastoralism at a high altitude. As Kurin writes, "Kellet interprets the shift to hilltop settlements during the Late Intermediate Period as an adaptation to climatic changes. He argues that high-altitude pastoralism was newly emphasized in the post-imperial [e.g., post-Wari] era as a risk reduction strategy in the face of increased aridity and drought, rather than due to instability catalyzed by Wari collapse. However, isotope geochemistry, ice and lake core data from the south-central Andes, and Laguna Pacucha in Andahuaylas suggest that the most intense period of drought in Andahuaylas began several hundred years after Wari's disappearance, after ca. A.D. 1250" (Kurin, "Bioarchaeology of Collapse," 31–32). In other words, the climatic shift that might have favored herding occurred about two hundred years after the Chankas relocated to the hilltops. Moreover, the Chankas continued to have the same diets during the Wari period and later; had there been a significant shift to herding and away from maize agriculture between A.D. 1000 and 1100, this would have been reflected in people's diets. As Kurin notes, "isotopic data gleaned from human dentition in Andahuaylas reveal no significant changes in climate-sensitive consumptive practices from late Wari through early post-Wari times. These data appear to indicate that environmental shifts did not significantly impact the availability of crucial crops like maize, which continued to form a substantial part of the diet in early LIP Andahuaylas" (17–18).

21. Kurin, "Bioarchaeology of Collapse," 288–89.

22. Bauer, Kellet, and Aráoz Silva, *Chanka*.

BIBLIOGRAPHY

Archival Sources

Archivo Departamental del Cusco (ADC), Cusco, Peru
Cabildo justicia ordinaria, legajo 2
Caja de censos, legajos 1, 2, 3, 6, 12
Colegio ciencias, legajo 45
Corregimiento—causas ordinarias, legajos 1, 2, 5, 16; causes criminales, legajos 10, 11; pedimientos y intendencia, legajos 1, 13
Protocolo notarial de Antonio Sánchez, protocolos 17, 19
Protocolo notarial de Andahuaylas, siglos XVII, XVIII, XIX
Archivo General de Indias (AGI), Seville, Spain
Audiencia de Charcas 64
Contaduria 1827
Contratación 253, 305B, 486, 941B, 5235
Escribanía de Cámara 503B
Indiferente 2090
Lima 200, 210, 211, 224, 226, 235, 238, 305, 308, 464
Patronato 93, 135
Archivo General de la Nación (AGN), Lima, Peru
Derecho indígena, legajos 3, 4
Lima, Títulos de propiedad, 1596, legajo 2
Real Audiencia, Causas criminales, legajo 154
Archivo Histórico Nacional, Madrid, Spain
Inquisición, 1652, expediente 8
Biblioteca Nacional del Perú (BNP), Lima, Peru
Ms. B-28
Ms. B771
Ms. C1861, C1871, C1883, C1925, C2478
Ministry of Agriculture, Andahuaylas, Peru
Títulos de la comunidad, Cachi
New York Public Library
Rich 75
Yale University Library, Manuscripts and Archives, New Haven, Connecticut
Latin American Manuscript Collection, series 1

Published Sources

Abercrombie, Thomas A. *Pathways of Memory and Power: Ethnography and History Among an Andean People*. Madison: University of Wisconsin Press, 1998.
Acosta, José de. *Historia natural y moral de las indias*. Vol. 2. 1590. Madrid: Pantaleon Aznar, 1792.
Acosta Rodríguez, Antonio. "Los doctrineros y la extirpación de la religion indígena en el arzobispado de Lima, 1600–1620." *Jahrbuch für Geschichte von Staat, Wirtschaft und Gesellschaft Lateinamerikas* 19 (1982): 69–109.
———. "El pleito de los indios de San Damián contra Francisco de Avila, 1607." *Historiografía y Bibliografía Americanistas* 23 (1979): 3–33.
Adorno, Rolena. *Guaman Poma and His Illustrated Chronicle from Colonial Peru: From a Century of Scholarship to a New Era of Reading*. Copenhagen: Museum Tusculanum Press, 2001.
———. *Guaman Poma: Writing and Resistance in Colonial Peru*. 2nd ed. Austin: University of Texas Press, 2000.
Aguilar, Mario I. *Religion, Torture, and the Liberation of God*. New York: Routledge, 2015.

Alaperrine-Bouyer, Monique. "Cruzar el océano: Lo que revelan los viajes a España de los mestizos peruanos en la segunda parte del siglo XVI." *Histórica* (Peru) 37, no. 2 (2014): 7–58.

———. *La educación de las elites indígenas en el Peru colonial*. Lima: Instituto de Estudios Peruanos, 2007.

———. "Saber y poder: La cuestión de la educación de las elites indígenas." In *Incas e indios cristianos: Elites indígenas e identidades cristianos en los Andes coloniales*, edited by Jean-Jacques Decoster, 154–63. Cusco: Centro de Estudios Regionales Andinos Bartolomé de las Casas, 2002.

Albornóz, Cristobal de. "Instrucción para descubrir todas las guacas del Pirú y sus camayos y haziendas." In *Fábulas y mitos de los incas*, edited by Henrique Urbano and Pierre Duviols, 161–98. 1582. Madrid: Historia 16, 1989.

Alcala, Luisa Elena. "La imagen del indio devoto: La codificación de una ideal colonial." In *Miradas comparadas en los virreinatos de América*, edited by Ilona Katzew, 227–49. Los Angeles: Los Angeles County Museum of Art, 2012.

Alciato, Andrea. *Los emblemas de Alciato traducidos en rhimas españolas*. Translated by Bernardino Daza. Lyon: Guilielmo Rouillio, 1549.

Allen, Catherine J. "'Let's Drink Together, My Dear!': Persistent Ceremonies in a Changing Community." In *Drink, Power, and Society in the Andes*, edited by Justin Jennings and Brenda J. Bowser, 28–48. Gainesville: University Press of Florida, 2008.

Anderson, Siwan. "The Economics of Dowry and Brideprice." *Journal of Economic Perspectives* 21, no. 4 (2007): 151–74.

Andrien, Kenneth J. *Andean Worlds: Indigenous History, Culture, and Consciousness Under Spanish Rule, 1532–1825*. Albuquerque: University of New Mexico Press, 2001.

Angles Vargas, Víctor. *Historia del Cusco (Cusco colonial)*. 2 vols. Cusco: Industrial Gráfica, 1983.

Arellano Hoffmann, Carmen. *Apuntes históricos sobre la provincia de Tarma en la sierra central del Perú. El kuraka y los ayllus bajo la dominación colonial española, siglos XVI–XVII*. Bonner Amerikanistische Studien 15. Bonn: Universität Bonn, 1988.

Arguedas, José María. *Deep Rivers*. Translated by Francis Horning Barraclough. 1958. Austin: Universtiy of Texas Press, 1981.

Avendaño, Fernando de. *Sermones de los misterios de nuestra santa fe católica, en lengua castellana y en la general del Inca*. Lima: Jorge López de Herrera, 1649.

Bailey, Gauvin Alexander. *The Andean Hybrid Baroque: Convergent Cultures in the Churches of Colonial Peru*. Notre Dame: University of Notre Dame Press, 2010.

Barnes, Monica. Afterword to *José María Arguedas: Reconsiderations for Latin American Cultural Studies*, edited by Ciro A. Sandoval and Sandra M. Boschetto-Sandoval, 251–64. Athens: Ohio University Center for International Studies, 1998.

———. "Un análisis de la iconografía y la arquitectura andinas en una iglesia colonial: San Cristóbal de Pampachiri." In *Mito y simbolismo en los Andes: La figura y la palabra*, edited by Henrique Urbano, 183–214. Cusco: Centro de Estudios Regionales Andinos Bartolomé de las Casas, 1993.

———. "The Chicha Project." *South American Explorer*, 1980, 10–15.

———. "The Yawar Fiesta of Pampachiri, Apurímac, Peru." *NAOS* 10, nos. 1–3 (1994): 13–18.

Barr, Jane. "The Influence of Saint Jerome on Medieval Attitudes to Women." In *After Eve: Women, Theology, and the Christian Tradition*, edited by Janet Martin Soskice, 89–102. London: Marshall Pickering, 1990.

Barroso, Maria Do Sameiro. "Bezoar Stones, Magic, Science, and Art." In *A History of Geology and Medicine*, edited by C. J. Duffin, R. T. J. Moody, and C. Gardner-Thorpe, 193–207. London: Geological Society, 2013.

Bauer, Brian S. *Ancient Cuzco: Heartland of the Inca*. Austin: University of Texas Press, 2004.

Bauer, Brian S., Lucas C. Kellet, and Miriam Aráoz Silva. *The Chanka: Archaeological Research in Andahuaylas (Apurimac), Peru*. Los Angeles: Cotsen Institute of Archaeology Press, 2010.

Bauer, Brian S., and Charles Stanish. *Ritual and Pilgrimage in the Ancient Andes: The Islands of the Sun and the Moon*. Austin: University of Texas Press, 2001.

Berquist Soule, Emily. *The Bishop's Utopia: Envisioning Improvement in Colonial Peru*. Philadelphia: University of Pennsylvania Press, 2014.

Blair, R. J. R. "Neurobiological Basis of Psychopathy." *British Journal of Psychiatry* 182, no. 1 (2003): 5–7.

Boone, Elizabeth Hill. "Pictorial Documents and Visual Thinking in Postconquest Mexico." In *Native Traditions in the Postconquest World: A Symposium at Dumbarton Oaks*, edited by Elizabeth Hill Boone and Tom Cummins, 149–99. Washington, D.C.: Dumbarton Oaks, 1998.

Bray, Tamara L. "Andean Wak'as and Alternative Configurations of Persons, Power, and Things." In *The Archaeology of Wak'as: Explorations of the Sacred in the Pre-Columbian Andes*, edited by Tamara L. Bray, 3–22. Boulder: University Press of Colorado, 2015.

———. "The Commensal Politics of Early States and Empires." In *The Archaeology and Politics of Food and Feasting in Early States and Empires*, edited by Tamara L. Bray, 1–16. New York: Kluwer Academic / Plenum, 2003.

Brinkley, C. A., W. A. Schmitt, and J. P. Newman. "Semantic Processing in Psychopathic Offenders." *Personality and Individual Differences* 38, no. 5 (2005): 1047–56.

Brooks, William E., Luisa Vetter Parodi, Armando V. Farfán, and David Dykstra. "Lead in Ancient Peru: The Curamba Smelter and Lead Sling Bullets." *JOM: Journal of the Minerals, Metals, and Materials Society* 64, no. 11 (2012): 1356–64.

Brown, Kendall W. "Workers' Health and Colonial Mercury Mining at Huancavelica, Peru." *The Americas* 57, no. 4 (2001): 467–96.

Brundage, Burr Cartwright. *Empire of the Inca*. Norman: University of Oklahoma Press, 1985.

Burga, Manuel. *Nacimiento de una utopia: Muerte y resurrección de los incas*. Lima: Instituto de Apoyo Agrario, 1988.

Burger, Richard L., and Lucy C. Salazar, eds. *The 1912 Yale Peruvian Scientific Expedition Collections from Machu Picchu: Human and Animal Remains*. New Haven: Department of Anthropology, Yale University, 2003.

Burger, Richard L., and Nikolaas J. van der Merwe. "Maize and the Origin of Highland Chavín Civilization." *American Anthropologist* 92, no. 1 (1990): 85–95.

Burkholder, Mark A. *Spaniards in the Colonial Empire: Creoles vs. Peninsulars*. London: Wiley-Blackwell, 2013.

Burns, Kathryn. *Into the Archive: Writing and Power in Colonial Peru*. Durham: Duke University Press, 2010.

Cabello Balboa, Miguel. *Miscelánea antártica*. 1586. Lima: Universidad Nacional Mayor de San Marcos, 1951.

Campbell, Leon G. "Ideology and Factionalism During the Great Rebellion, 1780–1782." In *Resistance, Rebellion, and Consciousness in the Andean Peasant World, Eighteenth to Twentieth Centuries*, edited by Steve J. Stern, 110–42. Madison: University of Wisconsin Press, 1987.

Cañizares-Esguerra, Jorge. *How to Write the History of the New World: Histories, Epistemologies, and Identities in the*

Eighteenth-Century Atlantic World. Stanford: Stanford University Press, 2002.

Carrillo Cázares, Alberto. "Tratados novo-hispanos sobre la guerra justa en el siglo XVI." In *Las teorías de la guerra justa en el siglo XVI y sus expresiones contemporáneas,* edited by Gilles Bataillon, Gilles Bienvenu, and Ambrosio Velasco Gómez, 47–91. Mexico City: Universidad Nacional Autónoma de México, 1998.

Carrión, Alejandro. *Antología general de la poesía ecuatoriana durante la colonia española.* Quito: Banco de los Andes, 1992.

Carver, Jonathan. *The New Universal Traveller.* London: G. Robinson, 1779.

Castillo, María Elena. "Guzmán ordenó asesinar a campesinos en Soras." *La República,* September 12, 2013. http://www.larepublica.pe/12-09-2013/abimael-guzman-ordeno-ase-sinar-a-campesinos-en-soras. Accessed March 9, 2015.

Cecconi, Arianna. "Dreams, Memory, and War: An Ethnography of Night in the Peruvian Andes." *Journal of Latin American and Caribbean Anthropology* 16, no. 2 (2011): 401–24.

Charles, John. *Allies at Odds: The Andean Church and Its Indigenous Agents, 1583–1671.* Albuquerque: University of New Mexico Press, 2010.

———. "Testimonios de coerción en las parroquias de indios: Perú, siglo XVII." In *Los indios ante los foros de justicia religiosa en la Hispanoamérica virreinal,* edited by Jorge E. Traslosheros and Ana de Zaballa Beascoechea, 111–26. Mexico City: Universidad Nacional Autónoma de México, 2010.

Chuchiak, John F., IV. "The Sins of the Fathers: Franciscan Friars, Parish Priests, and the Sexual Conquest of the Yucatec Maya, 1545–1808." *Ethnohistory* 54, no. 1 (2007): 69–128.

Cieza de León, Pedro. *Obras completas.* Vol. 2, *Las guerras civiles peruanas.* Edited by Carmelo Saenz de Santa Maria. Madrid: Instituto Gonzalo Fernández de Oviedo, 1985.

———. *El señorío de los Incas.* 1544. Madrid: Historia 16, 1985.

Cleckley, H. M. *The Mask of Sanity.* St. Louis: Mosby, 1982.

Cobo, Bernabé. *Historia del Nuevo Mundo.* Biblioteca de Autores Españoles 91 and 92. 1653. Madrid: Ediciones Atlas, 1964.

Coello de la Rosa, Alexandre. *Espacios de exclusión, espacios de poder.* Lima: Instituto de Estudios Peruanos, 2006.

Cole, Jeffrey A. *The Potosí Mita, 1573–1700: Compulsory Indian Labor in the Andes.* Stanford: Stanford University Press, 1985.

Concha Pacheco, Angela María, and Edgar Villafuerte Acuña. "Espacios de inclusión y exclusión: Etnias, ayllus y cofradías en la conformación de la doctrina ecclesiástica de Cocharcas, 1570–1614." *Cuadernos de Investigación Universitaria* (Cusco) 1 (2013): 45–70.

Concolorcorvo [Alonso Carrió de la Vandera]. *El lazarillo de ciegos caminantes desde Buenos-Ayres hasta Lima.* Lima: Impresa de la Rovada, 1773.

Cook, Alexandra Parma, and Noble David Cook. *Good Faith and Truthful Ignorance: A Case of Transatlantic Bigamy.* Durham: Duke University Press, 1990.

Cook, Noble David. *Demographic Collapse: Indian Peru, 1520–1620.* Cambridge: Cambridge University Press, 1981.

———, ed. *Tasa de la visita general de Francisco de Toledo.* Lima: Universidad Nacional Mayor de San Marcos, 1975.

Cooke, Colin A., Holger Hintelmann, Jay J. Ague, Richard L. Burger, Harald Biester, Julian P. Sachs, and Daniel R. Engstrom. "Use and Legacy of Mercury in the Andes." *Environmental Science and Technology* 47, no. 9 (2013): 4181–88.

Cornblit, Oscar. *Power and Violence in the Colonial City: Oruro from the Mining Renaissance to the Rebellion of Tupac*

Amaru (1740–1782). Cambridge: Cambridge University Press, 1995.

Covarrubias Orozco, Sebastián de. *Emblemas morales*. Madrid: Luis Sanchez, 1610. Reprint, Madrid: Fundación Universitaria Española, 1978.

Curatola Petrocchi, Marco, and José Carlos de la Puente Luna. "Estudios y materiales sobre el uso de los quipus en el mundo andino colonial." In *El quipu colonial: Estudios y materiales*, edited by Marco Curatola Petrocchi and José Carlos de la Puente Luna, 9–30. Lima: PUCP, 2013.

Dadson, Trevor. "Private Libraries in the Spanish Golden Age: Sources, Formation, and Function." *Journal of the Institute of Romance Studies* 4 (1996): 51–91.

Davies, Keith A. *Landowners in Colonial Peru*. Austin: University of Texas Press, 1984.

Decoster, Jean-Jacques. "La dualidad andina revisitada: En torno a la operación de las formas sociales en contextos rituales." In *Cultura andina: Cosmovisión, arqueología*, edited by Jesús Washington Rozas Álvarez and Delmia Valencia Blanco, 253–65. Cusco: CUD, CIUF, FUNSAAC, 2012.

Donahue Wallace, Kelly. *Art and Architecture of Viceregal Latin America, 1521–1821*. Albuquerque: University of New Mexico Press, 2008.

Durston, Alan. "Apuntes para una historia de los himnos quechuas del Cusco." *Chungará* (Arica) 42, no. 1 (2010): 147–55.

———. *Pastoral Quechua: The History of Christian Translation in Colonial Peru, 1550–1650*. Notre Dame: University of Notre Dame Press, 2007.

Duviols, Pierre. *La lutte contre les religions autochtones dans le Perou colonial: "L'extirpation de l'idolatrie" entre 1532 et 1600*. Lima: Instituto Francés de Estudios Andinos, 1971.

———. *Procesos y visitas de idolatrías, Cajatambo, siglo XVII*. Lima:

Instituto Francés de Estudios Andinos, 2003.

Earle, Rebecca. "'If You Eat Their Food . . .': Diets and Bodies in Early Colonial Spanish America." *American Historical Review* 115, no. 3 (2010): 688–713.

Eco, Umberto. *The Mysterious Flame of Queen Loana: An Illustrated Novel*. Translated by Geoffrey Brock. Orlando: Harcourt, 2005.

Egaña, Antonio de. *Historia de la Iglesia en la América Española: Hemisferio Sur*. Madrid: Biblioteca de Autores Españoles, 1966.

———, ed. *Monumenta Peruana*. Vol. 7. Rome: Monumenta Historica Societatis Iesu, 1981.

Elferink, Jan G. R. "The Use of Poison and Malevolent Magic in Criminal Practices Among the Incas." *Colonial Latin American Historical Review* 8, no. 3 (1999): 339–60.

Elías, Julio María. *Copacauana-Copacabana*. Copacabana: Santuario de Copacabana, 1978.

Engel, Emily A. "Visualizing a Colonial Peruvian Community in the Eighteenth-Century Paintings of Our Lady of Cocharcas." *Religion and the Arts* 13, no. 3 (2009): 299–339.

Erasmus. *Apologia ad monachos quosdam hispanos*. Basel: H. Froben, 1528.

Estenssoro Fuchs, Juan Carlos. *Del paganismo a la santidad. La incorporación de los indios del Perú al catolicismo (1532–1750)*. Lima: Instituto Francés de Estudios Andinos, 2003.

Fane, Diana. *Converging Cultures: Art and Identity in Spanish America*. New York: Brooklyn Museum, 1996.

Figuera, Guillermo. *La formación del clero indígena en la historia eclesiástica de América, 1500–1818*. Caracas: Archivo General de la Nación, 1965.

Fogelman, Patricia. "Una 'economía espiritual de la salvación': Culpabilidad, purgatorio y acumulación de indulgencias en la era colonial." *Andes* (Salta) 15 (2004): 1–26.

Flores Galindo, Alberto. *Buscando un Inca: Identidad y utopía en los Andes*.

Mexico City: Consejo Nacional para la Cultura y las Artes, 1993.

Fracchia, Carmen. "Constructing the Black Slave in Early Modern Spanish Painting." In *Others and Outcasts in Early Modern Europe: Picturing the Social Margins*, edited by Tom Nichols, 179–96. Aldershot: Ashgate, 2007.

García Bernal, Jaime. "La Biblioteca del Convento de la Merced Calzada de Sevilla." In *Gaillard—Fondos y procedencias: Bibliotecas en la Biblioteca de la Universidad de Sevilla*, 139–57. Seville: Universidad de Sevilla, 2013.

Garcilaso de la Vega. *Primera parte de los "Comentarios reales."* Lisbon: Pedro Crasbeeck, 1609.

Gareis, Iris. "Repression and Cultural Change: The 'Extirpation of Idolatry' in Colonial Peru." In *Spiritual Encounters: Interactions Between Christianity and Native Religions in Colonial America*, edited by Nicholas Griffiths and Fernando Cervantes, 230–50. Birmingham: University of Birmingham Press, 2001.

Garrett, David T. *Shadows of Empire: The Indian Nobility of Cusco, 1750–1825.* Cambridge: Cambridge University Press, 2005.

Gauderman, Kimberly. *Women's Lives in Colonial Quito: Gender, Law, and Economy in Spanish America.* Austin: University of Texas Press, 2003.

Gibbs, Laura, trans. *Aesop's Fables.* Oxford: Oxford University Press, 2002.

Gilbert Santamaría, Donald. *Writers on the Market: Consuming Literature in Early Seventeenth-Century Spain.* Lewisburg: Bucknell University Press, 2005.

Ginzburg, Carlo. *The Cheese and the Worms: The Cosmos of a Sixteenth-Century Miller.* Translated by John Tedeschi and Anne Tedeschi. Baltimore: Johns Hopkins University Press, 1992.

Glave, Luis Miguel. *Vida, símbolos y batallas: Creación y recreación de la comunidad indígena.* Lima: Fondo de Cultura Económica, 1993.

Godoy, Ricardo A. "The Fiscal Role of the Andean Ayllu." *Man*, n.s., 21, no. 4 (1986): 723–41.

Golte, Jürgen. *Repartos y rebeliones: Tupac Amaru y las contradicciones de la economía colonial.* Lima: Instituto de Estudios Peruanos, 1980.

Goñi Gaztambide, José. *Historia de la bula de la cruzada en España.* Madrid: Vitoria, 1958.

González, Olga M. *Unveiling Secrets of War in the Peruvian Andes.* Chicago: University of Chicago Press, 2011.

González Sánchez, Carlos Alberto. *New World Literacy: Writing and Culture Across the Atlantic, 1500–1700.* Translated by Tristan Platt. Lewisburg: Bucknell University Press, 2011.

Graubart, Karen B. *With Our Labor and Sweat: Indigenous Women and the Formation of Colonial Society in Peru, 1550–1700.* Stanford: Stanford University Press, 2007.

Griffiths, Nicholas. *The Cross and the Serpent: Religious Repression and Resurgence in Colonial Peru.* Norman: University of Oklahoma Press, 1996.

Guaman Poma de Ayala, Felipe. *Nueva corónica y buen gobierno.* Vols. 2 and 3. Edited by John V. Murra, Rolena Adorno, and Jorge L. Urioste. Ca. 1615. Madrid: Historia 16, 1987.

Guerra, Juan Carlos de. *Ensayo de un padrón histórico de Guipúzcoa según el orden de sus familias pobladoras.* San Sebastián: Joaquín Muñoz Baroja, 1928.

Gutiérrez de Santa Clara, Pedro. *Historia de las guerras civiles del Perú.* 1548. Madrid: Libreria General de Victorian Suárez, 1905.

Hagen, Kristine T., and Sophie C. Yohani. "The Nature and Psychosocial Consequences of War Rape for Individuals and Communities." *International Journal of Psychological Studies* 2, no. 2 (2010): 14–25.

Hampe Martínez, Teodoro. *Cultura barroca y extirpación de idolatrías: La biblioteca de Francisco de Avila (1648).* Cusco: Centro de Estudios

Regionales Andinos Bartolomé de las Casas, 1996.

———. *Santidad e identidad criolla: Estudio del proceso de canonización de Santa Rosa.* Cusco: Centro de Estudios Regionales Andinos Bartolomé de las Casas, 1998.

Harrison, Regina. "Pérez Bocanegra's *Ritual Formulario*: Khipu Knots and Confession." In *Narrative Threads: Accounting and Recounting in Andean Khipu,* edited by Jeffrey Quilter and Gary Urton, 266–92. Austin: University of Texas Press, 2002.

———. *Sin and Confession in Colonial Peru: Spanish-Quechua Penitential Texts, 1560–1650.* Austin: University of Texas Press, 2014.

Hastorf, Christine A. "Steamed or Boiled: Identity and Value in Food Preparation." Special issue, *Journal for Ancient Studies* 2 (2012): 213–42.

Hernáez, Francisco Javier. *Colección de bulas, breves y otros documentos relativos a la Iglesia de América y Filipinas.* 2 vols. Brussels: Alfredo Vromant, 1895.

Hernández Méndez, Rodolfo Esteban. "Acercamiento histórico a los bulas de la Santa Cruzada en el reino de Guatemala." *Revista Estudios del Instituto de Investigaciones Históricas y Antropológicas,* 1998. http://www.afehc-historia-centroamericana.org/index.php?action=fi_aff&id=355.

Hirstein, William. "What Is a Psychopath? The Neuroscience of Psychopathy Reports Some Intriguing Findings." *Psychology Today,* January 2013. https://www.psychologytoday.com/blog/mindmelding/201301/what-is-psychopath-0. Accessed July 27, 15.

Horace. *Epistles, Book I.* Edited by Roland Mayer. Cambridge: Cambridge University Press, 1994.

Huertas Vallejos, Lorenzo. "Historia de la producción de vinos y piscos en el Perú." *Universum* (Talca) 19, no. 2 (2004): 44–61.

Hughes, Ann Nickerson. *Religious Imagery in the Theater of Tirso de Molina.*

Macon: Mercer University Press, 1984.

Hyland, Sabine. *Gods of the Andes: An Early Jesuit Account of Inca Religion and Andean Christianity.* University Park: Pennsylvania State University Press, 2010.

———. "Illegitimacy and Racial Hierarchy in the Peruvian Priesthood: A Seventeenth-Century Dispute." *Catholic Historical Review* 84, no. 3 (1998): 431–54.

———. *The Jesuit and the Incas: The Extraordinary Life of Padre Blas Valera, S.J.* Ann Arbor: University of Michigan Press, 2003.

———. "Ply, Markedness, and Redundancy: New Evidence for How Andean Khipus Encoded Information." *American Anthropologist* 116, no. 3 (2014): 643–48.

———. *The Quito Manuscript: An Inca History Preserved by Fernando de Montesinos.* New Haven: Department of Anthropology, Yale University, 2007.

Hyland, Sabine, Brian S. Bauer, and Carlos Socualaya Dávila. "The Acta de Uranmarca." In *The Chanka: Archaeological Research in Andahuaylas (Apurimac), Peru,* edited by Brian S. Bauer, Lucas C. Kellett, and Miriam Aráoz Silva, 151–56. Los Angeles: Cotsen Institute of Archaeology Press, UCLA, 2010.

Hyland, Sabine, Gene A. Ware, and Madison Clark. "Knot Direction in a Khipu / Alphabetic Text from the Central Andes." *Latin American Antiquity* 25, no. 2 (2014): 189–97.

Isbell, Billie Jean. *To Defend Ourselves: Ecology and Ritual in an Andean Village.* Long Grove: Waveland Press, 1985.

Itier, César. "Un sermón desconocido en quechua general: La 'Plática que se ha de hazer a los indios en la predicación de la Bulla de la Santa Cruzada' (1600)." *Revista Andina* 10, no. 1 (1992): 135–46.

Jones, Caroline. "Woman's Worth: A Western Misconception." *Nebraska Anthropologist* 26 (2011): 96–111.

Julien, Catherine. "Diego Maldonado y los chancas." *Revista Andina* 34 (2002): 183–97.

Juvenal. *The Sixteen Satires.* Translated by Peter Green. New York: Penguin Books, 1974.

Katzew, Ilona. *Casta Painting: Images of Race in Eighteenth-Century Mexico.* New Haven: Yale University Press, 2005.

Kellett, Lucas. "Chanka Settlement Ecology: Hilltop Sites, Land Use, and Warfare in Late Prehispanic Andahuaylas, Peru." Ph.D. diss., University of New Mexico, 2010.

Kroeber, Theodora. *Ishi in Two Worlds: A Biography of the Last Wild Indian in North America.* 50th anniversary ed. Berkeley: University of California Press, 2011.

Kurin, Danielle Shawn. "The Bioarchaeology of Collapse: Ethnogenesis and Ethnocide in Post-Imperial Andahuaylas, Peru (A.D. 900–1250)." Ph.D. diss., Vanderbilt University, 2012.

Larson, Brooke. *Cochabamba, 1550–1900: Colonialism and Agrarian Transformation in Bolivia.* 2nd ed. Durham: Duke University Press, 1998.

Lastra, Pedro. "Testimonial Portrait: Images of José María Arguedas." In *José María Arguedas: Reconsiderations for Latin American Cultural Studies,* edited by Ciro A. Sandoval and Sandra M. Boschetto-Sandoval, 234–50. Athens: Ohio University Center for International Studies, 1998.

Lee, Jessica H. *The Treatment of Psychopathic and Antisocial Personality Disorders: A Review.* London: Risk Assessment and Management and Audit Systems, 1999.

Lehner, Ulrich L. *The Catholic Enlightenment: The Forgotten History of a Global Movement.* Oxford: Oxford University Press, 2016.

Leonard, Irving A. *Books of the Brave: Being an Account of Books and of Men in the Spanish Conquest and Settlement of the Sixteenth-Century New World.* 1949. Berkeley: University of California Press, 1992.

Lockhart, James. "Encomienda and Hacienda: The Evolution of the Great Estate in the Spanish Indies." *Hispanic American Historical Review* 49, no. 3 (1969): 411–29.

Lohmann Villena, Guillermo. *Las minas de Huancavelica en los siglos XVI y XVII.* 1946. Lima: Pontificia Universidad Católica del Perú, 1999.

López Martínez, Héctor, ed. *Rebeliones de mestizos y otros temas quinientistas.* Lima: Villanueva, 1972.

Lynch, John. *Spain Under the Hapsburgs.* Vol. 2, *Spain and America: 1598–1700.* Oxford: Oxford University Press, 1969.

MacCormack, Sabine. *Religion in the Andes: Vision and Imagination in Early Colonial Peru.* Princeton: Princeton University Press, 1993.

Mannarelli, María Emma. *Private Passions and Public Sins: Men and Women in Seventeenth-Century Lima.* Translated by Sidney Evans and Meredith D. Dodge. Albuquerque: University of New Mexico Press, 2007.

Mannheim, Bruce, and Guillermo Salas Carreño. "Wak'as: Entifications of the Andean Sacred." In *The Archaeology of Wak'as: Explorations of the Sacred in the Pre-Columbian Andes,* edited by Tamara L. Bray, 47–74. Boulder: University Press of Colorado, 2015.

Markham, Clements R. *Markham in Peru: The Travels of Clements R. Markham, 1852–1853.* Edited by Peter Blanchard. Austin: University of Texas Press, 1991.

Martens, Willem. "The Hidden Suffering of the Psychopath." *Psychiatric Times,* October 7, 2014. http://www.psychiatrictimes.com/psychotic-affective-disorders/hidden-suffering-psychopath. Accessed April 21, 2015.

Martiarena, Laurie M. "The Social Life of Death: Mortuary Practices in the North-Central Andes,

Eleventh–Eighteenth Centuries."
Ph.D. diss., University of East Anglia,
2014.

Martin, Louis. "Anti-feminism in Early
Western Thought: St. Jerome,
Evolution, and Culture." *Politics and
Culture*, April 29, 2010. http://www.
politicsandculture.org/2010/04/29/
anti-feminism-in-early-western-
thought-st-jerome-evolution-and-
culture/. Accessed April 23, 2015.

Martín Casares, Aurelia, and Margarita
García Barranco. *La esclavitud negroafricana en la historia de España,
siglos XVI y XVII*. Granada: Editorial
Comares, 2010.

Martínez, María Elena. *Genealogical
Fictions: Limpieza de Sangre,
Religion, and Gender in Colonial
Mexico*. Stanford: Stanford
University Press, 2008.

Marzal, Manuel. *La transformación
religiosa peruana*. Lima: Pontificia
Universidad Católica del Perú, 1983.

McCall, Cheryl. "An American Woman
Discovers an Ancient Empire Lost
in the Mountains of Peru." *People*,
October 20, 1980, 40–45.

McCusker, John J. *How Much Is That in
Real Money? A Historical Price Index
for Use as a Deflator of Money Values
in the Economy of the United States*.
2nd ed. Worcester, Mass.: American
Antiquarian Society, 2001.

McEwan, Gordon F. *The Incas: New
Perspectives*. New York: W. W.
Norton, 2008.

Meddens, Frank. "The Chicha/Soras
Valley During the Middle Horizon;
Provincial Aspects of Huari." Ph.D.
diss., University of London, Institute
of Archaeology, 1985.

Meddens, Frank, and Cirilo Vivanco
Pomacanchari. "The Chanca
Confederation: Political Myth and
Archaeological Reality." *Xama*
(Argentina) 15–18 (2002–5): 73–99.

Metzler, Josef. *America pontificia primi
saeculi evangelizationis, 1493–1592:
Documenta pontificia ex registris et
minutis praesertim in Archivo Secreto
Vaticano existentibus*. 2 vols. Vatican
City: Libreria Editrice Vaticana, 1991.

Mignolo, Walter D. "Looking for the
Meaning of 'Decolonial Gesture.'"
E-misférica 11, no. 1 (2014). http://
hemisphericinstitute.org/hemi/en/
emisferica-111-decolonial-gesture/
mignolo. Accessed July 27, 2015.

Millones Figueroa, Luis. "The Bezoar
Stone: A Natural Wonder in the
New World." *Hispanófila* 171 (2014):
139–56.

Mills, Kenneth. *Idolatry and Its Enemies:
Colonial Andean Religion and
Extirpation, 1640–1750*. Princeton:
Princeton University Press, 1997.

Mirow, Matthew C. *Latin American
Law: A History of Private Law and
Institutions in Spanish America*.
Austin: University of Texas Press,
2004.

Mitchell, William P., and Barbara H. Jaye.
"Pictographs in the Andes: The
Huntington Free Library Quechua
Catechism." *Latin American Indian
Literatures Journal* 12, no. 1 (1996):
1–42.

Montesinos, Fernando. *Anales del Perú*.
Vol. 2. Edited by Victor M. Maurtua.
1642. Madrid: Imp. de Gabriel L. y
del Horno, 1906.

Monzón, L. de. "Descripción de la tierra
del repartimiento de Atunsora." In
Relaciones geográficas de Indias,
edited by Marcos Jiménez de la
Espada, 220–25. Biblioteca de
Autores Españoles 183. 1586. Madrid:
Atlas, 1965.

Moore, Sally Falk. *Power and Property in
Inca Peru*. New York: Columbia
University Press, 1958.

Moreno Cebrián, Alfredo. *El corregidor de
indios y la economía peruana del
siglo XVIII: Los repartos forzosos de
mercancías*. Madrid: Instituto G.
Fernández de Oviedo, 1977.

Mumford, Jeremy. "The Taki Onqoy and
the Andean Nation: Sources and
Interpretations." *Latin American
Research Review* 33, no. 1 (1998):
150–65.

———. *Vertical Empire: The General
Resettlement of Indians in the
Colonial Andes*. Durham: Duke
University Press, 2012.

Murphy, Jane M. "Psychiatric Labeling in Cross-Cultural Perspective." *Science* 191, no. 4231 (1976): 1019–28.

Murra, John V. "Cloth and Its Functions in the Inca State." *American Anthropologist* 64, no. 4 (1962): 710–28.

Nash, Elizabeth. *Seville, Córdoba, and Granada: A Cultural History.* Oxford: Oxford University Press, 2005.

Nébias Barreto, Herman. "Legal Culture and Argumentation in the Vice-Reign of Peru from the Sixteenth to the Eighteenth Centuries." *Clio Themis: Revue Électronique d'Histoire du Droit* 2 (2009). http://www.clio-themis.com/legal-culture-and-argumentation-in. Accessed July 27, 15.

Núñez Zeballos, Alejandro Málaga. "La Virgen Candelaria en el obispado de Arequipa: Origen y milagros." In *Incas e indios Cristianos: Elites indígenas e identidades cristianas en los Andes coloniales*, 347–58. Lima: Institut français d'études andines, 2002.

O'Phelan Godoy, Scarlett. *Un siglo de rebeliones anticoloniales: Perú y Bolivia, 1700–1783.* Cusco: Centro de Estudios Regionales Andinos Bartolomé de las Casas, 1988.

Pagden, Anthony. *The Fall of Natural Man: The American Indian and the Origins of Comparative Ethnology.* Cambridge: Cambridge University Press, 1982.

Pärssinen, Martti, and Jukka Kiviharju. *Textos andinos: Corpus de textos khipu incaicos y coloniales.* Madrid: Instituto Iberoamericano de Finlandia, 2004.

Penry, S. Elizabeth. "Transformations in Indigenous Authority and Identity in Resettlement Towns of Colonial Charcas (Alto Perú)." Ph.D. diss., University of Miami, 1996.

Pélach y Feliu, Enrique. *Nuestra Señora de Cocharcas.* Abancay: Editorial Andina, 1972.

Perez Bocanegra, Juan. *Ritual formulario e instrucción de curas para administración a los naturales de este reyno los santos sacramentos.* Lima: Gerónymo Contreras, 1631.

Perry, Mary Elizabeth. *Gender and Disorder in Early Modern Seville.* Princeton: Princeton University Press, 1990.

Peters, Edward. *Inquisition.* Berkeley: University of California Press, 1989.

Phipps, Elena. "Garments and Identity in the Colonial Andes." In *The Colonial Andes: Tapestries and Silverwork, 1530–1830*, edited by Elena Phipps, Johanna Hecht, and Cristina Esteras Martín, 16–41. New York: Metropolitan Museum of Art, 2004.

Piel, Jean. *Capitalismo agrario en el Perú.* Lima: Institut français d'études andines; Salta: Universidad Nacional de Salta, 1995.

Pike, Ruth. "Seville in the Sixteenth Century." *Hispanic American Historical Review* 41, no. 1 (1961): 1–30.

Platt, Tristan. "The Andean Experience of Bolivian Liberalism, 1825–1900: Roots of Rebellion in Nineteenth-Century Chayanta (Potosí)." In *Resistance, Rebellion, and Consciousness in the Andean Peasant World, Eighteenth to Twentieth Centuries*, edited by Steve J. Stern, 280–326. Madison: University of Wisconsin Press, 1987.

———. "Container Transport: From Skin Bags to Iron Flasks; Changing Technologies of Quicksilver Packaging Between Almadén and America, 1788–1848." *Past and Present* 214, no. 1 (2012): 205–53.

———. *Estado boliviano y ayllu andino: Tierra y tributo en el norte de Potosí.* Lima: Instituto de Estudios Peruanos, 1982.

Powers, Karen Vieira. *Andean Journeys: Migration, Ethnogenesis, and the State in Colonial Quito.* Albuquerque: University of New Mexico Press, 1995.

———. "The Battle for Bodies and Souls in the Colonial North Andes: Intraecclesiastical Struggles and the Politics of Migration." In *The Church in Colonial Latin America*, edited by John F. Schwaller,

121–47. Wilmington, Del.: Scholarly Resources, 2000.

Prado, Pablo de. *Directorio espiritual en lengua española y quichua general del inga*. Lima: Luis de Lyra, 1641.

Premo, Bianca. *Children of the Father King: Youth, Authority, and Legal Minority in Colonial Lima*. Chapel Hill: University of North Carolina Press, 2005.

Presta, Ana María. "Undressing the Coya and Dressing the Indian Woman." *Hispanic American Historical Review* 90, no. 1 (2010): 41–74.

Puente Luna, José Carlos de la. "Felipe Guaman Poma de Ayala, administrador de bienes de comunidad." *Revista Andina* 47, no. 2 (2008): 9–40.

Puente Brunke, José de la. *Encomienda y encomenderos en el Perú: Estudio social y político de una institución colonial*. Seville: Publicaciones de la Excma. Diputación Provincial de Sevilla, 1992.

Quintanilla, Lino. *Andahuaylas: La lucha por la tierra. Testimonio de un militante*. Lima: Mosca Azul, 1981.

Raheja, Gloria Goodwin. "'Crying When She's Born, and Crying When She Goes Away': Marriage and the Idiom of the Gift in Pahansu Song Performance." In *From the Margins of Hindu Marriage: Essays on Gender, Religion, and Culture*, edited by Lindsey Harlan and Paul B. Courtright, 19–59. Oxford: Oxford University Press, 1995.

Ramírez, Susan Elizabeth. *To Feed and Be Fed: The Cosmological Bases of Authority and Identity in the Andes*. Stanford: Stanford University Press, 2005.

———. *The World Upside Down: Cross-Cultural Contact and Conflict in Sixteenth-Century Peru*. Stanford: Stanford University Press, 1996.

Ramos, Gabriela, ed. *Death and Conversion in the Andes: Lima and Cuzco, 1532–1670*. Notre Dame: Notre Dame University Press, 2010.

———. *La venida del reino. Religión, evangelización y cultura en América, siglos XVI–XX*. Cusco: Centro de Estudios Regionales Andinos Bartolomé de las Casas, 1994.

Ramos Gavilán, Alonso. *Historia del célebre Santuario de Ntra. Sra. de Copacabana y sus milagros e invención de la cruz de Carabuco*. Lima: Geronymo de Contreras, 1621.

Rasnake, Roger Neil. *Domination and Cultural Resistance: Authority and Power Among an Andean People*. Durham: Duke University Press, 1988.

Regeser López, Steven, and Peter J. Guarnaccia. "Cultural Psychopathology: Uncovering the Social World of Mental Illness." *Annual Review of Psychology* 51 (2000): 571–98.

Reina Maldonado, Pedro de. *Norte claro del perfecto prelado en su pastoral govierno*. Madrid, 1653.

Robins, Nicholas A. *Mercury, Mining, and Empire: The Human and Ecological Cost of Colonial Silver Mining in the Andes*. Bloomington: Indiana University Press, 2011.

Rostworowski, María. "Peregrinaciones y procesiones rituales en los Andes." *Journal de la Société des Américanistes* 89, no. 2 (2003): 97–123.

Rowe, William. "Arguedas: Music, Awareness, and Social Transformation." In *José María Arguedas: Reconsiderations for Latin American Cultural Studies*, edited by Ciro A. Sandoval and Sandra M. Boschetto-Sandoval, 35–52. Athens: Ohio University Center for International Studies, 1998.

Said, Edward W. "Reflections on Exile." In *Reflections on Exile and Other Essays*, 173–86. Cambridge: Harvard University Press, 2000.

Saignes, Thierry. *Caciques, Tribute, and Migration in the Southern Andes: Indian Society and the Seventeenth-Century Colonial Order*. London: University of London, 1985.

Salles-Reese, Verónica. *From Viracocha to the Virgin of Copacabana: Representation of the Sacred at Lake*

Titicaca. Austin: University of Texas Press, 1997.

Sallnow, Michael. *Pilgrims of the Andes: Regional Cults in Cusco.* Washington, D.C.: Smithsonian Institute Press, 1987.

Salomon, Frank. "Collca y sapçi: Una perspectiva sobre el almacenamiento inka desde la analogía etnográfica." *Boletín de Arqueología PUCP* 8 (2004): 43–57.

———. Introduction to *The Huarochirí Manuscript: A Testament of Ancient and Colonial Andean Religion*, translated and edited by Frank Salomon and George L. Urioste, 1–38. Austin: University of Texas Press, 1991.

———. "Testimonies: The Making and Reading of Native South American Historical Sources." In *The Cambridge History of the Native Peoples of the Americas*, vol. 3, *South America*, pt. 1, edited by Frank Salomon and Stuart B. Schwartz, 19–95. Cambridge: Cambridge University Press, 1999.

Salomon, Frank, and Sue Grosboll. "Names and Peoples in Incaic Quito: Retrieving Undocumented Historic Processes Through Anthroponymy and Statistics." *American Anthropologist* 88, no. 2 (1986): 387–99.

Salomon, Frank, and Armando Guevara-Gil. "A 'Personal Visit': Colonial Political Ritual and the Making of 'Indians' in the Andes." *Colonial Latin American Review* 3, nos. 1–2 (1994): 3–36.

Salomon, Frank, and Mercedes Niño-Murcia. *The Lettered Mountain: A Peruvian Village's Way with Writing.* Durham: Duke University Press, 2011.

Sánchez-Albornoz, Nicolás. *Indios y tributos en el Alto Perú.* Lima: Instituto de Estudios Peruanos, 1978.

Santana Perez, Juan Manuel. "Sobre el encierro de los pobres en los tiempos modernos." *Espacio, Tiempo y Forma*, 4th ser., 9 (1996): 339–57.

Sarmiento de Gamboa, Pedro. *The History of the Incas.* Translated and edited by Brian S. Bauer and Vania Smith. 1572. Austin: University of Texas Press, 2007.

Seligmann, Linda J. *Between Reform and Revolution: Political Struggles in the Peruvian Andes, 1969–1991.* Stanford: Stanford University Press, 1995.

Sempat Assadourian, Carlos. "Sobre un elemento de la economía colonial: Producción y circulación de mercancías en el interior de un conjunto regional." *Eure* 3, no. 8 (1973): 135–82.

Serulnikov, Sergio. *Subverting Colonial Authority: Challenges to Spanish Rule in Eighteenth-Century Southern Andes.* Durham: Duke University Press, 2003.

Silverblatt, Irene. "Family Values in Seventeenth-Century Peru." In *Native Traditions in the Postconquest World*, edited by Elizabeth Hill Boone and Tom Cummins, 63–89. Washington, D.C.: Dumbarton Oaks, 1998.

———. *Moon, Sun, and Witches: Gender Ideologies and Class in Inca and Colonial Peru.* Princeton: Princeton University Press, 1987.

Socolow, Susan Migden. *The Women of Colonial Latin America.* Cambridge: Cambridge University Press, 2000.

Soldi, Ana María. "La vid y el vino en la costa central del Perú, siglos XVI y XVII." *Universum* (Talca) 21, no. 2 (2006): 42–61.

Solórzano Pereyra, Juan de. *Política indiana.* Vols. 1 and 2. Madrid: Compañía Iberoamericana de Publicaciones, 1972.

Spalding, Karen. "The Crisis and Transformation of the Invaded Societies: Andean Area (1500–1580)." In *The Cambridge History of the Native Peoples of the Americas*, vol. 3, *South America*, pt. 1, edited by Frank Salomon and Stuart B. Schwartz, 904–72. Cambridge: Cambridge University Press, 1999.

———. *Huarochirí: An Andean Society Under Inca and Spanish Rule.* Stanford: Stanford University Press, 1984.

———. "Social Climbers: Changing Patterns of Mobility Among the Indians of Colonial Peru." *Hispanic American Historical Review* 50, no. 4 (1970): 645–64.

Staller, John E. *Maize Cobs and Cultures: History of Zea mays L.* New York: Springer, 2009.

Stanfield-Mazzi, Maya. "The Possessor's Agency: Private Art Collecting in the Colonial Andes." *Colonial Latin American Review* 18, no. 3 (2009): 339–64.

Stavig, Ward. *The World of Túpac Amaru: Conflict, Community, and Identity in Colonial Peru.* Lincoln: University of Nebraska Press, 1999.

Stephenson, Marcia. "From Marvelous Antidote to the Poison of Idolatry: The Transatlantic Role of Andean Bezoar Stones During the Late Sixteenth and Early Seventeenth Centuries." *Hispanic American Historical Review* 90, no. 1 (2010): 3–39.

Stern, Steve J. "The Age of Andean Insurrection, 1742–1782: A Reappraisal." In *Resistance, Rebellion, and Consciousness in the Andean Peasant World, Eighteenth to Twentieth Centuries*, edited by Steve J. Stern, 34–93. Madison: University of Wisconsin Press, 1987.

———. *Peru's Indian Peoples and the Challenge of Spanish Conquest: Huamanga to 1640.* Madison: University of Wisconsin Press, 1982.

Szeminski, Jan. "Why Kill the Spaniard? New Perspectives on Andean Insurrectionary Ideology in the Eighteenth Century." In *Resistance, Rebellion, and Consciousness in the Andean Peasant World, Eighteenth to Twentieth Centuries*, edited by Steve J. Stern, 166–92. Madison: University of Wisconsin Press, 1987.

Taylor, Bruce. *Structures of Reform: The Mercedarian Order in the Spanish Golden Age.* Leiden: Brill Academic, 2000.

Taylor, William. "Santiago's Horse: Christianity and Colonial Indian Resistance in the Heartland of New Spain." In *Violence, Resistance, and Survival in the Americas: Native Americans and the Legacy of Conquest*, edited by William B. Taylor and Franklin Pease G. Y., 153–89. Washington, D.C.: Smithsonian Institution Press, 1994.

Theidon, Kimberly. *Intimate Enemies: Violence and Reconciliation in Peru.* Philadelphia: University of Pennsylvania Press, 2013.

Thomson, Sinclair. *We Alone Will Rule: Native Andean Politics in the Age of Insurgency.* Madison: University of Wisconsin Press, 2002.

Tirso de Molina [Gabriel Téllez]. *El condenado por desconfiado.* Edited by Daniel Rogers. 1615. New York: Pergamon Press, 1974.

———. *Historia general de la Orden de Nuestra Señora de las Mercedes.* Edited by Manuel Penedo. Vol. 2. 1637. Madrid: Provincia de la Merced de Castilla, 1973.

Turner, Francis. "Money and Exchange Rates in 1632." http://www.1632.org/1632Slush/1632money.rtf. Accessed April 23, 2015.

Uribe-Uran, Victor M. "Innocent Infants or Abusive Patriarchs? Spousal Homicides, the Punishment of Indians, and the Law in Colonial Mexico, 1740s–1820s." *Journal of Latin American Studies* 38, no. 4 (2006): 793–828.

Urton, Gary. "From Knots to Narratives: Reconstructing the Art of Historical Record Keeping in the Andes from Spanish Transcriptions of Inka Khipus." *Ethnohistory* 45, no. 3 (1998): 409–38.

Valderrama, Pedro de. *Exercicios espirituales para todos los dias de la Cuaresma.* Seville: Francisco Pérez, 1603.

Valdivieso, José de. *Doze actos sacramentales, y dos comedias divinas.* Toledo: Juan Ruiz, 1622.

van Goozen, Stephanie H. M., Graeme Fairchild, Heddeke Snoek, and Gordon T. Harold. "The Evidence for a Neurobiological Model of Childhood Antisocial Behavior."

Psychological Bulletin 133, no. 1
(2007): 149–82.

Vargas Ugarte, Rubén. *Historia del culto
de María en Iberoamérica y de sus
imágenes y santuarios más celebra-
dos*. Buenos Aires: Editorial Huarpes,
1947.

Villanueva Urteaga, Horacio. *Cajamarca:
Apuntes para su historia*. Cusco:
Editorial Garcilaso, 1975.

Viqueira, Carmen. "Los hospitales para locos e 'inocentes' en Hispanoamerica
y sus antecedentes españoles."
*Revista de Medicina y Ciencias
Afines* 22, no. 270 (1965): 1–33.

Wachtel, Nathan. *Le retour des ancêtres:
Les Indiens Urus de Bolivie, XXème–
XVIème siècle*. Paris: Gallimard,
1990.

Walker, Charles F. *The Tupac Amaru
Rebellion*. Cambridge: Harvard
University Press, 2014.

Wardle, Huon. "A Cosmopolitan
Anthropology?" *Social Anthropology*
18, no. 4 (2010): 381–88.

Weingarten, Kaethe. *Common Shock:
Witnessing Violence Every Day*. New
York: Dutton, 2003.

Weinstein, Donald, and Rudolph M. Bell.
*Saints and Society: The Two Worlds
of Western Christendom, 1000–1700*.
Chicago: University of Chicago
Press, 1982.

Weismantel, Mary. "Ayllu: Real and
Imagined Communities in the
Andes." In *The Seductions of
Community: Emancipations,
Oppressions, Quandaries*, edited by
Gerald W. Creed, 77–100. Santa Fe:
School of American Research Press,
2006.

———. *Food, Gender, and Poverty in the
Ecuadorian Andes*. Philadelphia:
University of Pennsylvania Press,
1988.

Wernke, Steven A. *Negotiated Settlements:
Andean Communities and
Landscapes Under Inka and Spanish*

Colonialism. Gainesville: University
Press of Florida, 2013.

Wightman, Ann M. *Indigenous Migration
and Social Change: The Forasteros
of Cuzco, 1520–1720*. Durham: Duke
University Press, 1990.

Williamson, S., T. J. Harpur, and R. D.
Hare. "Abnormal Processing of
Affective Words by Psychopaths."
Psychophysiology 28, no. 3 (1991):
260–73.

Zavala, Melina. "Emblemas Morales." In
*Emblem Scholars, Emblematica
Online*, edited by Mara R. Wade.
University of Illinois, 2013.
https://emblematicaonlineuiuc
.wordpress.com/research-re-
sults/research-papers-2/
emblemas-morales/.

Zemon Davis, Natalie. "On the Lame."
American Historical Review 93, no. 3
(1988): 572–603.

———. *The Return of Martin Guerre*.
Cambridge: Harvard University
Press, 1984.

Zuidema, R. T. "Guaman Poma and the Art
of Empire: Toward an Iconography
of Inca Royal Dress." In *Transatlantic
Encounters: Europeans and
Andeans in the Sixteenth Century*,
edited by Kenneth J. Andrien and
Rolena Adorno, 151–202. Berkeley:
University of California Press, 1991.

———. *Inca Civilization in Cuzco*.
Translated by Jean-Jacques Decoster.
Austin: University of Texas Press,
1990.

Zulawski, Ann. "Migration and Labor in
Seventeenth-Century Alto Peru."
Ph.D. diss., Columbia University,
1985.

INDEX